TIME TO
DEFEAT *the*
DEVIL

1 Kings 20:43

TIME TO DEFEAT *the* DEVIL

CHUCK D. PIERCE

CHARISMA
HOUSE

Most CHARISMA HOUSE BOOK GROUP products are available at special quantity discounts for bulk purchase for sales promotions, premiums, fundraising, and educational needs. For details, write Charisma House Book Group, 600 Rinehart Road, Lake Mary, Florida 32746, or telephone (407) 333-0600.

TIME TO DEFEAT THE DEVIL by Chuck D. Pierce
Published by Charisma House
Charisma Media/Charisma House Book Group
600 Rinehart Road
Lake Mary, Florida 32746
www.charismahouse.com

Unless otherwise noted, all Scripture quotations are from the New King James Version of the Bible. Copyright © 1979, 1980, 1982 by Thomas Nelson, Inc., publishers. Used by permission.

Scripture quotations marked AMP are from the Amplified Bible. Old Testament copyright © 1965, 1987 by the Zondervan Corporation. The Amplified New Testament copyright © 1954, 1958, 1987 by the Lockman Foundation. Used by permission.

Scripture quotations marked CJB are from the Complete Jewish Bible. Copyright 1998 by David H. Stern. Published by Jewish New Testament Publications, Inc. All rights reserved. Used by permission.

Scripture quotations marked KJV are from the King James Version of the Bible.

Scripture quotations marked NAS are from the New American Standard Bible. Copyright © 1960, 1962, 1963, 1968, 1971, 1972, 1973, 1975, 1977, 1995 by the Lockman Foundation. Used by permission. (www.Lockman.org)

Scripture quotations marked NIV are from the Holy Bible, New International Version. Copyright © 1973, 1978, 1984, International Bible Society. Used by permission.

Scripture quotations marked NLT are from the Holy Bible, New Living Translation, copyright © 1996, 2004. Used by permission of Tyndale House Publishers, Inc., Wheaton, IL 60189. All rights reserved.

Cover design by Justin Evans
Design Director: Bill Johnson

Visit the author's website at www.gloryofzion.org.

Library of Congress Cataloging-in-Publication Data:

Pierce, Chuck D., 1953-
  Time to defeat the devil / Chuck D. Pierce. -- 1st ed.
    p. cm.
  Includes bibliographical references.
  ISBN 978-1-61638-278-0 (trade paper) -- ISBN 978-1-61638-423-4 (e-book) 1.
Spiritual warfare. I. Title.
  BV4509.5.P565 2011
  235'.4--dc22

                          2011002209

12 13 14 15 16 — 9 8 7 6 5
Printed in the United States of America

Contents

Chapter 1

THERE IS A MOMENT FOR CHANGE

I DO NOT HAVE time for many outlets or hobbies. My life is mostly travel, ministry, prayer, and family. At one time I painted on canvas. That was an enormous outlet. I still do some yard work when I have a Saturday and observe that Pam, my wife, is behind on maintenance. I travel 70 percent of the time, so that is usually my excuse when people ask me what I do. I actually sleep very little (a five-hour-a-day sleep pattern) and spend much of the night (and day) praying for people. I listen daily for my prayer list to form. Usually the Lord keeps ten people on that list each day. These are people in the throes of transition, ensnared by the enemy, or *on the verge*. My delight is to seek and know God and worship Him on a daily basis.

THERE IS A MOMENT FOR CHANGE AND VICTORY

One diversion I do enjoy is bowling. Actually, I have bowled for forty years. All of my sons bowl, some better than others, and as a ministry we bowl in city, regional, and national competitions. Our teams are Christian influences (most of the time) when we compete.

So why would I be starting this book this way? Recently, we were in competition on a regional level. In the first game of the nine-game competition, my son John Mark bowled a perfect game, a score of three hundred. He has performed this feat several times, so the perfect score was not the real issue. During the game, the Spirit of God impressed me deeply with these words: "There is a moment for change and victory." I looked at my score—one hundred seventy. I really could not grasp what I was hearing.

Here at Glory of Zion we have corporate prayer on Tuesday mornings.

During our next Tuesday prayer, I heard the voice of God speaking again, "There is a moment for change and victory." I wasn't leading in the prayer meeting, and this revelation from heaven appeared not to fit, so like Mary, I just pondered this statement.

Tuesday nights, we have five teams in a very competitive regional league. The league is called "The Money League." This league pays quarterly and is more lucrative than most leagues in the area. I bowl with one of the owners of a pro shop in our area. She and her husband are great friends of ours. She is a devout Jew. So she understands G-d and recognizes His reality.

In the last game of the night, when we were only a few pins behind, I kept missing my mark. I heard the Spirit of God say again, "There is a moment for change and victory." Immediately I knew! Sometimes you know—*you just know!* If we were to increase our winnings and supply line, I would have to change. However, the Spirit of God was saying, "I already have the time for this change and the grace for you to shift."

After we lost by six pins and I was leaving the alley, I looked at Dora and her husband, Fred, one of the best bowlers I know, and said, "I plan on relearning this game. Yes, I have done this for forty years one way, but there is a moment for me to change, and now is the time." I knew I would have to change my entire game—my approach, my rotation, the ball, my stance, my release, my timing, and most importantly, my brain. However, I knew that there was a moment, and I did not want to miss this change, even if I had to fail at the beginning to increase at the end.

I am a right hander, but I learned to throw the ball as a left-hand bowler. When you are right-hand dominant and you bowl like that, you throw a back-up ball. This ball looks like a left-hander's ball, but you are using your right hand. Now God was saying, "There is a moment for change and victory if you will allow Me to reorder your thoughts and movement. If you submit, you will increase! You can continue to try to back up or face forward, reposition, and learn to go forward in a new way."

For the mind to break out of the last season's mentality, there is war. Whether bowling or worshiping or learning a new system or way of doing things, there is war! The war is over a greater portion, an increase, a new way to prosper.

As you read this book, pursue this concept in every area of your life; be prepared to enter into your future. Be expectant! When I asked John Mark, "Why do you bowl so well?" he said, "Every time that I begin a game, I see myself bowling three hundred! I may not always bowl a perfect game, but I *expect* to do so!" In the next chapter, we will discuss expectations.

BELIEVE THAT *YOU CAN* AND YOU WILL

Time and space are two of the most interesting and difficult concepts to grasp as you move through your life journey. We are in time, but God is not. Though some of us may feel that we were born out of time, we have been set in time and place to understand our Creator and what He created us to accomplish. Acts 17:26 says, "He has...determined their pre-appointed times and the boundaries of their dwellings." When you are *in time* correctly, you can grasp God and His purpose for your life.

Times are changing, and we must stay in God's timing to prosper in a world where the *god of this age* desires to mold you into the blueprint of the day and cause you to look like the world around you. But we are called to have transformed minds and be linked to the *Head*—not to bring up the rear in producing the changes around us. Even righteous Lot was vexed because of his environment in Sodom. When we are at the right place at the right time we can break out of vexing, confusing, mind-altering powers that war against the covenant of holy God and all of the blessings He is ready to pour upon us.

In this season, you must know your belief system. *What* do you believe in? *Whom* do you believe in? Everyone has some sort of belief system that they develop for their life. Mine is the Word of God. In this season we must rehearse the Word. What revelation has come to you? That is what you use to war in the world around you. We must meditate on what God says until the power of that revelation enters our bloodstream and cell structure. We also must learn to worship and minister in our homes. Doing so will allow our gifts to be activated in a new way in small groups. When the time comes that we are not free to worship publicly in our church buildings, we will already know how to continue worshiping in our homes. Take the points below and use them to speak into your life and the environment around you.

I Believe the Bible Is the Word of God

I am asked often, "What do you believe?"

This summarizes my belief system: Hebrews 4:12 says, "For the word of God is living and powerful, and sharper than any two-edged sword, piercing even to the division of soul and spirit, and of joints and marrow, and is a discerner of the thoughts and intents of the heart." Romans 10:17 says, "So then faith comes by hearing, and hearing by the word of God." Therefore I contend that if faith comes by hearing and hearing by the Word of God, then for those who are lost, faith to be saved comes by hearing the Word of God, and for those who are already saved, faith to continue on to spiritual maturity comes by hearing the Word of God.

I believe Father God came as Spirit and hovered over a virgin and impregnated her. I believe the Son was then born to this virgin named Mary and grew in stature and favor with man. I believe that He came unto His own but His own did not receive Him. I believe that He overcame the power of sin in this world and withstood all temptations that would be known to man. He presented who Father was to mankind. He then submitted Himself to Father's plan, for me. He was then sacrificed, that I could be redeemed from the power of sin. I believe that He overcame death, hell, and the grave and now sits at the right hand of the Father. I believe His Spirit dwells among us to give us the same power to overcome all temptation, sin, and decay of the world.

I believe that I can be a son and receive a full inheritance from Him. I believe that the miracle-working power that was displayed by Jesus Christ, the Messiah, as He rose from the dead is now working in the world today. It is available to each and every one who will submit to the cross he or she has been given. This power enables us to unlock our futures and walk in overcoming victory.

I believe His power is working in the earth to align and redeem nations, forming a joyful house of prayer for each ethnic group. I believe this power continues to work to make Gentiles and Jews into one new man who will be presented to the Father. I believe that if I give my best, monthly, to Him, I will move from blessing to blessing until blessings overtake me.

War With Your Prophetic Word

The Word of God endures forever (Isa. 40:8; Ps. 119:89). The world cannot overcome the power of God's life-giving Word when released through the spirit of man. The Spirit of God breathing on His Word makes His Word life and power. This Word is not bound by time but transcends from generation to generation and beyond. The deeds of the Word can be shared as a testament from one person and will affect the generations to come. The Word produces works—divine revelation and requirements that we believe will manifest. The Word is synonymous with *speech, command, promise,* and *prophecy.* Therefore we must speak the Word or utter our belief. Prophetic utterance is vision being released. "Where there is no vision [no redemptive revelation of God], the people perish" (Prov. 29:18, AMP). Vision produces faith. Within our vision is the allotment for our provision.

Faith Develops and Increases

Faith is linked with an object. This book centers on a holy living God who sent His Son as His perfect reflection for us to believe, just as the prophets have prophesied and the Scriptures have been written. We do not seek God just for information; we seek God so we can respond and relate to Him. God is not important unless He is the *supreme* importance of our life.

Faith is not the same as belief. *Faith* is sensitivity, understanding, engagement, and attachment. We can gain more understanding of the object of our faith, or we can resist His plan and lose what we once acquired. A good example is the generation that left Egypt (Ps. 78:14–32; Isa. 63:17). Faith includes faithfulness, strength of waiting, the acceptance of His concealment, and the defiance of history (Isa. 26:13). Faith is preceded by awe or fear—the beginning of wisdom (Prov. 9:10). Without faith, we cannot please God.

Faith is like the numbers of a combination lock. We have many promises, but without combining and mixing those promises with faith, we cannot open up the way to enter the promise. Every time our faith soars, we gain a secret that is like one of the numbers that is necessary to open the combination lock. The secrets of God are with those who fear and reverence Him in worship. Psalm 25:12–15 says:

> Who is the man that fears the LORD?
> Him shall He teach in the way He chooses.
> He himself shall dwell in prosperity,
> And his descendants shall inherit the earth.
> The secret of the LORD is with those who fear Him,
> And He will show them His covenant.
> My eyes are ever toward the LORD,
> For He shall pluck my feet out of the net.

We must learn to see the miracles that are daily with us. There are signposts all along our path. By faith, signs illuminate and keep our path bright. These signposts are like streetlights that guide us through a dark neighborhood. Because "faith cometh," we must open our eyes to where we are going (Prov. 14:15).

Our faith is linked with the submission of our will. We must learn how to let His will prevail. The will wars against faith. Until the will is yielded, you cannot secure your desire. Our faith is not just our concern but is also His concern. Only in His *light* do we see *light*.

Through His Word, we have power to overcome the enemy's plan. This season is supernatural! I am a pray-er and love to meet corporately with others to pray. Each time we meet for corporate prayer, we discuss what the Lord was saying from heaven and prophesying to us during the week. Then we pray. We *watch* and *war* with this revelation. First Timothy 1:18 admonishes us, "According to the prophecies previously made concerning you...you may wage the good warfare."

God's people must leave *religion* and their natural way of battle and enter this supernatural season with sharpened weapons. This is a season of breaking new ground, a time for us to gain new vision. For you to see the necessary action for breakthrough, you must extend your hand through the darkness and into the heavenly realm. You will touch God in a new way. That divine touch is like lightning connecting from one world to this world. You become God's lightning rod. The Lord will give you strength by touching you with His *hand*. He will release the *sword of revelation*, which will connect with you to do war. Every dark, evil, watching force cannot hide when His light invades the realm of Earth and illuminates your spirit with revelation. Revelation produces faith, and faith overcomes.

LIFT YOUR HANDS FOR A FRESH TOUCH

Prophecy is the life flow of God's voice and heart to His people and the earth realm. Recently I heard Him say, "Do not let your hands grow slack at this time. Slack hands will not be able to grab the weapon that is needed to defeat the enemy. I am bringing new strength into your hands. Your hands will be free as you ready yourself for the battle ahead. There's a new watchman call that I'm placing upon My people, and they will stand, observe, and see in ways they've not seen before. They will know the order when things are not in order. You must be able to watch and see the slightest 'out of order' issue that would keep Me from moving you and yours forward. Don't major on minors but see with My eyes, for I am setting many *bodies* in order. One of these is yours! I am setting groups in order. I am setting towns in order, and I am setting cities in new order. This is not a time for slack hands. This is not a time for manipulation and rearrangement or justification. You must see the way I see things; otherwise you will find yourself saying, 'What happened to the glory in my boundaries?' Raise up your slack hands now, and I will energize them, and you will be ready for the battle ahead."

I am writing this book to help us understand how to take a word like this and enter a new level of freedom and victory. This book is the third of a series. The first two books, *Interpreting the Times* and *Redeeming the Time,* helped us to understand time. This third book is to extend a call to you. This call is for you to prosper. This call is for you to soar above all the atmospheric forces around you that would rob your faith and vision. This call is to withstand and overcome the vexing power of an enemy who opposes God in you—*the Hope of Glory*! Throughout this book, I want to encourage your spirit man to rise up and be filled with His Spirit. Look at your hands now and say, "NOW IS THE TIME FOR YOU TO PROSPER!" This book is like a war manual that will help you stay free from the enemy's vexing power as you journey through life.

War in Time

This installment of the Time trilogy will teach you how to *war in time.* Your battles are now! Your battle is not in the past. Some of what you are warring through originated in your past. But God is one who reconciles our past so that our *now* opens up to our future. He will bring your past in front of you so your defeats in a former season will now become the victories and triumphs for your future. This book is meant to educate and encourage you on how the enemy attempts to deflate your spirit man so you cannot soar in the heavenlies with the One who paid the price to make you free to rise to your royal state.

In a crisis season, the strategies of heaven must invade your sphere of authority! Everyone has a portion. You have been positioned in a sphere of authority. You must understand your sphere of authority and know how to operate with others in that sphere. It is from this sphere that you will watch the formation of your *new. A sphere* is a circuit of motion, revolution, or orbit. A sphere is also defined as a vast expanse where your heavenly realm appears. My favorite definition of *sphere* is "a circuit of action, knowledge, or influence that is both linked to the functional area of your involvement and every territory that is affected by you exercising authority." Within this expanse is an order of society that you can influence. In 2 Corinthians 10, Paul talks about what his sphere of influence includes and where he does not have certain authority to rule. This is where you enter the *new*!

For you to see what is happening new around you, you must shake off all discouragement, disillusionment, and disinterest. You must tell your emotions not to resist the *new*. You must believe that God has more for you. In other words, your latter can be greater than your former! You must go up into a new spiritual realm. Actually, you must *go beyond* where you have been in the past.

As you read this book, I will be addressing each of the points that I will briefly outline below.

TEN KEY REVELATORY WAR POINTS

1. How to enter the new season that has begun

It takes a war to break out of one season and enter another. We all go through transition times. (I write several chapters on this in the other two Time books.) Every transition time has three phases, and each phase has a warfare element involved. John the Baptist was a transitional prophet between the old covenant and new covenant. He announced in the wilderness who was coming. Jesus served the world transitionally between the wilderness of the old covenant and through the warfare of the cross of redemption up to the time when the Holy Spirit came to be our advocate in the world. In our lives, transitional times are filled with warfare but lead to the breaking of a new day (Ps. 110).

The Word of God is written from a Hebrew perspective. In Hebraic terms, we have entered a season linked with the *number 70*. This book is being written as we proceed into 2010. In the Hebrew perspective, the year is 5770. (This will be explained in detail as you read.) The number 70 in Hebrew is *ayin*. In Hebrew, *ayin* means "eye." In the season of *ayin,* or "the eye," God will create new vision in you for your life, family, ministry, and land where you are positioned. All seventies are linked with breaking captivity from one season and entering a realm of greater freedom. As you refresh and clear your conscience, you will *see* clearly. Holy Spirit is ready to give us Father's eyes to see the world around us. I will explain other seasons as you proceed in the book.

2. How to see and open your eyes to a greater dimension of the demonic realm

You will see beyond the dark structures that attempt to produce fear in your life. You will move in faith against what you have discerned and view your battles from God's heavenly perspective. You will say, "I now see what was attempting to discourage and stop me from advancing." When you see these foes in a new way, you will not be overwhelmed. Remember, Elijah saw the "word and the demon gods" that Jezebel was aligned with and ran from his position of authority. (See 1 Kings 19:1–3.) His actions postponed the Lord's plan to change the government of Israel. You will learn to *see* and take your stand against what has opposed you from having victory.

3. How to hear the Spirit of God

You will begin to perceive the prophetic revelation you need to break forth. While you are praying, *Yeshua,* who is at the right hand of the Father, will open the way for you to have an audience with the King. He will hear and respond. You will become alert and look again at what He has already said to you in the past seasons. He will refresh you with His voice, and you will gain the revelation you need now to see a manifestation of His grace and promise in your life. You will progress in your spiritual life and process. The Spirit of God is ready to manifest in new ways.

4. How to colabor with angels and ministering spirits

God has released engineering and conducting angels. The Spirit of God wants many things engineered (as in construction) and conducted (as in electricity) in this season. We are entering into a new building season. *To build* means to add "sons and daughters" to what is being built. There is a new apostolic leadership arising to lead the body of Christ into this kingdom season. The apostolic leaders who are being raised up today will be downloading heaven's building plan for His kingdom projects. Invite these angels as messengers to bring God's plans. Angels will be ministering to us with fire in this new season. We will see great demonstrations of power, including unusual miracles.

5. How to receive your new assignment and go forth into new mission fields

God will be sending some of His people into dark structures. Do not fear the darkness. He will give you *night vision* to see a path of righteousness through any unrighteous structure. This will be like moving in the Gulf Stream through normal ocean currents. The Gulf Stream is a warm stream that originates in the Gulf of Mexico, goes through the Florida Straits, and then moves into the colder waters of the Atlantic Ocean. God is parting waters. Dark spirits that have stopped us from advancing in certain areas to bring forth the harvest commission of the Son will now let go of harvest gates. First Corinthians 16:9, which says, "For a great and effective door has opened to me, and there are many adversaries," will become a reality in this season. The Word of God will enter places that have been closed and groups of people who have resisted freedom. Demon forces will part like the Red Sea and will be held back while God's children go into their new assignments.

6. How to see and get into the next move of God

Do not look at just *jumping in the river* in this season, but go to the source—the place where the river is beginning. Go to the high places. Topple old thrones of iniquity, follow the river down, and break all dammed structures. Find the supply sources that have been withheld from you in the last season. God is opening your eyes to see those in need. A new move of God initiated by compassion is being released in the earth. This move will be filled with healing power. Entire neighborhoods, tribes, and cultures will experience a power release. Heaven will and is now invading your atmosphere and is filling your mouth with the Word that will transform cultures, structures, and territories.

7. How to express joy in a new way

There is a shout rising from us that will cause God to meet us with His shout. He will open the fountains of the deep to release the revelation about how we are to enlarge our tents and walk forward in this season. There is a shout deep in your belly where the *springs of living waters* exist. Play skillfully with this shout as it rises and flows from your mouth. (See Psalm 33.) There is a new *drink* (spring) bubbling up within us that will expel bitterness, pain, and sorrow. How do we get joy unblocked and flowing in a new way and gain strength for our future? This is *not* a time to grieve. His joy will be your strength! When the Lord had determined to relieve Saul of his kingly duties, Samuel grieved over the loss of what could have been. Therefore the Lord asked Samuel a question: "How long will you grieve?" Grief moves us from shock to denial through the pain and guilt of the past season. We move up and down the emotional scale from anger to depression to bargaining to reflection to loneliness. We forget that God's plan is for "joy to come in the morning"!

8. How to gain new vision and see your provision

God will open our eyes to things we could not see in the last season so that He can activate the vision within us and finish what He has begun in us. He is Alpha and Omega. Alpha will show you how to begin what needs to be finished. Omega will show you how to walk things to the end. Poverty and infirmity blind our vision. Therefore, you will overcome and disconnect these two demonic spirits' handshakes and enter into new thought processes.

9. How to have a renewed mind and a restored, alive human spirit filled with Holy Spirit

There is a path of freedom. There is a path of deliverance that leads to your destiny. God is making our minds new. The crowns you received in the last season need to be cast at His feet. Those crowns were meant to be given to our Lord and not worn into this season. He is fitting us and giving us new crowns to present to Him. He is putting new turbans on our heads and developing a new mind-set for a new season. Your spirit was meant to soar! We must learn to have a soaring spirit.

10. How to understand the enemy's vexing power

How do you detect a curse working against you? How do you discern a vexing power that is stopping the anointing within you from flowing and breaking you into the prosperity that God has for you? How do you break the powers that have fragmented you and kept you from expressing God's plan of wholeness and His holy character in your life? You will see Babylon arise in a new way. Do not fear. The kingdoms of the world are becoming His. This will happen as we are sent, as Daniel was, to be the greatest influencers in the Babylonian system. Dark watchers exist to co-labor with familiar and familial spirits in our lives. You will see the dark watchers. You will be delivered from familial spirits that are holding iniquitous family patterns in place.

CHAPTER 2

SEE YOUR FUTURE AND GO BEYOND

R EVELATION IS EXPRESSED through human words by voice and
vision. Prophetic revelation expresses the heart and mind of Father
God in heaven. Law was fulfilled and life expressed through Jesus's
example! When we speak heaven's words, we change our atmosphere
and create an event. Change comes. Your message produces change. This
change becomes an overcoming testimony against the enemy's blockades.

The real war in days ahead will come over how we fellowship. True fellowship revolves around revelation. We will have to learn how to operate
in decentralized fellowship. In other words, we won't all be going to church
every Sunday. That form of worship is changing rapidly. However, we will
express a kingdom that the world has never fully grasped. Corporate worship gatherings in certain territories will break through into new levels
of revelation—not extra-biblical revelation (the Bible has been canonized
and is the established Word of God). However, this revelation will give us
insights into how our territory can experience the glory of God. A curse
is defined as "the absence of the glory of God." This revelation will show
us what is warring for God's glory in the regions of the earth.

Governments of the world cannot fully change until the government
of God here on Earth aligns itself and represents the order of God. That
means leaders in the church must get their act together! I see many
denominations or wineskins of the past fading and becoming irrelevant by 2016. There have already been many changes, and these will only
accelerate over the next ten years. We have become aware of God's foundational plan of apostles, prophets, evangelists, pastors, and teachers. We
are learning how to interact with each other. We are letting go of old
methods of operation and embracing new ways of worship.

I believe there is revelation coming that will cause the Word to become even more applicable for this age, while also giving us strategies to defeat the enemy. Many of what are now corporate warfare worship gatherings will turn into times of travail, and the result will be changed nations. As we come together and worship in such settings, we will gain new strategies for how to govern in our spheres of authority.

God's Covenant for Prosperity

To prosper means "to advance or gain in anything good or desirable." To prosper means you have successful progress in any enterprise, business, or undertaking. To prosper means that you obtain your desire. Success from a Hebrew perspective means that there is already *help on your road* so you will accomplish your destined goal.

God's plan from the beginning was for us to prosper. So many people have problems with the concept of prosperity. In the Western world, *prosperity* and *making money* seem to be synonymous. God's prosperity was part of the garden plan! He planted a garden, put man in the garden, and told man to watch and cultivate the garden. His goal was that the glory and prosperity of the garden would increase and cover the whole earth. That is still His plan of fullness. To this day, the only thing that wars with this plan is the serpent or adversary. Jesus came to overthrow the power of the wrong communion that occurred between man, woman, and the serpent in the garden. Jesus's work on the cross was a full work of redemption. Father's sacrifice of His Son defeated the serpent's voice. Jesus's resurrection broke the serpent's headship. However, mankind must enter in to this full victory on a daily basis. We each still have a garden or portion that we have been given to prosper in.

One of the most incredible truths revealed by God to mankind was the covenant that He made to Abraham. Abram, who became Abraham, became His offspring. Many years later, God, through His own Son, *Yeshua*, then offered all mankind the ability to enter this inheritance. Those who would be grafted into the power of this inheritance that was created from God and Abraham's union would have access to all the blessings of the agreement that was made between the two. Through the family of Abraham, God had an incredible plan to bless mankind.

Abraham, the father of Israel (his grandson Jacob's new name), was the firstborn prototype of prosperity. Israel was first denoted in Exodus 4:22 when God said, "Israel is My son, My firstborn." The Lord then brought *all* of Israel out of Egypt by armies. Even in Egypt, the people prospered for a season. Though they fell into slavery, when He brought them out by armies, a great plunder of Egypt came with His covenant people. This plunder would be used to form what was necessary for God's people to worship in the future.

Deuteronomy 8:18 says, "And you shall remember the Lord your God, for it is He who gives you power to get wealth, that He may establish His covenant which He swore to your fathers, as it is this day." That means that Adonai will give you the power to get wealth today, just as He did then. In the New Living Translation we find a little different aspect of this verse: "Remember the Lord your God. He is the one who gives you power *to be successful*, in order to fulfill the covenant he confirmed to your ancestors with an oath" (emphasis added). Success means that on your road God has already made available what you need to accomplish His purpose for your life.

The covenant that God made with Abraham was beyond any that had been seen or formed in the earth realm. This covenant was not limited to the confines of time or space. There are times when God limits the generational flow of blessings and curses for ten generations. However, this was not so with Abraham. Abraham's blessings were open-ended to all who would bless Abraham and his offspring as a nation. In today's world, many want God's blessings, but they do not want to be grafted into the covenant plan of God through Abraham.

God's intent was to bless all nations. However, the only thing that can secure blessings for a nation is for that nation to stay in right relationship to the Abrahamic covenant. Nations and people do not have to be related to Abraham to experience the promise of prosperity. Through the Lord Jesus Christ they can be rightly related and claim Abraham as their father and watch the fullness of their destined blessings unfold (Rom. 4:11–12; Gal. 3:29).

Expect Your Blessings to Manifest

You can succeed! I could use quotes from some of the greatest *success speakers*—Christian and non-Christian—to discuss what it takes to succeed. However, let me remain with God's plan for prosperity and success as biblically recorded. Granted, He does not always give us one formula to become rich, but He does have a plan for each of us to prosper. Many times the Lord uses prophets to speak to others so they gain revelation on how to succeed.

For instance, take Elijah. Once he told a tired widow who was ready to die to feed her last meal to a prophet. This resulted in her withstanding a three-and-a-half-year famine, and she and her son were blessed. Or consider Elisha. He told a wealthy woman to build a room for a prophet, and she was blessed. She longed for a child, and her womb was opened. Her child died later but was resurrected. She hid for seven years during famine, yet all that was taken from her was restored. Elisha also told a general in the enemy's army of Samaria to dip in dirty water seven times, and he was blessed.

Then there was the unknown prophet in 2 Chronicles 20. Jehoshaphat was in the greatest trial of his reign as king. A confederacy of nations was aligning to destroy him and all of Judah. He cried out to the Lord for help. God chose to bring the needed revelation to a prophet, who told him, "If you will take the choir down to the Brook Ziv and get set up and sing, God will overtake the enemy" (author's paraphrase). Jehoshaphat moved by faith. The result? The enemy was defeated, and for three days his people picked up the spoil or supplies for their future needs. The word of the Lord was, "Believe His prophets, and you shall prosper" (2 Chron. 20:20).

Jesus blessed a young boy's lunch, and seven thousand people were blessed. He changed water to wine because they needed wine at a wedding feast. He spoke and the dead were raised. A centurion told Jesus that he would trust whatever Jesus said to heal his servant who was sick back home. I could go on and on with story after story from Bible history. The issue is very simple: *What will He say, and how will you receive His word for your faith to become active and see your blessings manifest?* He knows when someone touches Him by faith. Faith, success, and blessings go hand in hand.

I believe one of the most important concepts that a child of God (or really anyone, as a matter of fact) needs to understand is the *power of blessings*. When you are warring for your inheritance, which is a reality, what you are really contending over is your garden or promised land dominion. Within Abraham's covenant promise was the boundary of the future. This boundary was not just land but everything in the land. The Lord even shared with Abraham a timing sequence. He told him that when the iniquity of the Amorites became "full," His people could go into the boundaries of what was promised and experience a transfer. God has a perfect timing to remove the prosperity of a group who depends upon themselves and the empowerment of their gods. He then transfers their material blessings to His people's stewardship.

LEARN HOW TO *SEE* YOUR BLESSING

We are much more visual as a society in the world today. We now live in a season to *see*. What you should see first are the *blessings* that are there for you in heavenly places. In any season, you want to press toward unlocking and entering into all the blessings that God has ordained for you. God wants to increase your ability to see.

I sense that we are a people who miss much of what we should see. Therefore, I hear the Lord saying, "Look again!" He wants you to see *beyond*—to see in ways you have not seen! I will explain this in the next chapter, "Break Into His Cycles of Blessings."

An important dimension of one's life is to see *eye to eye* with the person you are communicating with, whether in business, ministry, family, or any relationship. Most importantly, you want to see eye to eye and face-to-face with the One who created you, who knows you best, and who knows your future. *God wants to give you clear vision!* This is an important time to see your vision clearly. Proverbs 29:18 warns us that "where there is no vision, the people perish" (KJV). Lack of vision will destroy your motivation. Without vision you fall into passivity and discouragement. Having a clear vision keeps you moving forward toward your goal. So ask God to restore and refresh your vision for your future.

You have an enemy who does not want you to see! Because of this, you must see how the adversary is opposing you. Therefore see the strategies Satan would use to hold you in bondage this year. In the chapters that follow, we will learn how to see word curses and casualty covenants. We will also see how to break curses and escape from old cycles. We will also see how the enemy wants to hold you in a wilderness season. Therefore we will learn to break out of captivity and make our way through the wilderness, gathering all the blessings that the wilderness holds for us.

How Do You *See* the Blessing God Has Prepared for You on Your Path?

One of the most important things any Christian can know is that God *has* blessings prepared for you. Many Christians are confused about God's blessing. Some are not sure God wants to bless them. Some are not sure what God's blessing is. I've heard Christians say silly things like, "God blessed me with infirmity and poverty to make me holy!" Some Christians actually call infirmity and poverty *blessings*, but that's not what God calls them. Yes, all things work together for our good when we love God and are devoted to His purpose. However, we must learn to gather God's blessings when we are in testing times by learning to overcome what attempts to rob us of them or shorten our time to experience blessings. In the Bible, when God talks about infirmity and poverty, He calls them curses. Infirmity and poverty are not blessings given by God to make you holy. You can cause these to work for your good and produce blessings for you. Most of the holy men and women of the Bible were both healthy and prosperous. The result of the church's confusion about blessing is that many Christians live under a curse when God wants them to walk in His blessing.

Blessing is a word we often use without understanding what it means. I looked it up in several Bible dictionaries and couldn't find one good definition, so I asked Dr. Robert Heidler, the scholar I work with, to give me his definition. This is what he said: "*Blessing* is the increase of that which is good, beneficial, and pleasant in life. On the other hand, the *curse* is the increase of that which is bad, harmful, and unpleasant in life." I believe a good way to define *a curse* is "anything that is lacking or that is absent of the presence of God."

The good news is that God *wants us* to live in His blessing. From the beginning of His plan of redemption, the heart of redemption has been the restoration of His full blessing. I want to suggest that you read *Redeeming the Time*, an incredible book on how time has been bought back on our behalf.

Blessing has always been God's desire. Back in the Garden of Eden, His perfect plan for Adam and Eve was only blessing. They experienced no part of the curse until one day they listened and participated in a plan to have something they desired that was not in God's best plan for their lives. This caused them to miss the mark that God had established for their communion. When we deviate from God's plan, this is called *sin*. Sin separated them from the source of all blessing. God's *goal* for us is to experience His blessing forever. In heaven there will be fullness of blessing. There is a place where there will be "no more sickness, crying, or pain." (See Revelation 21:4.)

Here on Earth there is sickness, poverty, sorrow, and pain. Jesus wants us to intercede that God's will be done on Earth as it is in heaven. The process of redemption is to bring us out from under the curse and into the experience of His blessing right here on Earth. God's original *plan* for us was blessing, and His ultimate *goal* for us in heaven is blessing. Therefore, Jesus taught His disciples to press in and ask for the will of God, which is blessing in heaven, to be brought into the earth. This means that we can know the same blessings here on Earth that will be in heaven.

How Do We Walk by Faith?

In the next chapter we will talk about the "shout of the Lord" that dwells in you. This is a shout that defies the enemy and creates an expectation of manifested faith. We must expect blessings to come to us by our activating our faith. By faith, thank God that Jesus took upon Himself all of the curse you deserved. By faith, declare God's blessing is now your portion! Because of what Jesus did on the cross, your portion now includes healing, provision, and peace. By faith, reject discouragement and fear. Ask God for His strategy to overcome. Satan still wants to inflict the curse. (He comes to steal, kill, and destroy; that's what he does.) To enter God's blessing, we need to learn how to stand against enemy. There is a battle but *expect* to win! By faith, set your eyes on the goal, see your path clearly, and move forward.

God wants us to *see* the blessing He has prepared on your path. That's one of the ministries of the Holy Spirit. I do not want to end up teaching on the tabernacle of Moses. However, we find this is a shadow and type of what we are to look forward to as God's glory manifests in our lives. Let me just give a brief overview.

There's an interesting lesson we can learn from Moses's tabernacle. If you study the tabernacle, you discover that in the holy place there's a seven-branched lamp stand called the *menorah*. The Bible tells us that the menorah was a symbol of the *Holy Spirit*. In the holy place we find the *table of showbread*. The table of showbread symbolizes God's provision for His people. Every week, twelve loaves of bread were set out on the table—one loaf for each tribe. *This was a recognition of God's gracious provision!* The menorah was the only means of illumination in the holy place. God's *provision* could only be seen in the light of the menorah, the Spirit of God. Without the ministry of the Holy Spirit, you cannot *see* the provision God has prepared for you to enjoy.

The Holy Spirit gives you light to see your provision. Legalism and religion will always leave you in poverty, but the Holy Spirit will enlighten your eyes to *see* the path to your blessing. The Holy Spirit gives faith and vision. He releases creativity and direction. He reveals the path to move forward and receive the full blessing God has for you. So if we want to experience God's blessing, we need to draw close to the Spirit. Receive His revelation and follow it.

In the last chapter we talked about blessings. *We must expect blessings!* Psalm 62:5 (AMP) says, "My soul, wait only upon God and silently submit to Him; for my hope and expectation are from Him." We need to *expect God*!

The key to our life is to see the blessings that a holy God ordained for us before the foundation of the earth. He formed you in your mother's womb. He ordained blessings for you. He longs for you to submit your life to Him, come into a relationship with Him, and see into a realm beyond your natural daily surroundings. He longs for you to become a supernatural child of God, be grafted into His cycle of blessings, commune with Him on a daily basis, and walk in freedom and joy. His desire is for your spirit man to be free.

You Have an Inheritance

Inheritance means that you have a portion. God has given each of us an incredible inheritance. It's an inheritance of covenant blessing that He prepared for all who know Him. God spent two thousand years, from Abraham to Jesus, giving the Jews a revelation of Himself and preparing a people who would understand how to walk in His blessing. That's an inheritance God intended His church to share also.

Our God is a God of order and wisdom. In His covenant plan, He promised Abraham land, children, and prosperity. He determined the boundaries of the land He promised. He planned the timing for Abraham's inheritance to be transferred and occupied by His children. Eventually He changed the name of Abraham's grandson from *Jacob* to

Israel, the name of the land of promise. He identified Himself as the God of Israel. His heart and rulership were relegated to a people and a place. Jacob had sons, who became twelve tribes, who were each a part of the whole land of Israel. Each son had a redemptive destiny. When this redemptive destiny arises in the generations to come, the land and people will express God's original intent to the whole earth. Nations and people who bless this people and land, called *Israel*, will be blessed. Through the sacrifice of Yeshua, our Messiah, we have been grafted into this promise and can be blessed with all the covenant blessings of the original promise to Abraham.

If Your Place Is God's Place, You Live in Blessings

There are times when the place that was ordained for your *best* is not the place you are dwelling. Though the people were ordained for Canaan, because of drought and covenant necessity they were destined to dwell in Egypt for four hundred years. The land of Canaan remained intact, overrun by enemy hosts, but waiting for occupation. The identity of God's people was *submerged* during the exile time in Egypt.

Joseph, one of the twelve brothers of Jacob, through circumstantial distress and family betrayal, had preceded the whole clan to Egypt. He was favored, prospering, and serving to secure Egypt during a time of regional famine. God had used very difficult situations to get him positioned for the covenant sake of His kingdom purpose. Jehovah had paved the way for the entire family to have a *good* place during a trying time. However, Joseph said, "So it shall be, when Pharaoh calls you and says, 'What is your occupation?' that you shall say, 'Your servants' occupation has been with livestock from our youth even till now, both we and also our fathers,' that you may dwell in the land of Goshen; for every shepherd is an abomination to the Egyptians" (Gen. 46:33–34).

Though they were shepherds, and sheep were part of their lives, they were to keep this portion of their identity disclosed. Many times we are not allowed to be who we really are. Joseph was concerned that if Pharaoh saw how strong his brothers really were, he would reject them from the land. This people were a prosperous people and had been blessed by God to multiply. And multiply they did.

One way that our spirit man gets vexed is when we do not fully disclose who we are. This may be prudent in the beginning of a relationship, but the soul and the heart cry out for freedom to *be*. We will discuss this fully in later chapters.

Many of our promises remain intact while we are diverted in other phases of our lives. But there comes a time when the place we are in, which is not the place we have been allotted, does not satisfy the desires of our heart. I believe this happens because a Holy God knitted within us His desire. There comes a time when the place we presently live in can become unkind to us if it is not God's perfect, original intent for our life. How we express our identity is limited when we are in a place that is not God's best. *A submerged identity longs to be released from captivity.*

Our freedom is expressed fully when we are in the right place at the right time. If your identity has been layered with expectation and demands that are contrary to God's purpose, you cry. You cry loudly! A cry rises from the depths of your being and says, "I know I have a *future* and an *expected end*. Lord, hear me and open up a way for me to find the best You have for me!" He hears your cry and develops a way for you to escape and overcome.

When God brought this people out of slavery in Egypt to move toward the Promised Land, He brought them out by armies. Each tribe was a warring army with a redemptive gift. Without each tribe warring for their portion, the full plan of God for the land could not be fully manifested in the earth. "The earth is the LORD's, and the fullness thereof" (Ps. 24:1, KJV). The earth groans for freedom and expresses the fullness of God when the people are free in God.

When God is ready for us to move, we must move with Him. While in the wilderness, the children of Israel moved toward their promise as they heard the trumpet sounding. The ark of His covenant, or His presence, was central and shifted them toward their destiny. There was an order in their movement. Three of the twelve tribes moved together. *Judah,* the apostolic, warring leadership tribe who understood sound, moved first. Then came *Issachar*, the Torah tribe, who would bear the burden for victory and wages. This tribe understood time and could interpret the *Word of God* in time. They were connected to *Zebulun*, the wealth tribe, because provision for the journey and the supply for victory were important. There is an order, a place, a time, and a sound that get us positioned for our future. To move into freedom, we must be aligned properly.

Jesus, Yeshua, our Messiah, was out of the tribe of Judah. His obedience of submission brought about the fullness of Father's plan to redeem man. He became the Passover lamb to bring all of mankind out of slavery and death. When the people of Israel rejected Him as their Savior, He turned His heart toward the Gentiles. He grafted us into this glorious covenant that God made with Abraham. His plan, the new covenant, allowed the redemptive quality of each tribe to come alive in us. This will allow us to see His plan for Israel fulfilled and His glory cover the whole earth. Through the Gentiles receiving grace and power to become sons of God, Israel is now becoming jealous and turning toward its Messiah. There will be no wall between Jew and Gentile in the future—they will be One. All nations in the earth can now become His inheritance. The time has come to harvest the nations and develop one new man, Jew and Gentile.

THE TIME IS NOW TO SEE YOUR TODAY AS YOUR *TOMORROW*

We need to be filled with the expectation of God moving in our lives. I woke up one morning recently, and the Lord said, "See your today as your tomorrow." I was awakened by the Lord to these words: "My people are weary. I will give them new strength to enter the next place that I have for them. How they move by faith today is how they will walk into victory tomorrow!"

There comes a time for each of us to enter our new day and new way. There came a point in the history of Israel when Moses had died, and Joshua was crossing the people over into the promise that had been waiting on them. There came a moment when Joshua told the people that their today would create God's best tomorrow: "And Joshua said to the people, Sanctify yourselves [that is, separate yourselves for a special holy purpose], for tomorrow the Lord will do wonders among you. Joshua said to the priests, Take up the ark of the covenant and pass over before the people. And they took it up and went on before the people" (Josh. 3:5–6, AMP).

Here are five key points to understand:

1. There is a time in your life when you are being directed to a pathway you have never gone down before.

2. There is a moment of *crossing over* into your covenant identity.

3. If you sanctify yourself today, then you are assured to enter into victory tomorrow.

4. You must watch the presence of God closely. As His presence moves, you move.

5. God has put the right leaders in place to help you enter into what you have been waiting and watching for in your life. Know those leaders.

I feel that there is a portion of our promise that remains. We have grown weary obtaining one portion, but there is a greater portion that remains. We need new strength for this new portion. Stop now and ask yourself, What remains for me to enter into and occupy?

Today Is the Day for a New Faith Action in Your Life

Mix faith with the Word you are trusting to be performed. If you mix in faith today, you will see a manifestation tomorrow. Allow the Lord to bring your *hope* back into time! Here is an encouraging word for you. The Lord says:

> Hope deferred makes the heart grow weary. Today is the day that I have come to break weariness from you—out of your bones. I have come to cleanse your atmosphere of despair. If you will arise and shake off the weariness, I will restore the hope in your heart that has been captured. You've slept, and you've lain in your bed long enough. Arise from the depression that has held you prostrate. The spring coils of your bed will no longer allow you to rest. Your comfortable padding and *rest place* will rise up and throw you forward into a new place.
>
> Today is the day that I AM sweeping across your nation to break the agreement of weariness and slumber that is holding the land captive. I must restore celebration and praise in My people before the land can rejoice again. Rise and pick up your mat! Your healing will be in the next moment and next place or room that you move into. Come up off your sick bed and move into the living room that I have prepared for you. Breathe and begin to live again.
>
> *Watch for Me.* Turn and look full circle around you. There's a way out of this hard place that is threatening to captivate you. There's a way out to keep you from getting your head knocked off. If you'll just get flat and bend down a little lower, then you can get through this hard place. You still have your head up too high. Get down a little lower and you'll make it out. If I can bring a camel through the eye of the needle, I can get you through this hard place. Bend down, then *rise up* and shine again.
>
> There are places that I need to meet with you. I know your comings and goings and your times of intersections. I know your routines and your stopping places. I know when you will be at certain places to do certain things. I am nearer to you than you know. I have an unexpected rendezvous planned for you. In days ahead I will meet you at a place, unexpectedly. *Watch for Me!* I will manifest unexpectedly in your routine places. When I do, I will reveal something to you that you didn't think I knew. Get ready, for new revelation is coming to you of who you are and who I AM. You have been thirsty, and I have ways to give you drink to quench your

longings. I have water you know not of. I will reveal Myself to you. From this revelation, you will not be able to hold your mouth shut of the wondrous things I will perform on your behalf. You will become My spokesperson and tell many how I met you unexpectedly and performed a wonder for you.

Always remember that on a daily basis God is watching our faith response to Him. His eye is upon you. Here are some key points to remember:

1. The Word spoken *today* will manifest tomorrow (Exod. 8:10).

2. The test you are experiencing *today* will become a testimony tomorrow (Ps. 66).

3. If you refuse to submit and humble yourself *today*, then you will be brought lower tomorrow (Exod. 9–10).

4. If you ready yourself *today*, then you can move forward tomorrow (Exod. 19:15).

5. If you deal with your fear *today*, then He will overtake your enemies tomorrow (Josh. 11:6).

6. If you will seek God *today* through fasting and worship, then He will send you forth to overcome your blockades tomorrow (Judg. 20).

7. When you disobey *today*, you risk losing your all tomorrow (1 Sam. 28:18).

8. If you lose your stand *today*, you will run tomorrow (1 Kings 19:2–3).

9. Hear the word of the prophet *today* and gain your strategy for victory! God will battle tomorrow, and you will prosper (2 Chron. 20).

10. Gain favor with the King *today*, and the enemy will be yours tomorrow (Esther 5).

11. When you have an opportunity *today*, GIVE (Prov. 3:28)!

12. Don't worry *today*; He knows your tomorrow (Matt. 6:30; James 4:13–14).

OUR FAITH TODAY CAN GIVE US VISION FOR TOMORROW

The concept of time—past, present, and future—and place is very important. One of my favorite scriptures is Acts 17:24–28:

> God, who made the world and everything in it, since He is Lord of heaven and earth, does not dwell in temples made with hands. Nor is He worshiped with men's hands, as though He needed anything, since He gives to all life, breath, and all things. And He has made from one blood every nation of men to dwell on all the face of the earth, and has determined their preappointed times and the boundaries of their dwellings, so that they should seek the Lord, in the hope that they might grope for Him and find Him, though He is not far from each one of us; for in Him we live and move and have our being, as also some of your own poets have said, "For we are also His offspring."

When we are in the *right* place at the *right* time, God extends our horizon line so we can see into our future. Many Christians forget that God ordained us to see the future and communicate what we see so many may know how to find their way in a changing world. God does not do anything without first telling His prophets. Your *today* is your tomorrow! Faith foresees.

Now faith is the assurance (the confirmation, [a]the title deed) of the things [we] hope for, being the proof of things [we] do not see and the conviction of their reality [faith perceiving as real fact what is not revealed to the senses]. For by [faith—trust and holy fervor born of faith] the men of old had divine testimony borne to them and obtained a good report. By faith we understand that the worlds [during the successive ages] were framed (fashioned, put in order, and equipped for their intended purpose) by the word of God, so that what we see was not made out of things which are visible.

—HEBREWS 11:1–3, AMP

When you allow the Lord to extend your horizon line beyond today, tomorrow becomes a faith dimension that will become a reality. We have a great portion *that can be obtained by faith.*

By faith, we can see the world the way God meant it to be. We can see our future as we walk in the present. We can allow the Lord to bring our past into our present, reconcile our mistakes, and remove the hindrances that have vexed our spirit man. We then gain strength that keeps us moving into the future.

So how does time and place work on our behalf to cause our reactions, mistakes, lost hopes, misplaced desires, missed opportunities, and overall colossal messes to be redeemed, or *bought back*? That was the question we answered in *Redeeming the Time. To redeem* means "to buy back or to be released from prison." We have been in a buying-back season. As we progress into our future, we must receive the prize for our battles. We talked about how we leave our past season, reconcile our losses, and move into the future. Let me remind you that you can form a relationship with a Redeemer who can redeem your days, help you overcome bad situations, and open up your new day ahead. Remember: the sun will come out tomorrow, a new day will break, and you will see a new horizon line that has formed on your behalf.

As you read this book, I want you to learn to see into the future. This is an ability that the Spirit of God gives each of us so our vision remains sure.

Interpret Your Times

I also wrote a book titled *Interpreting the Times* (Charisma House, 2008). God wants us to understand and interpret our times so we can prosper in every season and have wisdom to advance. God is *beyond* time, but because of His love for us, He reaches down and intervenes *in* time. A big part of walking in God's blessing involves seeing time from God's perspective and recognizing how His cycles operate.

The pagan world saw time as endlessly repeated cycles leading nowhere. The church has focused on time being linear, with a clear beginning and end. But in reality, both are part of God's plan. Our lives operate in cycles. God is moving history to a clear destination, but in the process, He uses cycles to move us forward and draw us closer to Him. When you learn how time operates, how you fit into time, and how God works through time, you can move forward and fulfill your destiny in the earth!

God's has the best for our life cycle. The enemy wants to interrupt our life cycle and interject sin that becomes an iniquity that shifts us out of God's best. Iniquity can form a cycle that twists our life's purposes. This is how our spirits become vexed. I will explain this more fully in chapters to come. I will explain how you can build a *sanctuary of time filled with God's presence.* From this sanctuary you can understand the process of time that is directing your life. To stay in God's processes you must keep in line with the appointed times of God for your life.

CHAPTER 3

BREAK INTO HIS CYCLES OF BLESSINGS

U NDERSTANDING THE TIMES and seasons is key to walking in victory. To be an Issachar prophet means that you live in tune with
God and know how to flow with His covenant plan. When the power
of grace enters into time, many situations are rearranged. There is not
an understanding of the full concept of judgment in the body of Christ.
When God is ending one season and beginning another or taking us
through transition, He has to end or bring to death some old situations.

As I said earlier, to experience the fullness of God's covenant blessings we must understand His covenant with man through His Son. By
yielding our human spirit to the Spirit of our Messiah, we are grafted
into a land, and a people, called Israel.

Unfortunately, because of the root of anti-Semitism, the church
rejected much of that blessing. I will explain this further. The good news
is, God is restoring what we lost. We learn how to restore the blessing
of our lost biblical inheritance when we embrace the Jewish roots of our
Christian faith. God is not calling Christians to try to be Jews, but He
does want us to receive the blessings He gave *through* the Jews. That's
true Christianity, the kind of Christianity the apostles knew. We have
been grafted into this glorious covenant and have access to all the promises and blessings of the covenant.

When you embrace the Jewish roots of our Christian faith, your lost
biblical inheritance can be restored and your *lost* future can be seen.

BE LIKE THE TRIBE OF ISSACHAR

In *Interpreting the Times*, I wrote about the tribe called Issachar. Issachar
was the ninth son of Jacob and the fifth son of Leah. In the wilderness,

the tribe of Issachar was positioned strategically with *Judah* and *Zebulun* (Num. 2:5; 10:14–15). *Zebulun*, the tenth son of Jacob and the sixth and last of Leah, meant, "dwelling, habitation." *Zebulun* was the tribe of war, ships, and trade. *Judah* was the fourth son of Jacob and Leah. His name meant "may He [God] be praised." Judah prophetically was always *destined to go first* as the war tribe that would conquer.

The Issachar tribe had several distinct characteristics in its DNA. You can see now why the scripture from 1 Chronicles 12:32 (AMP) had such significance at the time: "And of Issachar, men who had understanding of the times to know what Israel ought to do, 200 chiefs; and all their kinsmen were under their command." The tribes were in a tremendous conflict and transition. The government was changing. They were moving from the government of the house of Saul to the government of the house of David. David was of Judah. Issachar could give great insight on how to make this shift.

In the last chapter, we discussed blessings and prosperity. By knowing the times, you can enter into prosperity.

> Now Reuben went at the time of wheat harvest and found some mandrakes (love apples) in the field and brought them to his mother Leah. Then Rachel said to Leah, Give me, I pray you, some of your son's mandrakes. But [Leah] answered, Is it not enough that you have taken my husband without your taking away my son's mandrakes also? And Rachel said, Jacob shall sleep with you tonight [in exchange] for your son's mandrakes. And Jacob came out of the field in the evening, and Leah went out to meet him and said, You must sleep with me [tonight], for I have certainly paid your hire with my son's mandrakes. So he slept with her that night. And God heeded Leah's [prayer], and she conceived and bore Jacob [her] fifth son. Leah said, God has given me my hire, because I have given my maid to my husband; and she called his name Issachar [hired].
>
> —GENESIS 30:14–18, AMP

The people of the tribe of Issachar would become servants to many, work for wages, and live a comfortable life. By understanding times, you will prosper and see your blessings!

God's Appointed Times

Most Christians don't know that God has His own calendar, although God's timetable is clearly revealed in the Bible. This calendar was followed by the Jews in the Old Testament, by Jesus, by the apostles in the New Testament, and by the early church for hundreds of years. During the Dark Ages, the church turned from God's calendar and adapted the pagan Roman calendar. As a result, we lost many of the blessings of heaven that God wanted to pour upon us in time. The *good news* is, *God is restoring His appointed times*!

The appointed times of God are not some legalistic burden. As a believer in Jesus, you are free to celebrate them or not. (Don't get legalistic!) But when we *choose* to align our lives with the appointed times of God, we enter His cycle of blessing. His times are built around the harvest feasts. Once we understand these times, we go from increase to increase.

I Saw an *Hourglass*

Recently I was in a conference when the Spirit of God gave me a vision. I saw an *hourglass*. I began to shout, "He's making each of us into an hourglass! We're becoming His hourglass. You are becoming an hourglass. God is making His people an hourglass." The Lord began to impress me with the following:

> There are many narrow places that I AM sending you to and some narrow ways that I'm calling you through. You're going to be cinched up till I can pull you through My eye, through the pupil of My eye to the other side. Many have been confused when they have seen My body in the past, but now they will look at you and tell the time they are living in. For you will reflect My time and My way.

Those in the world will say, "By them I am determining my day." People will say, "What time is it?" But you will say, "Look at me and you will see!"

We are becoming God's hourglass, God's timetable in the earth! When people look at us, they will see what time it is in eternity. The Lord is setting His watch, synchronizing the timetables of the earth. He is setting His clock. He is setting His watch. He's turning us like we would turn an hourglass. The past, the present, and the future are all aligning. We, the body of Christ, are stepping in His time. He is squeezing our regrets from us. The past is leaving us, and we are becoming free at last. I hear Him encouraging us by saying:

I am straining every nerve in you to pull out a praise sound that I've not heard. My people have praise in their fibers, and the enemy has captured their garment of triumph that I released from heaven. Watch Me strain your nerve structure to produce a new garment of praise. You might say, "I don't know if this praise fits me, for I've been used to expressing myself another way." Watch Me cinch you into this new way of expression. Before long you'll say, "My, I've been transformed, and now I look different." I'm cinching you— girding your waist so Truth and Spirit become one. I'm pressing every last valuable drop out of you. You think that you're empty, but you're not quite empty yet. There's more in you to be poured out. You're going to have to dig deep. It's almost like putting on a compression garment that is so tight that it moves everything up higher.

LIFT UP YOUR EYES AND *LOOK BEYOND*

This is a time to go beyond or take the matter at hand in our lives to a deeper measure of understanding. The only way we can do this is to *see* from God's perspective. I love the Book of Isaiah. One Scripture portion that is so important to understand is from Isaiah 55:1–3, 8–12 (AMP):

Wait and listen, everyone who is thirsty! Come to the waters; and he who has no money, come, buy and eat! Yes, come, buy [priceless, spiritual] wine and milk without money and without price [simply for the self-surrender that accepts the blessing]. Why do you spend your money for that which is not bread, and your earnings for what does not satisfy? Hearken diligently to Me, and eat what is good, and let your soul delight itself in fatness [the profuseness of spiritual joy]. Incline your ear [submit and consent to the divine will] and come to Me; hear, and your soul will revive; and I will make an everlasting covenant or league with you, even the sure mercy (kindness, good-will, and compassion) promised to David....For My thoughts are not your thoughts, neither are your ways My ways, says the Lord. For as the heavens are higher than the earth, so are My ways higher than your ways and My thoughts than your thoughts. For as the rain and snow come down from the heavens, and return not there again, but water the earth and make it bring forth and sprout, that it may give seed to the sower and bread to the eater, so shall My word be that goes forth out of My mouth: it shall not return to Me void [without producing any effect, useless], but it shall accomplish that which I please and purpose, and it shall prosper in the thing for which I sent it. For you shall go out [from the spiritual exile caused by sin and evil into the homeland] with joy and be led forth [by your Leader, the Lord Himself, and His word] with peace; the mountains and the hills shall break forth before you into singing, and all the trees of the field shall clap their hands.

This is about *seeing beyond*. The prophets tells us that the Lord's ways are not our ways, and if we will see beyond our circumstances and go beyond our present thought patterns, we will begin to have vision of what He is doing in our lives. His way of doing things is so far beyond ours. His light is more powerful than any darkness around us. His truth is so much stronger than any spirit of error that could attempt to lead us astray. Holy Spirit is greater than the spirit of the evil one, who attempts to deviate us from God's best. The Lord's blood and Spirit work together in our living bodies to keep us having His perspective as we encounter the trials of earth.

Lift up your eyes and look beyond! We're going into a place called *beyond*. Take a deep breath; we're going to a place called *beyond*. You've not been there before. Since you've not been there before, you're going to have to be willing to move in new ways, dance in new ways, hear in new ways, see in new ways, feel in new ways, touch in new ways, and taste in new ways. You're going beyond! I once taught on going to the place called *there*. That's not this place. Rather, there is a place called *beyond*.

My brother, Keith, who never misses church, called one Sunday and said, "I'm going to stay home today because of sickness."

I said, "Great. You will go beyond where you normally go (on the first row), and you'll enter into what we enter into in your home." It is vital that we each understand how God is orchestrating our paths to the place called *beyond*.

Let's go to Isaiah, starting at chapter 50. There comes a time when God comforts you over your past. He tells you to look back at it for a while. Don't go there, but do look back at it. Then He says, "Look ahead into where I'm taking you. My Word is very near to your mouth. I'm going to put My words in your mouth because I am changing the heavens (Isa. 51). I'm changing the heavens, and you're going to replant them."

You must think differently. You are a spiritual being. You are already beyond *here* if you have yielded your spirit man to the Lord Jesus Christ. Our problem is that we can see *here*, but we don't see *beyond*. Then, Isaiah 52 says, "Awake, awake, put on, put on this new thing that I'm going to have you wear into the beyond" (author's paraphrase). You have to remember this is all in the context of Isaiah 43, which says, "I'm doing a new thing. Can you see it?" (author's paraphrase). The prophet then takes them through an incredible process of getting the people to the point that they can begin to see. The prophet had been prophesying, "You're going to be in captivity seventy years, but then I'll do a new thing. Will you be able to see it after seventy years? Or will you get so used to Babylon that you can't see My new thing?" That's the danger in America right now. We're so used to Babylon, with its system of religion and materialism. The two cohabit to blind God's people. That's how Antichrist will take over the pulpit, and we might even receive it. That's the imminent danger if we don't go beyond.

Here is an exegesis of several passages in Isaiah. In the midst of their situation, the Lord gets them to a place and says, "Listen; quit worrying about your warfare, because no weapon formed against you is going to prosper. So sing through your last barrenness." He says, "Sing through your last barrenness and sing yourself into a new tent (Isa. 54), and once you get there, no weapon can prosper against you." This is why the Word has to be built into us so strongly. We receive incredible revelation in this ministry of the Glory of Zion because He's taking us beyond our thought processes of where we've been, bringing us into a new place of submission—like Hagar in Genesis 21. He says, "I can visit you even in your running. I can turn you around as a nation and move you forward." He's taking us beyond!

Isaiah 55 says this: "Seek the LORD while He may be found" (v. 6). He says, "What I'm going to do for you now is to invite you into a place of abundance that you've never stepped into before. You've had plenty in the wilderness. You've had plenty in Babylon, but now I'm going to invite you into a place of abundance, a place beyond where you've been."

This is where we're headed in the next ten years. You have to make this choice along your path: *Do I stay, or do I go?* Will I go through the tent to get to the abundance or stay where I am? God has a journey for you to go into your abundance. If you're unwilling to go on that journey, you won't enter into seeing beyond. It doesn't mean you won't receive in measure, but you won't see beyond.

"Seek Me while I may be found; call on Me while I'm near, because I'm going to have the wicked forsake their way." Do you realize what God is saying in Isaiah 55:7? "I'll have the wicked and unrighteous man give up his way and his thoughts, and he will return to the Lord."

And the Lord is telling His people, "You have to enter the place called *beyond* and *abundance*, because I'm going to have the wicked give up the way they're thinking, and they are going to start coming after Me, *and you already need to be there.*"

He goes on to say, "This is the part you're not getting about Me. My thoughts are not your thoughts (v. 8). My ways are not your ways. For as the heavens are higher than the earth, My ways are higher than your ways." You are struggling through the way as best you can. But hear me—the Lord is saying this to you: "You're struggling through your way the best you can, but My way is not your way, and My way of thinking isn't the same way you're thinking. Seek Me while I can be found, because I'm going to start meeting with the wicked; I'm even going to start meeting with the unrighteous and sinners. They're going to come seeking Me, and I want you to already know what I'm doing."

The earth is the Lord's and the fullness thereof, but the heavens are higher than the earth. Therefore, when you walk out into the heavens, remember what the Lord has said: "My ways are different than your ways. You can build this sanctuary building, but you can't create the atmosphere that I can create." You must understand that God can fill every structure with His glory, and also know that Satan will try to gain access to every structure. It doesn't matter what structure it is. It doesn't matter if it's your home or what we call the *sanctuary*—the enemy tries to gain access to every structure.

Then the Lord says: "For as the rain comes down, and the snow from heaven, and do not return there, but water the earth, and make it bring forth and bud, that it may give seed to the sower and bread to the eater…" (v. 10). He could also say it this way: "Once I open that treasury of heaven and pour it out, I don't take it back. How you steward the water of the rain and snow and the treasury that I pour out is your choice, in every generation. When I open the treasury, I give it. I give it. I give it. I have already poured the seed; you already have the seed for your future." It is the same principle with His Son. Once He gave Him, He didn't take back the work His Son completed. Once He gives, He doesn't take back. He gives until the end of what He gave has its work, and its work is completed.

You already have the seed. It's already there. Once He opens the heavens, He pours it on you, and you have it. But then He says this: "So shall My word be that goes forth from My mouth; It shall not return to Me void, but it shall accomplish what I please, and it shall prosper in the thing for which I sent it" (v. 11). He is saying, "Once I send it, I'm taking you beyond. Once I open it up over you, I'm going to take you beyond what you have seen manifest. Once My Word is spoken, even if it was spoken forty years ago, or just because you didn't see it, it doesn't mean that now you can't go beyond into it. Once you went into captivity, seventy years prior, but that doesn't mean you can't go beyond captivity. If your bloodline got captured, it doesn't mean you can't go beyond. Once My Word is loosed, once My heavens give you a seed, that seed can go beyond. It can come in one form and manifest in another form."

Go beyond! Move into the new season seeing! In other words, "I'm sending My Word beyond. My Word is going to manifest beyond what you have seen in the past."

Chapter 4

DOORWAYS TO GOING BEYOND

Here are fifteen issues related to "going beyond."

1. Go beyond and into the next level of prophetic destiny (John 1).

I believe God is assembling a group who is saying, "We want that place called *beyond*!" Look at the prophet John. No one has been greater in the earth than this man who prophesied and said, "I am the voice of one crying in the wilderness: make straight the way of the Lord." Do you know what he was saying? He was going all the way back to Isaiah 40, hundreds of years earlier, and was quoting what had been prophesied. That's how God works in our midst. All of a sudden He will have something spoken into your life that has already been said concerning you, maybe even by Great-Grandpa, that you didn't even know was said. It was locked up and stored in the heavens. Then all of a sudden, like the rain and snow, He unlocks it and pours it down. Some of you think it's all about you connecting right now, when it's really about you receiving.

John said, "I baptize with water, but there stands One among you whom you do not know. It is He who, coming after me, is preferred before me, whose sandal strap I am not worthy to loose" (John 1:26–27). "He will baptize you with the Holy Spirit and fire" (Luke 3:16). In other words, you're receiving a baptism now, but there's one beyond where you presently are.

Here's the problem of getting that new baptism: you are going to have to recognize the Word that is dropping in your path, because that's what the Bible says is lighting your path. Some of you might not have had one prophetic word given over you until God quickened one to you from this book. When you receive a prophecy, that word begins to light your path, even if you were in total darkness before now. That's how the Spirit of God works.

The Spirit of God recently told me this: "You have to come and have a heart to get to know My Son. You have to know Him, because in knowing Him you'll see what I'm like and see what you're like. I sent Him and created you in My image, and by seeing Him and getting to know Him, you can begin to understand Me. But there's more to it than that. You can get to know who My Son was and can even study the Word like the Pharisees did and still not yield your heart to Him."

Jesus said to the Pharisees, "You search the Scriptures backward and forward, but you never come to know My Spirit." The Son, who is seated in the heavenly places, who has given His Spirit, says, "You must also know My Spirit and what My Spirit is capable of doing in you, or your spirit will never form properly. If it does not form properly, it will never come into the strength I've ordained for it. It will not be able to strengthen your soul, and you will be unable to ascend in new ways to accomplish My will."

John was saying, "I'm baptizing you one way, but you're going to have to have another one. You have to go beyond this baptism!"

2. Go beyond your last relational alignment and follow into the new (John 1).

If I chose to say, "This year we're going to just teach the fundamentals," you would not want to align with me. This is not what God is saying over these next ten years. You would be foolish to align with me if I did not press into the new. But I say this: In this season we are going to see! It's a season of seeing, and the only way we'll get there is to go beyond where we presently are. You might say, "I knew Him in the last season, in the season called *Samekh*, but now I'm going to relate to Him in the season called *Ayin*." That's when you have to make decisions over your relationships. That's what causes wineskins to change. Another wineskin might have presented the *Samekh* season better than Robert Heidler and I have, but it's no longer that season. If you choose to get in that wineskin, it will have life for about three and a half years, but it won't have the life that will take you through the next ten years. This is what Philip and Andrew told John: "You've been prophesying that this Man can take us beyond, and we're going to go with Him." They did, but John didn't.

Philip and Andrew honored John for going as far as he did, but they shifted that relationship and started forming a new relationship with Jesus for the next season. And the Lord said to them, "Come and see. Just follow along with Me, because you don't have it yet, and I haven't shown it yet. Therefore, all we can really do is to start where we are now, and go beyond. If you two want to go with Me, we can go beyond—together."

3. Go beyond your last understanding of healing (John 9:7).

The disciples had gotten to a place where Jesus was teaching them, moving with them, and they began moving into a place of freedom. When I was getting before the Lord over these scriptures, I had this thought: We want the next drink of wine, but not last season's wine. I'm talking about revelation here. We want to enter into a new level of revelation, but we get to a place where we start having problems, because some of us are *Word* people. We have lots of Word in us. We know the Word of God. We know the statues of the Lord. We've studied it back and forth, and some of us can *read* it without opening the Bible. But there is a danger. Jesus and the disciples were walking along when they saw a man in his thirties who had been blind from birth (John 9). The disciples asked Jesus, "Rabbi, who sinned, this man or his parents, that he was born blind?" (John 9:2).

Jesus said, "Neither one of them." That statement violates everything they knew. He said, "Neither one of them. It is for My glory that I'm doing this, and while there's still light, I'll be doing these things." He healed this blind man, and it surpassed anything the disciples had been taught in the Word. They knew nothing about this aspect of the Word, which had to do with the glory realm beyond where they had ever been.

This can be a huge danger for all of us. We sometimes try counseling, teaching, or attempting to make *the blind man* understand what a mess he is in, but it has nothing to do with that. Based on our old, methodical understanding, if someone were blind, deliverance ministers might try to deliver that person of generational iniquity or some sin he or she committed, as opposed to just saying, "The reason she's blind is for the glory of the Lord. Just get up!"

4. Mary went beyond her comfort zone: "Whatever He says to you, do it" (John 2:5).

Jesus and the disciples had been invited to a wedding. Jesus's mother, Mary, was also in attendance, and said to her Son, "The wine has run out for the last season."

The Son said, "What's that got to do with Me, woman?"

Mary basically told the person in charge of the wedding feast, "Whatever He tells you to do, do it, or we'll be stuck halfway through this celebration without celebrating the way we've come to celebrate." Remember, Jesus could not do anything unless Father told Him to, and He didn't see Father doing anything—*until Mary prophesied it.* The moment Mary prophesied and said, "We have to have wine, and whatever He tells you to do, do it," Father came into action and told the Son, "Act on that prophecy."

Some of this was not just God moving. Some of this was God saying, "I'm waiting for you to prophesy something so I can come down and make a shift and so My Spirit can begin to move in a new way." Go beyond! Mary went beyond her comfort zone. She went beyond her understanding of who Jesus was and activated Him in the earth. Then Father agreed with her, and the manifestation came. The disciples were there with Jesus, and after they saw the manifestation of His glory, they believed in Him (John 2:1–11). He did it so they would believe. He had to take them beyond where they believed. You can't get into this next season by merely believing the way you do now!

5. Go beyond your last duty. Remove all distractions, and listen for the wind of Holy Spirit (Luke 10:38–42).

Sometimes the reason Jesus comes to your house is to see how you're moving beyond your duty. He went to Martha's house. It was her house, not Mary's, and Martha had the responsibility for the house. It is important for you to understand you have certain responsibilities, and it's more difficult for you to go beyond in the midst of those responsibilities.

I have responsibilities. I have a book due. After leaving a ministry engagement early one Friday, I could have gotten off the plane and run home and started writing, but I could also hear Linda Heidler saying, "Are you sure you're not forgetting Shabbat this year?" Then I had to make a choice: Would I get distracted with ministry and messages, or would I enjoy Shabbat with my wife? I don't even know what we did. I actually think I just sat and stared—I was such a zombie after a very heavy ministry schedule. That's what happened to Martha. She had responsibility over this house, as well as for the most important person in the region. She wasn't in the *old thing* but actually was following after the *new thing* and wanted the new thing to enjoy all the amenities of her home.

Martha's thinking was valid. Most of us think like that. I don't want people coming over to my home with our table messed up. Take note that the Lord pulled aside from what He was doing to deal with her. He might have gotten up and gone into her kitchen (and don't think Jesus can't show up in your kitchen!) and basically said, "Martha, you're missing this thing. You're trying to get the dishes done and keep everything in order because we're at your house, and that's not what I'm about this time. Mary's getting it, and you're mad at Mary now because you're distracted and anxious over Me being here. If you're anxious over what I'm going to be doing, you can't get what I'm going to be doing. Martha, you're going to have to go beyond your responsibility, and not just with the dishes. If you can't lay down the responsibilities for a while, you will miss the moment, and you won't be able to go beyond into the whole season."

Similarly, He is saying to us, "You're going to have to go beyond the responsibility you have for your kids, for your house, for your business. You're going to have to come on in at the right moment and hear Me, because I'm going to give you marching orders over how to be responsible in the next season." Some of us have great responsibilities, inside and outside of the *house*, but at certain times He says, "If you don't get beyond your day-to-day responsibilities, you will miss what I'm saying. You might be the key to what I am saying and whom I'm saying it to!"

6. You have to go beyond your last drink and believe (John 2).

I see this with renewals. I'm a renewal person. I can't think of one renewal I've missed since the late sixties. I've received abuse from religious structures because I've gotten into every one of them. I recently went to Lakeland again. I've never spoken against the renewals for any reason. But you have to go beyond your last drink. If you don't, you're not going to get the next level of faith and glory that God is trying to show you.

7. Go beyond your last revelation (Matt. 16:13–20).

Nobody could get more revelation than Peter, but he didn't get it when Andrew brought him to Jesus. A lot of you need to be honest. You don't get it when you first hook in, but you know something's drawing you. Peter started following, but he didn't get it until about two years and eight months into his time with Jesus. Then all of a sudden he *got it*. He went beyond what he knew, and Father connected with him. Peter said, "I know who you are. You are the Christ, the Messiah; You are the One."

Jesus said, "Only Father could have shown you that," and then He prophesied to him. Peter went beyond but only stayed beyond about ten minutes—and that's legitimate. You can get it when someone is prophesying it on Sunday, but then by Tuesday you're saying, "What was that? Did somebody say something?" It's legitimate. Don't over-judge Peter. Know that you have to go beyond your last revelation.

8. Go beyond your last sifting (Luke 22:31).

Because Peter couldn't get it and keep it, the Lord had to prophesy to him again. Peter had gotten it and received the prophecy for the generations ahead but was then called *Satan* within fifteen minutes. After that, he had to have another prophecy. No one wants to end on that note. You don't want to end *in your mind*. Jesus could have said, "Peter, you are so mind-full. Your emotions and your way of thinking are so tangled up in the world that you can't keep your heavenly perspective." Peter had hooked in with Satan's thinking, and Jesus could have continued by saying, "And I'm going to call you his child." So, He had to give Peter another prophecy.

In verse 31, Jesus even reverts to Peter's former name, *Simon*, because he couldn't keep his new identity. When you can't keep your new identity, you go back to looking like who you were. "And the Lord said, 'Simon, Simon! Indeed, Satan has asked for you, that he may sift you as wheat. But I have prayed for you, that your faith should not fail; and when you have returned to Me, strengthen your brethren" (vv. 31–32). In other words, Jesus could have said, "Peter, you only have one shot at your beyond. You're going to have to strengthen your brothers. If you ever go another way, he has you. Satan asked for you, and I don't have a choice but to give you to him. He is going to sift you like wheat, so everything in you is going to be separated out. But when you come through this place, and you get beyond your sifting, you will strengthen your brothers. It's on the road to beyond."

If you can't keep and secure the revelation God's bringing to you, there is a place called *sifting* on your road. Basically, Jesus said, "Peter, when you get past this place called *sifting*, all you can do then is to strengthen your brethren. If you try to go another route, Satan's going to have you." This is why I do what I do.

9. Go beyond your understanding of resurrection and the last glory demonstration you've seen (John 11).

Let's go back to Martha again. She never got past her distractions to get it, even though He told her to. Now, her house (which she was responsible for) had a death in it, and Jesus waited until there was no longer any hope in this house. In other words, He waited until Lazarus was *good and dead*.

Four days into it, Lazarus had been buried. He was no longer in the house but was stinking, shut up in the grave. When Jesus came, Martha went to him and accused, "If You had been here, this wouldn't have happened." We are always doing this to the Lord, because we continue to look at Him based upon where He has been rather than based upon where He's taking us. Jesus could have said, "Martha, you should have gotten this *resurrection* thing by now. I love you, your sister, and your brother, and I've been visiting your home for quite a while, but you don't get resurrection." But when Jesus said, "Your brother will rise again," Martha responded, "I know that he will rise again in the resurrection at the last day."

Then Jesus declared, "I am the resurrection and the life. He who believes in Me, though he may die, he shall live" (John 11:25). In other words, He could have said, "Martha, listen to Me. Resurrection power is in your midst today. You understand resurrection for the future, but you don't get it for today, and I am grieved over it."

Mary came to Jesus and said, "Lord, if You had been here, my brother would not have died" (v. 21). Here's the difference between Martha and Mary's statements: Mary fell at His feet and spoke, instead of accusingly yelling at Him on the path. In a nutshell, that's the true difference between Martha and Mary. They each had a distinct personality, and He loved each of the sisters, but one of them knew how to touch Him. And because she knew how to touch Him, He took them both *beyond*. I think that's the place we're going. Do we really know how to touch Him so we can see Him in a whole new perspective? You know the rest of the story. Mary touched His heart. He removed the rock, the death, the grave clothes, the decay, and a whole new order came. They all saw it. That's the place I hear the Lord asking us if we will go to.

10. Go beyond your last trauma and death experience (Luke 24).

We have to see how He took a group beyond the prophecy of a previous season. These believers heard John prophesy in the last season but didn't see the prophecy of the baptism of fire and were seeking after it. "So shall My word be that goes forth from My mouth; it shall not return to Me void" (Isa. 55:11). John seeded it, and the Lord would open it up at the right time. His Word does not return void.

When Jesus died, it threw them all off, because they couldn't get the prophecies. This is a synopsis of what Jesus told some of them on the road to Emmaus: "If you could have just known the Scriptures, you could have gotten this, but you couldn't see beyond the trauma and what you expected to happen."

This is one reason that I admire my wife so much. When she was still barren, the Lord gave her a promise that she would have twins. She had twins, and after they died she said, "I'll go beyond this. I don't know how I'll go beyond, but I'll go beyond it."

I asked her, "Does this mean we'll have twins again?" She answered, "No, it's a new season. But I will see beyond into a new season where what that word truly means has manifested." That's what the men on the road to Emmaus couldn't do. He'll take you beyond your last trauma and death experience and open your eyes into a realm that you couldn't see or understand from the old place you were in.

That's also what happened to my friend Marty Cassady in the tent on our land for the Head of the Year gathering in 2009. The Lord reached down into the tent and touched her because she had been surrounded by death for fifteen years. He took her beyond all that.

He says to us, "I can put you into a place called *abundance*, into a place called *life*, where you're seeing into a realm you've never seen before. Let Me take you past the death of that child…Let Me take you past the loss in that relationship…Let Me take you past the loss of that business…Let Me take you past the loss that you've experienced and take you into a new realm."

11. Go beyond your last ability to fear and forgive (John 20).

In John 20, after Jesus died, those things He said began to manifest. On the first day of the week, the disciples were all together, because they thought all they had left was each other. There are times when all you have left to walk with are those whom God has given you. I want to end up with those He's given me. Remember, He prophesied that. He said, "I won't lose one of you who truly wants to follow after Me."

The disciples locked the door because they believed that the same ones who killed Jesus would come and kill them (v. 19). They were filled with fear. The door was locked, they were assembled, and Jesus came and stood in the midst of them, saying, "Peace be with you." He came through a closed, locked door. Are you aware that even if you lock yourself away He can still come in and say, "We can go beyond this place"? He can say to us, "You might think this is where you're going to hide out, but I am going to come right on through, into that locked-up place you have sequestered yourself in, trying to become a nun or a monk. I will find you and bring you right out again, because I want you to go beyond. There is no need to try to isolate yourself in a season of seeing, because I'll make you so miserable in that place that you'll get sick of everything you're seeing there. It will cause you to say, 'I've got to get out of here.' Your identity is not in that hidden place."

He showed up in the room the disciples were hiding in and said, "I'm taking you beyond your last ability and where fear is gripping you." Are you aware that the fear you're engulfed in is related to what you're capable of doing? Some of your fear is because you're relying upon yourself to pull things off, and you can't do it. He said to them, "Let Me bring you past that fear, and let Me commission you to go and forgive." That was the only way they could move forward, and the same holds true for us. You won't get to your *beyond* unless you can get past the signpost called *forgiveness*. You have to get past sifting, fear, and forgiveness, and then you can go beyond.

12. Go beyond the last understanding of your call (John 21).

This is the hardest one. The disciples went beyond, but then they went right back to what they used to do. Are you aware that's a very dangerous place for all of us right now? We're faced with the choice of going beyond where we've been or going back to the season from three and a half years ago. The disciples went back to fishing. They took up their business again. But Jesus met them in the business! Don't be deceived or get into the religious lie that you can't prosper if you are not doing what you're supposed to be doing. He can prosper you even when you're not doing what you're supposed to be doing. He can allow you to prosper. He helped His disciples prosper in their business.

After they recognized Him and had eaten breakfast, Jesus talked with Peter. It could have gone something like this: "Peter, let's talk about your call. Remember, I let Satan sift you. Do you feel like you've been sifted enough, or do you want to go to round two?" That's what He was saying. Peter had one shot at moving beyond, but Jesus would have let him stay in the fishing business. He would also have let him be sifted again. When Jesus asked Peter, "Do you love Me?" Peter answered, "Yes, Lord." Jesus said, "But do you really love Me?" Peter answered, "Yes, Lord." Jesus asked again, "But do you really love Me?" Peter answered, "Lord, only You know that." Peter had answered every question in what he thought was the right way, and he'd done this before and still ended up in a mess.

Jesus could have said to Peter, "If you do love Me, do you remember that prophecy I gave saying that you would be sifted like wheat and then you'd have to strengthen your brothers? You're going to have to go back into your call. You'll have to go beyond your last three and a half years and into a new type of call."

You would think Peter would have fallen on his face and said, "Here I am, Lord!" But what he actually said was, "What's going to happen with John?" Jesus answered him and basically said, "What is that to you? I'm asking you if *you* will go beyond." Jesus was not talking about shirking responsibility but was asking this: "Will you keep following Me, even if they decide not to?"

13. Go beyond your last place of repentance (Acts 2).

Between Jesus's death and Pentecost, Peter finally repented. He finally turned over all of his thoughts. That's what he didn't do when he had the first revelation of who Jesus really was. You can come to a revelation of who Jesus is but never turn over your way of thinking. Peter turned over his way of thinking, and in the midst of it, he came out differently. He came out beyond his sifting, beyond his fear, beyond his unforgiveness, and beyond his thinking (Isa. 55). He came out beyond the last prophecy and into a place called *new*. Then God fell on him, and the Spirit came down. Peter multiplied three thousand times over and came into a place called *abundance* because his thinking process had shifted. He was no longer in the place he once was.

14. Go beyond your present connections (Acts 10).

During Peter's process, God was working on other people. He was working on a Gentile, Cornelius, and Gentiles weren't even supposed to be worked on. But He's God. Isaiah prophesied He would work on Gentiles, and hundreds of years later, He was doing it! He said to Cornelius, "You're going to meet with Peter." If Cornelius had protested, not wanting to meet with *those crazy people*, the Lord could have said, "But Cornelius, I'm working on you!" The Lord took Cornelius past his present connections because he went beyond all the issues along his path, and God could bring in a new connection. Peter had already been worked on, even by the devil, and was almost ready for this new Gentile connection. Peter was almost at that place called *beyond*.

15. Go beyond your present legal, religious condition (Acts 10).

Meanwhile Peter, praying up on a housetop, got good and hungry. He was so hungry that in the midst of his hunger, God gave him a vision and then spoke to him. God told Peter that a man on whom He had been working for a little while, a Gentile, was coming to meet him. Peter might have had a few hesitations about meeting this man, who was known to his religious mind-set as *unclean*. This is one of our real issues. In the last season, the church came full circle, but today we're trying to be so clean we are not completely sure God can bring our divine connections to us.

What God did in the vision was lower a sheet filled with things that Peter knew from Leviticus as forbidden and unclean—things he should not even touch. The Lord said to Peter, "Rise, Peter; kill and eat" (Acts 10:13). Peter answered, "Not so, Lord! For I have never eaten anything common or unclean" (v. 14).

After Peter thought about the vision a while, the Lord told Peter He was bringing people into his life in his last season who were unclean, and he would have to be with them if he was to do what God was calling him to do. Peter had to get past all his legalistic constraints and the way the Word was given to him in that other season, because those the Lord was bringing to him didn't know anything about the Word or those constraints. If Peter couldn't kill and eat the animals in the vision, he would judge those whom the Lord was bringing to him.

God wasn't telling Peter to sin but was telling him he had to go beyond his sight and form of worship. The Lord could have said to Peter,

"I'm going to bring some new people into your worship system who will change your whole way of worshiping in the future. Peter, if you don't get past this vision, you won't get into My new structure."

Peter probably said, "Oh, my," and thought about the vision within himself before he finally got it. He then had the dubious task of telling the followers of the risen Jesus about the new structure and explained how they also were going to have to shift. It wasn't the Pharisees he was going to be dealing with but the other disciples. He was going to have to tell the other eleven, "You have to make a shift, or we will miss it."

Some of you have been pressing to get it, but now you're going to get it. Like Peter, we could say, "Lord, I've been through enough to know I don't want to go back through it again." Peter had even seen His Spirit fall like fire and the manifestation of the second word. With Peter, we must all say, "Lord, I'm willing to get past a lot of the narrow thinking I've had so I can bring others in. Lord, keep me focused; take me into a new place. Take me beyond. Take me into the place for this new season!"

LOOK AGAIN

This season is really about *seeing*. The Lord's goal is for you to see *eye to eye* with Him. He desires for you to look into His face and then see His reflection in all you do. When you see eye to eye from Zion, you sing forth what heaven is singing and saying over you. This causes you to see circumstances differently. Many circumstances, situations, insights, and even enemy structures that you looked at in the last season will now be seen differently in this season. Remember, Elijah's servant had to keep *looking again* until he saw the cloud of rain, or manifestation of God's will, appear in the atmosphere (1 Kings 18:41–45).

Elisha's servant could not see God's help when they were surrounded by their enemies, the Syrians (2 Kings 6). Elisha prayed for his servant and told him to look again. The servant then saw the horses and chariots of heaven surrounding their enemies. At first he could not see God's help, but after Elisha prayed, he saw!

Things are becoming *seeable*! Remember when Jesus took the blind man of Bethsaida by the hand and led him out of the city. This blind man needed healing. Jesus spit on his eyes and then told him to look. The man could only see men as trees, walking. Jesus lifted the blind man's head up, and since he was only partially seeing, He took the next plan of action. He laid hands on his eyes and then said, "Look again!" This time the man saw clearly. In our life, we see many things from one perspective. However, this is a time to *look again*! When we look again, things become clear and precise. All confusion leaves. There is an opportunity for each of us to see differently! He is determined for you to see your future. His *eye is* watching over you. Watch with *Him* as the storms of life come and go in this new season. Look deep into every circumstance that comes your way. Celebrate Him daily. Allow His joy to be your strength to overcome every attack of the enemy!

CHAPTER 5

*PASS OVER—*GOD'S PLAN FOR FREEDOM

THE LAST THREE chapters were about *seeing beyond* and moving into the future that the Lord has for each of us. I mentioned that the people of Israel had come out of Egypt and had to learn to break the power of a submerged identity. We will now begin discussing the issues that can vex our spirits and keep us from seeing into a new realm. In this chapter we will see how the Passover points us to our own to *pass over* into the freedom God has for us and will identify those things we need to pass over. In chapter 6 we will learn how each of the plagues that God sent to Egypt has spiritual meaning for us today. And in chapter 7 we will learn about *the blood key* to freedom and see how it relates to a clear vision. Understanding the blood key is one of the components necessary in overcoming the enemy!

BECOMING AWARE OF GOD

To see beyond where we presently see, both spiritually and physically, we must become aware that God IS! The first step in doing so is to *lift up your eyes and see*. Psalm 121 (AMP) says: "I will lift up my eyes to the hills [around Jerusalem, to sacred Mount Zion and Mount Moriah]—From whence shall my help come? My help comes from the Lord, Who made heaven and earth. He will not allow your foot to slip or to be moved; He Who keeps you will not slumber. Behold, He who keeps Israel will neither slumber nor sleep. The Lord is your keeper; the Lord is your shade on your right hand [the side not carrying a shield]. The sun shall not smite you by day, nor the moon by night. The Lord will keep you from all evil; He will keep your life. The Lord will keep your going out and your coming in from this time forth and forevermore."

Religion's best premise is that man is able to surpass himself by entering into a relationship with the Creator of the world. However, relationship far exceeds religion. Religion is for a time in the earth. Relationship can be eternal. Man, who is part of this world, can have relationship with the One who is greater than this world. Man must have a sense of *mystery*. Once eternity is in man's heart, he has the ability to see beyond space and time. This mystery must be planted in the hearts of men. Once the mystery is there, you can see into a dimension that will always take you beyond the natural.

This is a time to *see* the greater purposes of God. When we lift our eyes, we come face-to-face, and we transform into the identity that our Creator has for our future. Each time we lift our eyes, we see into the dimension that will cause us to overcome in the future. We *see* as He *sees*!

What Is *Out There* That We Should Be Looking For?

When man was created, he was confronted with the presence of the Lord. Man learned to look for *His presence* on a daily basis as he worked and watched after the Garden. Relationship formed. Daily he looked for his Creator, to commune with Him. You want to *see* the *One* communing with you! There is a voice going before you that you want to learn to recognize so you always prosper, multiply, and are led toward the best.

The thing man and woman did not see correctly was the *serpent*. When you read the Book of Genesis, you can surmise that they were used to animals talking and communing with them in the garden. However, the serpent was different from the other animals. His voice enticed them to see into a realm that the One they were communing with had forbidden them to see into. The only way they could see into this realm was to eat of a fruit that was forbidden. Their desire for that fruit had to overcome their alignment with the One with whom they walked on a daily basis. I believe the serpent caused them to see the fruit from a seducing point of view or perspective. You can also perceive that the serpent convinced them that God, the One with whom they walked and talked, was holding from them something necessary for their future. This deceived them, clouded their vision, and set in motion an atmosphere of decay. We must see our enemy correctly if we are to advance.

We must see revelation and gain understanding. This is a key to our advancement! We must be able to analyze, separate, and determine how the information that is revealed to us is to be used for our progress. This is what I call *the revelation key*. Revelation creates vision. *Provision* is part of our *vision*. If we have vision, we have provision. Supply is needed for victory. From vision our supply lines form. We must see our opportunities. One of my favorite stories is about the blind man who began to yell, "Son of David, heal me!" He was blind, but he *saw* his opportunity of healing and did not let the opportunity escape him.

You Are Called to Pass Over Into Deliverance and Healing

In this chapter we are going to discuss *Passover*, or the act of passing over! Passing over into freedom should be a deep desire for each of us. Once we have passed over, we should feel called to see others pass over.

When I think of the call of God, I always think of Moses. Instead of enjoying a place of royalty in Egypt, Moses became a shepherd in Midian, taking care of his father-in-law's sheep. That was where God had prepared Him for forty years. Many of you are being prepared. Some of you have been in preparation for many years.

I am an intercessor. Even though I'm known by many around the world as an apostolic, prophetic leader in the body of Christ, I would have to determine that my ultimate call is intercession. The Lord spoke to me from Ezekiel 13:5: "You have not gone up into the gaps to build a wall for the house of Israel to stand in battle on the day of the LORD." This happened when I was in my late twenties. Of course, I did not understand the fullness of what this verse meant, but I did embrace the call. While I was in a denominational church, God began to bring people into my life to develop this call. Actually, God's initiation of my call occurred during my second year of college. I was at a Baptist Student Union State Convention in 1972. When the speaker gave the invitation, I heard these words form in my spirit: "I have called you for the healing of the nations." Although I had not fully determined the course I felt I should pursue in college, I was already studying courses related to premed. I went forward and surrendered to the words I heard by signing a missions card, although I had no understanding of the call. My mind definitely resisted the thought of studying for eight years and then ending up in a foreign nation as a medical missionary. I could not get away from this experience, even when I switched to the field of business the next year. My change in direction did not change God's plan.

THE CALL OF GOD IS PROGRESSIVE

The call of God is progressive: this actually means that you have a starting place, but God matures you into the fullness of His plan. God has a plan over the life of each one of us. He also has a plan for people groups and a plan for nations. When He was knitting us together in our mothers' wombs, that plan was being initiated.

The call of God is the highest part of God's plan for us individually. God then matures our individual call as we align corporately in the body of Christ. We were never made to be independent. God made us so that our gifts and destinies would *align* with others. The hand needs the arm, the eyes need the mind, and so on. Once we find our place in the body of Christ and we see that *room has been made for our gift*, our call is extended to the city and territory that we are a part of. As we become stewards, faithful to demonstrate God's covenant plan in every aspect of our life, He can extend our call even to a nation. Therefore, the functionality of our gift can increase and be used in a greater scope, function, or sphere of authority.

Over the last thirty or so years, I have watched the Lord develop His call in my life for the *healing of the nations*. He first assigned me to pray for my extended family, which had been scattered. The Lord showed me that if I would take my stand, He would restore my family. He then had me take a stand on behalf of a friend who was going in a wrong direction. God had me stand and intercede for this friend until he surrendered to the call of God to minister the Word. He then had me take a stand on behalf of the church that my wife and I were attending. This church then experienced growth, entered into a major building program, and the Lord began to visit and pour out His Spirit in a new way in the midst of the body.

The Lord then asked me to stand and pray for the church and nations of the former Soviet bloc countries. At this point, I stepped over into a dynamic of understanding the healing of the nations. I rallied pray-ers and worked with other organizations to see oppressed Christians in those areas released from prison. After the changes that occurred in these nations from 1989–1991, the Lord arranged circumstances so that I would meet a lady named Cindy Jacobs, who introduced me to Peter Wagner and Barbara Byerly. They then opened the door for me to become a prayer leader for the 10/40 Window, the most unevangelized area in the world. Since that time, God has assigned me to pray for many nations. My faith has increased as I have progressed in His calling to believe for the healing of the nations and the release of captives from Satan's dominion.

While Moses was pasturing Jethro's flock, he was called by God. A bush burned; Moses turned! The fire came; an angel spoke! God met Moses face-to-face. Moses was sent to deliver. Listen carefully, for His *call* is being released from heaven in a new way to us this day. Moses turned aside and looked. I am sure he *looked again* and then entered into a dimension that was beyond anything he had known. This dimension would lead him to overcoming personally and corporately. A people who were vexed under Egypt's slavery system of idolatry would now be delivered, offered a way of escape, and given the opportunity to enter their future.

Moses's call was key to the people passing out of slavery. In the Book of Revelation, the account of Moses is important to our future. They had to have a deliverer. The account of these events and how they apply to us are important to our advancement. Your participation in Passover will be one of the first steps to your freedom from vexation.

Passover Causes the Enemy to Pass Over

We have discussed how we are grafted into God's covenant with Abraham. Today Abraham, the Hebrew, which means "one who passes over," has a huge army that constantly is passing over. When we are grafted into the one who passes over through the One who passed over through the cross, we will always be able to pass over! Whew, what a statement! Through the blood of Christ, we are adopted (or grafted) into the covenant of God that insures us that we can pass over.

Biblically, one of the most important times of the year is known as Passover. Passover is a celebration of redemption and deliverance by the power of the blood. This feast celebrates Israel's deliverance from Egypt but also our deliverance from Satan and sin by the blood of Jesus, our Passover Lamb. In Exodus 12 we read they were to take a lamb and "...kill it at twilight. And they shall take some of the blood and put it on the two doorposts and on the lintel of the houses where they eat it. Then they shall eat the flesh on that night; roasted in fire, with unleavened bread and with bitter herbs they shall eat it....It is the Lord's Passover. For I will pass through the land of Egypt on that night, and will strike all the firstborn in the land of Egypt, both man and beast; and against all the gods of Egypt I will execute judgment: I am the Lord" (Exod. 12:6–8, 11–12.

When we understand the story of Passover, we can better overcome the demonic forces that hold us, as God's children, in bondage. In the Book of Exodus, Israel was in slavery in Egypt. Egypt was a proud country, the most advanced and powerful nation in the world. It was known for magnificent architecture, great learning, and military might. As Exodus begins, we find that the Egyptians had held Israel under cruel oppression for four hundred years. The Israelites had been beaten, worked to death, and seen their children murdered.

The good news was, *God had a plan for freedom.* (God *always* has a plan for freedom!) As Israel cried out to God, He put His plan into action. To understand God's plan for Israel, we need to understand what had happened in Egypt in the spiritual realm. Egypt was a land filled with temples and monuments built to honor false gods. The Egyptians worshiped those false gods and trusted in them for their prosperity and security. But false gods are nothing more than demons.

The Egyptians' false worship actually created demonic structures over the land that held it in bondage. That's what always happens. As idolatry and false worship enter a land, it forms demonic structures over the territory, which hold people in bondage. And it wasn't just the Israelites who were held in bondage; the Egyptians also lived under the cruel oppression of those demonic powers. In any land that has no Christian or Word-based heritage, a level of darkness and oppression exists that we've never experienced in America. Even for those involved in idolatry, it's not pleasant.

The land of Egypt was shrouded in that kind of darkness. Those demonic forces over Egypt created a sphere within which God's people could be held captive. So before Israel could be freed, the demonic structures over the territory had to be removed. God did that in a series of *power encounters* with those demonic forces, which we call the *plagues of Egypt.* The plagues of Egypt were confrontations with the demonic religious structures of the land designed to break their power. As we will see in the next chapter, the ten plagues were God's ten-step program to freedom for Israel. God wants to set you free from the bondage of the enemy as well.

Begin today to ask God to show you how the enemy has held you in bondage.

WHY PASSOVER TODAY?

So many have asked the simple question, *Why Passover?* In a world that is in one of the most historical seasons of realignment and change, God's people must reorder their lives and cry again, *"Let us go, that we may worship!"* In Exodus 12:13–14 (NAS) we read:

> The blood shall be a sign for you on the houses where you live; and when I see the blood I will pass over you, and no plague will befall you to destroy you when I strike the land of Egypt. Now this day will be a memorial to you, and you shall celebrate it as a feast to the LORD; throughout your generations you are to celebrate it as a permanent ordinance.

Passover is a celebration designed by God. This feast and event was given to increase our faith and prepare us to enter in the fullness His blessing. Passover was commanded by God for the Jews in the Old Testament to teach them the importance of redemption by the blood. But it was also observed by Christians in the New Testament to remember and understand God's redeeming work. The Bible tells us it is to be a *permanent* ordinance—a celebration for all time.

Many Christians don't realize that Passover is just as much a New Testament feast as an Old Testament feast. It's all through the New Testament. Jesus and the apostles all celebrated Passover. The original Lord's Supper was a Passover meal. The apostles taught the Gentile churches to celebrate Passover. In 1 Corinthians, Paul wrote to a predominantly Gentile church and said, "Christ our Passover also has been sacrificed. Therefore, let us celebrate the feast" (1 Cor. 5:7–8, NAS). For hundreds of years, Passover was the most important yearly celebration in the early church.

WHAT MAKES PASSOVER SO IMPORTANT?

Derek Prince once said that the most powerful faith declaration for deliverance is this: "I am redeemed by the blood of the Lamb out of the hand of the enemy!" He said that if you can make that declaration in faith, and keep on making it, something will happen. You will be delivered from the power of the enemy. That's really the message of Passover.

The Feast of Passover is a faith declaration that we are redeemed by the blood of the Lamb! It does something in us when we celebrate Passover. When we come together to remember God's great works of redemption and declare the power of redemption in our lives today, it *always* does something!

Passover is very important to God. But the enemy resists the whole concept of Passover. The enemy has worked diligently to steal Passover away. The good news is, *God is restoring Passover*. But it is a battle. The battle for Passover is the battle for the blood. Satan wants to give us a bloodless religion, because a bloodless religion has no power. The power is in the blood.

There's always a battle for Passover. We see it in church history. In the fourth century when the emperor Constantine tried to merge Christianity and paganism, it sounded like a good deal to many. He legalized Christianity so people could go to church without having to fear being thrown to the lions. Constantine didn't mind Christians having a celebration of Jesus's resurrection. But he did have an issue with Passover. He demanded that Christians *not* celebrate Jesus's resurrection at the time of Passover. At the Council of Nicea (A.D. 325), he declared, "This irregularity [observing Passover] MUST be corrected!"

At the council of Nicea, Constantine *outlawed Passover* and directed that Christ's death and resurrection be celebrated on "the Sunday following the first full moon after the vernal equinox," a time associated with the spring festival of the pagan fertility goddess *Ishtar*, also known as *Eastre!* (That's why in the church today we celebrate the resurrection at *Easter* instead of Passover.) Constantine's goal was to remove Jesus from the context of Passover.

THE BATTLE CONTINUES

Many in the church resisted Constantine's edicts, so for many centuries after Constantine, the battle for Passover continued. In the sixth century, for example, Emperor Justinian sent the Roman armies throughout the empire to enforce the prohibition on Passover. In his attempt to wipe out the "heresy" of Passover, thousands of men, women, and children were brutally murdered. Entire cities were massacred for refusing to stop celebrating Passover. Pressured by the government, the Roman church joined in the attempts to stamp out Passover. Notice some of the decrees passed against Passover by various church councils:

- *The Council of Antioch* (A.D. 345)—"If any bishop, presbyter or deacon will dare, after this decree, to celebrate Passover, the council judges them to be anathema from the church. This council not only deposes them from ministry, but also any others who dare to communicate with them." (The word *anathema* means "cursed." The church actually pronounced a curse on Christians who would celebrate Passover.)

- *The Council of Laodicea* (A.D. 365)—"It is not permitted to receive festivals which are by Jews."

- *The Council of Agde, France* (A.D. 506)—"Christians *must not* take part in Jewish festivals."

- *The Council of Toledo X* (seventh century)—"Easter must be celebrated at the time set by the decree of Nicea."

THE BATTLE FOR PASSOVER IS SEEN CLEARLY IN CHURCH HISTORY

That battle against Passover is nothing new. We see the same thing in the Bible: Satan *always* tries to steal away Passover because he knows the celebration of the blood releases power. Look what happened in Hezekiah's day (2 Chron. 29–30).

Hezekiah did what was right in the eyes of the Lord. He repaired and cleansed the temple, tore down the false altars, and restored the sacrifices and Davidic praise. Then Hezekiah sent word to all Israel and Judah, inviting them to come to celebrate Passover. Couriers went throughout Israel and Judah saying, "People of Israel, return to the Lord." The hand of God was on the people to give them unity of mind to carry out what the king had ordered. A very large crowd of people assembled in Jerusalem to celebrate the feast. They slaughtered the Passover lamb and celebrated the feast for seven days with great rejoicing while the Levites sang to the Lord every day, accompanied by instruments of praise. The whole assembly then agreed to celebrate the festival seven more days, so for another seven days they celebrated joyfully. "There was great joy in Jerusalem, for since the time of Solomon the son of David, king of Israel, there had been nothing like this in Jerusalem. Then the priests, the Levites, arose and blessed the people, and their voice was heard; and their prayer came up to His holy dwelling place, to heaven (2 Chron. 30:26–27).

The same thing was happening in Josiah's day (2 Kings 22–23). Josiah did what was right in the eyes of the Lord. In the eighteenth year of his reign, while repairing the temple, they found the Torah scroll in the temple. When the king heard the words of the Torah scroll, he tore his robes. He went up to the temple with all the people. He read in their hearing all the words of the covenant. Then all the people pledged themselves to the covenant. The king ordered them to remove from the temple all the idols made for Baal and Asherah and all the starry hosts. He tore down the quarters of the male prostitutes, which were in the temple. The king gave this order to all the people: "Keep the Passover to the LORD your God, as it is written in this Book of the Covenant" (2 Kings 23:21). In the eighteenth year of King Josiah, this Passover was celebrated to the Lord in Jerusalem. Not since the days of the judges who led Israel, nor throughout the days of the kings of Israel and the kings of Judah, had such a Passover been observed.

WE SEE A BIBLICAL PATTERN

In both of these accounts, God's people had drifted far from the Lord and turned to idolatry, and the blessing of God was lost. They turned back to God and sought Him, and the first thing God did was restore Passover. As they turned from pagan idols and celebrated Passover, they were restored to God and experienced great joy and blessing. That's an interesting pattern. Over and over again in the Bible, we discover that Passover had been *lost*! During the Old Testament era, and even among the Jews, generations lived and died without celebrating Passover. Why had Passover been lost? Satan had *stolen* it away! Satan always wants to steal Passover. As a new generation turned back to the Lord and began to read the Book of the Covenant, they read about Passover for the first time. It seemed strange to them. They said, "We've never done this!" (And that's exactly what we see in much of the church today.) But as the Holy Spirit moved on their hearts, they celebrated God's feast of redemption, and God's power and joy were restored.

THE FIRST PASSOVER NIGHT—A PROTOTYPE

On the original Passover night, everything pointed to Jesus. Every father in Israel was told to stand at the door of his house with a basin containing the blood of the lamb. He was to dip a branch of hyssop into the blood and smear the blood on the two doorposts of the house. Then he was to repeat the action and put the blood on the lintel over the door. If you can picture the motion he made with that blood-soaked branch of hyssop, you'll see he was making the sign of the cross.

On Passover night, every father in Israel made the sign of the cross in the blood of the lamb. And as a result, the family experienced redemption from the power of the enemy. God's deliverance always comes by His cross and by His blood. That's what Passover celebrates. You see, it was not by accident that Jesus died on Passover. God could have had Jesus die any time of year. But it was God's will for Him to die at Passover, so we would recognize that He is the Passover Lamb. In fact, Passover is so important to God that He chose to have the most important event in history (the death and resurrection of Jesus) take place at Passover. God went to great lengths to *connect* the sacrifice of Jesus to Passover. This is interesting: Constantine's goal was to *separate* the work of Jesus from Passover, but God's goal was to *connect* Jesus's work to Passover. God wants us to think of Jesus in the context of the Passover celebration.

Overcoming Strongholds and Tearing Down Iniquitous Thrones

I define a *stronghold* as "a thought process impregnated by a spiritual force that keeps a person in bondage." A *stronghold* is a fortress or anything you run into for protection. Second Corinthians 10:5 tells us that spiritual strongholds are formed by thoughts that raise themselves up above and against the knowledge of Christ. The foundation of a stronghold is a belief system or mind-set that is opposed to the truth of God.

Many times a stronghold forms in a time of distress, trauma, or need. The devil comes to your mind and begins accusing God before you. He then offers you a solution or way of escape that leaves God out of the process. This eventually leads to a greater bondage.

A stronghold is opposed to the *knowledge* of God. *Knowledge* means "a living and interactive experience," not a theoretical or merely intellectual understanding of God. True knowledge is linked with that which has been tried and proven true by personal experience. Satan will present you with a way of escape that does not involve intervention by a loving God. There is no possibility of personal interaction with God. On the foundation of this lie, a system of worship is built. We worship what we serve. When the devil presents his way of escape from our distress, we will do whatever is necessary to keep that way open to us. We will serve the system that keeps the lie in place.

Let God show you any strongholds that have developed in your life. Let Him reveal any place where the enemy has convinced you that God cannot intervene to help you. Let the truth of God uproot the lies of the devil so that demonic strongholds are demolished and you are free to worship the true and living God. (See 2 Corinthians 10:3–6; Exodus 12:12; Joshua 24:14.)

ARE WE UNDER THE SAME *BONDAGE* AS ISRAEL WAS IN EGYPT?

In Egypt, a system of worship had developed in which an elaborate network of gods and goddesses offered protection from every conceivable source of trouble. Israel had lived under this system of worship for four hundred years. To bring His people out at Passover, God had to prove over and over that He was above all the gods of Egypt. He had to demolish the stronghold that the gods of Egypt offered to the people. He had to show that He was a God who would intervene on behalf of His people. Through the plagues of Egypt, God showed Himself to be stronger than all of the gods of Egypt. He judged them by showing them to be lacking in power compared to Him. God wants to demolish the strongholds in our lives. He wants to prove Himself strong on our behalf. He is listening for the cry of His people and looking for hearts that are devoted to Him.

When the demonic powers in the heavens are worshiped by the people on Earth, an unholy agreement between heaven and Earth is formed, and a throne of iniquity is established. Just as God is enthroned on the praises of His people, demons are enthroned wherever they are worshiped. Whoever is enthroned has the right and power to rule. This was the problem in Egypt before the exodus. For Israel coming out of Egypt, it was necessary not just to break the power of the gods of Egypt but also to establish a new order of worship to the Lord. This was God's intent from the beginning. This is why He said, "Let My people go that they might worship Me." The nation could not be established in the Promised Land without the Lord being enthroned over them.

Thrones of iniquity can be over a geographical location, over a people group, or even over an individual life. Psalm 94:20 says that a throne of iniquity cannot be joined with God. The two cannot rule at the same time. Where God is enthroned by the praise and worship of His people, a throne of iniquity must fall. As God breaks us free from the powers of demonic forces, we must see that the key to becoming established in freedom is to worship God in a new way.

The Bible gives many examples of how thrones of iniquity were torn down. In Judges 6, Gideon was instructed to tear down his father's altar to Baal and erect an altar to God in its place. This Baal altar was evidently a corporate altar. When Gideon tore it down, the people were freed to turn to God, and the spirit that enabled the Midianites to steal their harvest each year was broken. In the nation of Judah, there were several revivals recorded during which idols were removed. One of the most notable was under King Hezekiah. Second Kings 18 and 2 Chronicles 30 record that the first thing he did upon becoming king was to tear down the idolatrous altars, cleanse the temple, and restore true worship. The thrones of iniquity were torn down, and God was enthroned in the land. They then celebrated the Passover. Because of this, 2 Kings 18:7 tells us that the Lord was with Hezekiah wherever he went, and he prospered. During his reign the Assyrian army came against Jerusalem, but God sent an angel who killed 185,000 of them in one night. Judah never fell to the Assyrians because the Lord's throne had been established over the land.

We must see the demonic power that God was confronting and overcoming. Let God set you free from the power of that spirit in your own life. Do as Gideon did and establish an altar of worship in its place. If you will do this, you will have a new freedom to worship. As we corporately worship from territory to territory, we will see God enthroned in a whole new way so that His will can be done on Earth as it is in heaven. His power to rule will be manifested wherever He is worshiped.

Chapter 6

GOD'S TEN-STEP PROGRAM TO FREEDOM FOR ISRAEL

THE EGYPTIANS PLACED great faith in their gods, but their gods were really demons. The Egyptians worshiped powerful, demonic entities that held them in terrible bondage. In the ten plagues of Egypt, God was not just bringing random destruction on the land. He was demonstrating the foolishness of trusting in these false gods. In Exodus 12:12, God said His purpose was to bring judgment on all the gods of Egypt. Each plague was a direct confrontation with one or more of the Egyptian deities. God wanted to show the Egyptians the futility of idolatry and give them an opportunity to turn to the true God.

As you read the following account and explanation of each structure and atmosphere being removed, you will better understand how spiritual warfare really is expressed in our lives. The account of the plagues and their use in history to free a people from the vexation of Pharaoh and the power of Egypt are just as applicable to us today. Layer by layer, darkness was removed so the people of God could see their way of escape.

Exodus 12:38 tells us that when Israel left Egypt, a "mixed multitude" went out with them. That's an indication that many Egyptians were convinced by the plagues of the power of the true God. Because of the plagues, many Egyptians chose to leave Egypt and align themselves with the God of heaven. Let's look at how God confronted the false deities of Egypt.

PLAGUE ONE—THE NILE RIVER TURNS TO BLOOD

In ancient Egypt, the Nile River was looked at as the source of life. It provided both food and water for the people. Each year it would flood and leave a layer of fertile silt in which their next year's crops would flourish. Two gods were closely associated with the Nile. One was the god *Hapi*, and the other was the god *Khenmu* or *Khnum*. Hapi was worshiped as the god of the Nile. He was thought to be responsible for the fish, birds, and fertile soil that the Nile River brought to the people of Egypt. Without the Nile River the people would have died, so Hapi was sometimes revered more than Ra, the sun god.

Along with Hapi, Khnum was also worshiped as a god of the Nile. He was called *the potter god*. He was believed to be the one who formed human bodies from the silt of the Nile on his potter's wheel. These two gods were viewed as the source of life. Khnum formed your body, and Hapi provided the food and water necessary for life to be sustained, so these two gods were, to the Egyptians, the source and sustainer of life. While we would never say that we believe we were created by a *potter* like Khnum or that our lives are sustained by a god like Hapi, we sometimes look at material things or even the forces of nature the way the Egyptians viewed these gods.

But God wants us to know that *He* is the source and sustainer! First, He turned the Nile to blood, making it a source of death instead of a source of life. In doing this, He demonstrated the powerlessness of the Egyptian gods. Then when He brought Israel out of Egypt, He miraculously provided them with food and water. He showed Israel that He is the true source and sustainer! That's something God wants us to know also. When Jesus was in the wilderness and Satan tempted Him to turn the stones into bread, Jesus replied, "Man shall not live by bread alone, but by every word that proceeds from the mouth of God" (Matt. 4:4). What do you look to as the source and sustainer of your life? Take a moment and meditate on the fact that your life came from God. He is the source of your life. By His word the heavens and the earth were formed. He formed you in your mother's womb. You are not an accident or a mistake. You are the work of God's hands.

The Lord is also the sustainer of your life. He is committed to you. He brings forth bread from the earth to give you strength. He blesses you with good things. It is by His word that the earth is fruitful and multiplies. The first form of idolatry that God wants to deliver us from is the belief that anything besides the Lord could be the source and sustainer of our lives. Ask the Holy Spirit to show you any mind-sets that cause you to look to or depend on anything other than God to provide what you need.

The first plague deals with the foundation of core values in our lives. It goes to the very heart of our belief system. If we do not settle the issue of where we came from and how we will survive, we will develop all kinds of idols to deal with our fears. To avoid idols, we must be rooted and grounded in truth.

Plague Two—the Plague of Frogs

The second plague God sent on Egypt was closely related to the first, since the frogs came out of the Nile. It wasn't unusual for frogs to come up from the Nile. Each year after the Nile flooded, frogs would begin to appear. They were looked at as a symbol of fertility and of new life springing forth from the Nile River.

God's judgment on Egypt was to bring forth a superabundance of frogs—more frogs than they wanted, more than they could stand. They were in their homes, their beds, and their food. Frogs were everywhere. And the goddess of the frogs was powerless to remove them. Sometimes God judges people by giving them the fullness of what they've been seeking, until they can't stand it anymore!

The goddess associated with frogs was *Heket*. She was a goddess of childbirth, creation, and grain germination. As a water goddess, she was also a goddess of fertility and childbirth, particularly associated with the later stages of labor. She was thought to be the wife of Khnum, the god who created men on his potter's wheel. The Egyptians believed she gave a child the breath of life before it was placed in the mother's womb.

If Hapi and Khnum were the source and sustainers of life, then Heket was the goddess who insured a future generation. Midwives worshiped Heket as the one who would help them to give a safe birth to children. It's interesting that the Hebrew midwives were known to *fear God* rather than *Heket* and would not kill the male children born to the Israelite women, in spite of Pharaoh's edict.

It was fear that drove the Egyptians to worship Heket—fear for their children and the future generations. To avoid the trap the Egyptians had fallen into, we must get rid of all fear concerning our children. Fear over their welfare or safety will lead us into idolatry over our children. If we are not sure that God is enough to protect them, we will hold them back from things God has for them to do. We will arrange our lives based on how we think we can best protect or provide for our children.

If you do not overcome this, then your fears concerning your children will become as numerous as the plague of frogs. When you go to bed at night, your fears will be waiting for you. When you step out of bed in the morning, your fears will already be there. Everywhere you look, you will see a new possibility of danger.

Psalm 127 is great for gaining a biblical perspective on children. It says that children are a gift and a reward from God. They are sent to be a blessing, not a burden. It also says that unless the Lord is watching over and guarding our homes, all of our efforts are in vain. Allow the Lord to expose any fear concerning your children. Commit your children to the Lord and trust Him to make you the parent that your child needs.

PLAGUES THREE AND FOUR—THE PLAGUE OF STINGING GNATS AND FLIES (OR SCARAB BEETLES)

In Exodus 8:16 (AMP), God told Moses to strike the earth, and the dust would become stinging gnats that would cover the land of Egypt. This was a direct confrontation with the Egyptian god *Geb*, who was believed to be the *god of the earth*.

Some translations say this was a plague of *lice*, which would be bad enough, but a better translation is probably "stinging gnats." These were tiny gnats, almost invisible, that would inflict a painful sting. And they were everywhere! Their stings sometimes became infected, producing a painful sore. Suddenly the Egyptians' faith in Geb was shaken. Instead of the earth bringing forth food to nourish them, it was bringing forth stinging gnats. And Geb, the god of the earth, had no power to stop them.

Overcoming Geb means to overcome the fear of death. Geb was worshiped because it was believed he had the power to hold you in the grave or release you into the afterlife. But if Geb lacked power over something as small as a gnat, then how could you trust him with your future after death?

It is interesting that this plague is associated with *stinging gnats*. Paul writes in 1 Corinthians 15:55 that because of Jesus's resurrection, death no longer has a "sting." The way to overcome the fear of death is not by worship of a false god, as the Egyptians did, nor is it through keeping the Law of Moses, as the Jews believed. The sting of death is overcome by faith in the resurrection power of Jesus.

He has tasted death for all of us and is the firstfruits of the promise of resurrection. We can only overcome the fear of death by faith, which is the evidence of things hoped for and the assurance of things not seen. Faith comes from hearing the Word of God, and faith works through love. Let faith rise up in you to overcome fear of death.

Plague Five—the Plague of Flies

After the plague of stinging gnats, the Lord threatened to send a plague of flies. Some translations say it was scarab beetles—also called dung beetles—but a more likely translation is "flies." Whichever insect it was, the Egyptians felt they didn't need to worry much about it, because one of their most powerful gods was in control of insects.

His name was *Khepri*, and both beetles and flies were supposedly under his control. He was thought to be such a powerful god that he even controlled creation and personally moved the sun across the sky each day. The Egyptians depicted Khepri with a dung beetle for his head. Dung beetles got their name from the fact that they could always be seen rolling balls of dung across the ground to their homes. (If anyone should have authority over flies, it should be a god with a dung beetle for a head!) As the dung beetle rolled a big ball of dung along the ground, so the Egyptians thought Khepri rolled the sun across the sky each day.

It is interesting that both flies and dung beetles have one thing in common, *dung*. They are both attracted to dung. So Khepri is a dung god! But the Egyptians thought he was mighty. They called Khepri *the self-created god*. They believed he hadn't been created as the other gods were but came into being on his own. They thought he was able to rise again by his own works and power.

Yet when God sent the plague, Khepri could provide no help. God's message to the Egyptians was, "Don't be so proud of your dung god!" That's His word to many today also. So often we're very proud of our own righteousness. We think we can try hard and be good enough to please God. In Philippians 3:8 Paul tells us that he counted his good works and self-righteousness as a pile of dung (literal translation)!

Overcoming the dung god means abandoning all pride in our works and our hope that they will accomplish anything toward our salvation. Reject the dung god of self-righteousness and come to the Lord in humility to receive His *grace*!

PLAGUE SIX—THE PLAGUE OF BOILS

This is a season in which we will see healings. The Lord revealed Himself to the people as Jehovah Rophe. God said, "If you listen, listen obediently to how GOD tells you to live in his presence, obeying his commandments and keeping all his laws, then I won't strike you with all the diseases that I inflicted on the Egyptians; I am GOD your healer" (Exod. 15:26, THE MESSAGE). If we will keep moving out of our old worship structure, we will see the Lord put healing in our midst. When the Lord dealt with the Egyptians in the sixth plague, the system of healing they used was affected.

In the plague of boils, God directly challenged the power of the Egyptian gods to heal. Egypt is often thought of as having been medically advanced for an ancient civilization. The reason for this is that the Egyptians were riddled with every kind of disease and infirmity. Healing and cures were very important parts of their lives. For them, healing was not a matter of medicine but of magic.

Different ailments, diseases, or injuries were attributed to different gods or goddesses who could either cause or prevent infirmity. There was a goddess associated with snake or scorpion bites. Another goddess could send or cure disease. Still another god was responsible for wounds or injuries. Each kind of ailment had a corresponding ritual, potion, and amulet to appease the god or goddess who could bring about healing. Physicians guarded the secrets and mysteries of healing. For all of this, the ancient Egyptians were not a healthy people.

One of their rituals for healing was particularly gruesome. It's said that they would offer a human sacrifice, burning the victim alive on a high altar, and then scatter the ashes into the air. It was believed that with every scattered ash the blessing of healing would descend upon the people.

When Moses took a handful of soot and tossed it into the air, it was a direct confrontation of this belief. It caused boils to break out that none of the Egyptian physicians or magicians could heal. The gods of Egypt were shown to be powerless.

When Israel left Egypt, one of the first promises God gave them was for healing. In Exodus 15:26, He said if they would listen to His voice and obey Him, He would not put any of the diseases of Egypt on them because He is the Lord their healer. God always has a way for healing. In Ezekiel 47:12, the Lord shows Ezekiel trees whose leaves are for healing. The Lord told Isaiah to put a poultice of figs on King Hezekiah to heal him. When Jesus was on the earth, He healed all who came to Him and authorized His disciples to do the same. Throughout history God has continued to demonstrate that healing comes from Him, whether it comes supernaturally through prayer or naturally through healing elements He has placed in the earth.

Overcome the superstition and fear of the Egyptians and look to Jehovah Rophe, the Lord who heals you!

PLAGUE SEVEN—HAIL

In Egypt, the goddess associated with the sky was *Nut*. She provided a barrier separating the forces of chaos from the ordered cosmos in this world. She was the wife of Geb, the earth god, and was looked at as the protector of the earth. Nut was especially noted as the goddess of the night sky, with the stars and constellations predicting the future. Nut was one of the most important goddesses. People believed that their protection from the destructive forces of nature was dependent on serving her. When hail came from the sky to destroy crops, animals, and people, the power of Nut to protect was shown to be ineffective.

In Job 38, God describes hail as being in a storehouse set aside for the day of war and battle. In sending this devastating hailstorm on Egypt, He was warring with the belief that security and protection from disaster would come from anyone but Him. He was particularly confronting the belief that serving the forces of nature or being guided by the stars would ever be the key in someone's life to insure balance and harmony or to bring peace and prosperity to the earth. We see this kind of thinking in many today whose desire to protect the environment has gone to such an extreme that they are serving the earth rather than stewarding it, as God instructed man to do. This mind-set is based on fear of lack rather than faith for abundance. This is also linked with daily horoscope readings.

Read Job 38–40 and let a new expression of worship of God as Creator rise up within you. Let Him show you how you are to steward whatever garden He has given you so that it becomes fruitful and multiplies. Let Him expose any fear of lack in you so that this can be uprooted and not bear the fruit of idolatry. Thank Him for creation. Take time to enjoy the blessing of creation. Worship Him as the God of creation. Only connect heaven and Earth by worshiping Jehovah!

PLAGUE EIGHT—LOCUSTS

In the plague of locusts, God was overcoming a host of Egyptian gods. *Shu* was the god who controlled the winds, so God sent the locusts in on the east wind. *Nephri* was the goddess who guarded the grain, and *Renenutet* was the goddess who guarded the harvest, so God sent locusts to devour the grain and wipe out the harvest. *Geb* was the god of the earth, so God sent locusts to strip the earth of all vegetation. *Heset* was the god of plenty, so God sent the locusts to remove the Egyptians' prosperity. These gods were all counted on to produce and secure a good harvest for prosperity.

God showed that only He can bring and secure our supply. We will not prosper apart from Him. The fear of lack and the desire for prosperity led the Egyptians to worship these gods. Fear and desire are two foundations of idolatry. Job 3:25 says that what we fear will come upon us. Desire leads to coveting. Ask the Lord to show you if you have fear of lack in any area of your life. He always has a source of supply and a plan for you to get what you need. In the wilderness, He gave the people bread when they did not plant or reap. He sent a wind that brought quail so they had meat. He is able to meet your need in very creative or even supernatural ways. Let faith in His ability displace your fear of lack.

Ask the Lord if you have an inappropriate desire that has led to coveting. When you covet something, you will be discontent unless you have it. You will not be able to rejoice when someone else is blessed. Ultimately, you will do anything—even enter into sin—to get what you covet. Let the Lord reveal any coveting that will lead to idolatry. If He reveals anything to you, the good news is that you can repent. Quickly confess this to the Lord, repent, and be cleansed so that you can move into His good plan for your life. Psalm 37:4 says that if we delight ourselves in the Lord, He will give us the desires of our heart.

Plague Nine—Darkness

The ninth plague God sent on Egypt was *darkness*. This was no ordinary darkness. Exodus 10:21 says that this darkness could even be "felt." Exodus 10:22 says that it was "thick darkness"—a total absence of light. The highest god of Egypt was *Ra*, the sun god, the bringer of light. An adversary to Ra was the god *Apep*, who ruled the darkness. What God sent on Egypt was actually a confrontation with both Ra and Apep. By sending a darkness that was deeper and longer than any they had ever known, the Lord showed His power over Ra. He showed that He could prevent the sun from shining on the Egyptians. But by allowing the sun to shine in Goshen, where the Hebrews lived, He showed His power over the Egyptian god of darkness. The Lord could bring light wherever He chose.

So the God of Israel demonstrated that He ruled both darkness and light. Psalm 139:11–12 says that the darkness and the light are the same to Him. In this ninth plague, God gave the Egyptians a clear choice between darkness and light. He gave them a vivid picture of the darkness they were in. He also gave them a clear avenue for change. They could choose the God of Israel and enter into the light.

The main thing that keeps us in darkness is fear—fear of calamity, confusion, and destruction. God wants us to know He has the power to overcome that darkness. He does that when we look to Him for the light of revelation. The Bible is full of promises that God will be our light in the darkness. He will cause our path to grow brighter and brighter. He has transferred us out of the kingdom of darkness and made us citizens of the kingdom of the Son of light. The ultimate victory of light over darkness came through Jesus, the Light of the world. Fear not! He rules both the light of the day and the dark of the night.

PLAGUE TEN—DEATH OF THE FIRSTBORN

The power of the blood frees us! Through plague after plague, God confronted the gods of Egypt. Yet Pharaoh still would not let the people go. One of the highest gods of Egypt was *Pharaoh* himself. He was viewed as a god and was not only the ultimate authority in the land but also demanded worship. He was the one who could decide to let the people go or force them to remain in Egypt. So this plague was directed at the thing most important to Pharaoh.

In Exodus 4:22–23, God assured Moses that this plague would bring release for the people. This plague was the most serious of all because it involved the death of the firstborn. All through the plagues, Pharaoh's advisors and the people of Egypt had begged Pharaoh to let the people leave, but he refused. This plague was designed to finally break Pharaoh's stubborn pride.

This plague seemed terribly harsh, but we need to see that it was really Egypt's own sin revisited upon them. As Egypt had murdered the children of the Israelites and thrown the newborns into the Nile, so the just punishment that God inflicted on Egypt was that their own children would be forfeited.

There was an offer of grace! No Egyptian had to see their firstborn die. God provided a way of escape for anyone who would receive it. It was found in the blood of the lamb. On the night of Passover, anyone who put the blood on their door would be spared the loss of their firstborn. God provided a way to avoid this plague, and it's likely that many of the "mixed multitude" who left Egypt with the Israelites took advantage of this provision.

But Pharaoh was so sure of his own power that he refused to give in. Pharaoh's confidence was in his own strength and in the protection of *Isis*, the goddess who guarded children. He believed the two of them together could overcome the power of God to harm his firstborn. But Pharaoh finally learned the futility of trusting in his own pride and in the gods of Egypt.

God doesn't want us to fall into Pharaoh's trap! He doesn't want us to trust in our own strength or any other power. God has a provision of grace for all who will receive it. In Egypt, God allowed a lamb to die in place of the firstborn. Many centuries later, this is still God's provision. He gave His firstborn Son, the Lamb of God, to die—not just for the firstborn but for all mankind.

Our victory over death does not come by the strength of our will or from any other supernatural power. It comes from the power of the blood of Jesus. First Corinthians 15:26 says that the last enemy we overcome is death. This was true for Israel coming out of Egypt, and it is true for us today. How we face that enemy and overcome depends on what we are counting on for our victory. Thank God that His Son died in your place.

CHAPTER 7

THE BLOOD KEY

S ATAN HATES PASSOVER because Passover is the celebration of Jesus. *When the church gave up Passover, it invented other celebrations of Jesus.* That is how we shifted the timing of our celebration to Christmas and Easter. It's not bad to celebrate Jesus on those other days (it's always good to celebrate Jesus), but the celebration of Jesus that *God* gave us is called *Passover*. Celebrating Passover is celebrating Jesus. As the Passover Lamb, He shed His blood to redeem us from the enemy. When His blood is on the *doorpost* of your life, God delivers you from the destroyer. So if you understand Passover, you automatically understand what Jesus did. Passover is the *Jesus celebration*.

As you continue to read, you will better understand *the blood key* and how Passover is the celebration of that key to abundant life. The more you understand Passover, the more you appreciate Jesus. If you don't understand Passover, you'll have a hard time fully understanding what Jesus did. As we celebrate Passover, we are declaring our faith in the power of His blood and His redemption. That's why one of strangest things is that Christians all over the world have accepted Satan's lie that Passover is not a *Christian* thing. Satan tries to steal away Passover because he knows the celebration of the blood releases power. When the celebration of Passover was stolen away, the power left, but when Passover is restored, the power *returns*.

The good news is, as I said before, God is *restoring* Passover today. All over the world churches are again celebrating Passover, and the power is returning. I invite you to celebrate the power of Jesus's blood. We are *redeemed* by the *blood of the Lamb* out of the hand of the enemy. If you would like to know more about Passover and see suggestions for celebrating it, I recommend the book *The Messianic Church Arising* by Dr. Robert Heidler, available from Glory of Zion International Ministries.

Life Is in the Blood

The blood circulates through the body. Circulation is a movement in a circle or through a circular course or through a course that leads back to the same point at which it began. The circulatory system or the cardiovascular system is a system that moves the blood through the organs of the body from cell to cell. This helps stabilize our body temperature. On average the body has five liters of blood. The heart, the lungs, and the blood vessels, which include arteries, veins, and capillaries, work together to create this circle of life flow. The lungs, the heart, and the rest of our system work from the flow of this blood. An adult's vessels would be equivalent to a one-hundred-thousand-mile highway! So when the heart is pumping blood, it is carrying its "thought system" throughout your entire body. All of your organs are responding to the way your heart thinks. How our blood flows through our body creates the way we express life. There is such a war in our blood because what is in our blood is creating the way our mind thinks.

This is why the Lord chose the blood to be the final sacrifice that would liberate us from captivity. As we discuss the redemptive event of Passover, I am hoping it helps you understand your own escape from captivity through the power of the exchanged blood of the Lord, Jesus Christ. By you submitting your spirit to be filled with His Spirit, you actually allow the power of the His blood to change your DNA structure and liberate you from an iniquitous past that occurred when your bloodline deviated from God's best. We will fully discuss this as we move through this book.

Passover, the Blood, and the Lamb— the Timetable of Passover

Let's compare the timetable of Jesus's crucifixion with the Passover celebration. According to the Torah, at the time of Passover a number of events had to take place in a specific order and at very specific times:

1. *The Passover Lamb had to be selected on a specific day.*
   Exodus 12 instructs that the Passover lamb be chosen *on the tenth day of the first month.* By the time of Jesus, only lambs from Bethlehem were considered eligible to serve as Passover lambs. So the lamb born in Bethlehem was chosen and brought into Jerusalem from the east (down the Mount of Olives) and entered the city through the sheep gate. *On the tenth day of the first month,* Jesus, the Lamb born in Bethlehem, came down the Mount of Olives and entered Jerusalem through the sheep gate. (This is called His *triumphal entry.*) As He entered, the people waved palm branches and shouted, "Blessed is he that comes in the name of the Lord! Save us, son of David!" By mass acclamation, Jesus is designated as Israel's Messiah. The crowds had chosen their Passover Lamb.

2. *The Lamb then had to be examined.* The Torah instructed that once the lamb was chosen, it had to be carefully examined for blemishes. Only a perfect, spotless, and unblemished lamb would suffice for the Passover. After arriving in Jerusalem, Jesus went to the temple to teach. While there, He was approached by the Pharisees, Sadducees, Herodians, and the teachers of the Law. Each group posed difficult questions, trying to trap Him. Essentially, they were looking for any blemish that might disqualify Him as Messiah. But no one can find fault with Him. He was without blemish.

3. *The leaven (impurity) must be cast out.* The Torah instructs that before the feast, all leaven (impurity) must be cast out of every Israelite home. Each mother took a candle and searched out impurity, removing it from her house. This regulation is still observed today. Passover is a time to cleanse every house. Every observant Jewish family carefully cleans their house before Passover. Every trace of impurity is removed. After Jesus arrived in Jerusalem, He entered the temple and cast out the moneychangers. He was following the biblical instruction to prepare for Passover by cleansing His Father's house.

4. *The Lamb is taken to the altar for public display.* On the morning of the *fourteenth day of the first month*, when all has been set in order, the lamb is led out to the altar. At nine o'clock that morning, the lamb is bound to the altar and put on public display for all to see. On the morning of the *fourteenth day of the first month*, when all had been fulfilled, Jesus was led out to Calvary. At nine o'clock that morning, just as the lamb was being bound to the altar, Jesus was nailed to the cross and put on public display at Calvary.

5. *The Lamb was slain at a specific time.* At exactly *three o'clock in the afternoon*, the high priest ascended the altar. As another priest blew a *shofar* on the temple wall, the high priest cut the throat of the sacrificial lamb and declared, "It is finished!" At *three o'clock in the afternoon* on that high holy day, at the moment the Passover lamb was killed, Jesus cried with a loud voice, *"It is finished,"* and gave up His spirit. In Greek, "It is finished" is *tetelistai.* It means "the debt has been paid in full"!

THE CELEBRATION OF JESUS

Do you see how God chose to connect Jesus with Passover? It's no wonder John introduces Jesus by saying, "Behold the Lamb." It's no wonder Paul writes, "Christ, our Passover Lamb, has been sacrificed" (1 Cor. 5:7, NIV). *Do you see that Passover is all about Jesus?*

- He came as the *Lamb* of God.

- His blood redeems us.

- By His blood, judgment is turned away.

- By His blood, the power of the enemy is broken.

- By His blood, we are released from bondage and oppression.

- By His blood, we are set free to enter into God's promise.

NOT WITHOUT BLOOD

Marty Cassady is one of my dearest friends and is as deep in her relationship with the Lord as anyone I know. She shared the following with me:

In Revelation, the apostle John saw a door standing open in heaven and then heard the invitation, "Come up here!" Jesus Himself offers another invitation for us: "Open the door of our hearts!" When we act upon this invitation, He says He will come in and dine with us. In John 10, Jesus describes Himself as the door. Anyone who enters by Him will be saved. Just imagine—entering the realms of heaven, dining with the Lord, and entering a place in the Lord, the El Shaddai, the Shadow of the Almighty, where all is secure.

All of these directives, invitations, and promises are impossible to obtain without another door. We see that door in Egypt when we hear and SEE the Lord speaking to Moses of a freedom to come. Death would produce the freedom. From the invasion of death into captivity, the Lord was about to give His people a way of escape. God chose Moses and Aaron to receive instructions. He then commanded them to call the elders together. They shared, as best they could, with the limited understanding of what was about to happen with the leaders. Death was coming on a scale they had never seen before. Their lives would be saved by only one thing—the blood on the doorposts of the homes of those who would trust Him for deliverance from a political and spiritual captivity. They told the people to take a lamb, not just any lamb, but a lamb without blemish, and kill it. This lamb would become the Passover lamb.[1]

The people of Israel could not have fully understood the significance of the actions they were instructed to take. All they could do was to trust and obey. They could not have known that down through the centuries that night would be celebrated and re-created in countless homes as a reminder of God's love and provision. The blood of the lamb without blemish was to be placed on their doorposts in Egypt and would become the first Passover celebration. Death would pass over where the blood was. And so began the lesson that life and freedom were given to them only by a life given in their place. Their choice was life or death. But their gift of life was *not without the blood*! First Peter 1:18–19 says, "…knowing that you were not redeemed with corruptible things, like silver or gold, from your aimless conduct received by tradition from your fathers, but with the precious blood of Christ, as of a lamb without blemish and without spot."

THE POWER OF THE BLOOD KEY

If there is one thing that the church has lost today, it is an understanding of the power of the *blood covenant*. A worshiper who understood covenant fully believed he would interact by the divine Spirit of God, and that interaction would allow the Spirit to move through his blood. When the Lord sacrificed His blood for us and overcame death, hell, and the grave, He left His Holy Spirit in the earth to comfort, teach, and direct us. The Holy Spirit is the only restraining force of evil in and around us. When Jesus introduced the Last Supper, He did this to keep our memory aligned with His sacrificial act. He also did this so we would stay aligned with each other in covenant.

Covenant was sealed by the *cutting* of a person or sacrificial animal into two parts, which occurred when God made covenant with Abraham. Covenant was a bond of life fellowship. When Jeremiah started prophesying about the new covenant (Jer. 31), he was talking about a spiritual circumcision or cutting that would occur in our hearts that would allow the Spirit of God to enter our bloodstream and renew our spirit and give us a new spirit.

Hebrews 13:20 says, "Now may the God of peace who brought up our Lord Jesus from the dead, that great Shepherd of the sheep, through the blood of the everlasting covenant." In the early church, the blood covenant bonded you to someone who was not related to you by birth. Your possessions were their possessions (Acts 4:32–35). You committed your all to them and even died for them if that was necessary. That was what caused the early church to multiply so quickly.

In *The Power of the Blood,* H. A. Maxwell Whyte writes:

> While the Bible does not tell us of the chemical composition of the red and white corpuscles, yet it does tell us something which is absolutely basic to the mystery: *the life of the living creature is in its blood.* Thus, in Leviticus 17:11 we read, "For the LIFE of the flesh is IN the blood." But life is almost as mysterious as blood, and very little is understood about it.[2]

He goes on to say that when the Lord breathed into this chemical composition some of His own spiritual life, that life was held in the chemical substance we call blood.

> So, you see, blood is not life, but it carries life.... The life of man is carried in his bloodstream. Life itself is spiritual, but it must have a physical carrier, and this carrier is the blood.... Blood can even be frozen, but the life which is in it is unaffected by this freezing process. Jesus was the only begotten of the Father (John 1:14) and His body was formed and fashioned wonderfully in the womb of Mary His mother; but the LIFE that was in Jesus Christ came alone from the Father by the Holy Spirit. Therefore, this life which flowed in the veins of the Lord Jesus Christ came from God. No wonder He said,

"I am the LIFE." God imparted His own life into the bloodstream of Jesus....If we can clearly understand the meaning of the word "atonement," we have discovered tremendous truth. God has provided a substance by which we can cover things we no longer want; God guarantees not even to see our sins after we reckon by faith that the Blood of Jesus has covered them. When God sees blood, He does not see sin.[3]

We are told in Leviticus 17:12 that not only is the life in the blood, but the blood is the only substance that can make an atonement, or covering for our souls. The sinner, therefore, on accepting a substitute (in Old Testament times it was a clean animal), beholds the substitute dying in his place...for there is not life in the flesh without blood. The Son had offered His LIFE in His BLOOD for all mankind and all shed blood speaks to God....To plead the blood of Jesus is to confess to God that we are depending wholly on His mercy....At Passover in Egypt it took blood to turn the battle in favor of God's people.[4]

There has always been a war in the church over the celebration of Passover. As we already discussed, Constantine forbade this celebration, knowing that it was fine for Christians to have the *name* but not the *empowerment* of the blood of the One they worshiped. The war will always be over the blood of our Lord and how we worship Him. This threatens an enemy that desires to gain power in the earth realm. The anti-Christ force is always against the blood of the Lord Jesus Christ. We must discern this anti-Christ force. As John said, "He must increase, but I must decrease" (John 3:30). His Spirit must increase in our blood.

As anti-Christ forces increase in the blood of mankind, they will attempt to war with anyone who is carrying the life force of Jesus Christ within them. There is a major shift in war. We are moving from the concept of imperialistic warfare, where nations and leaders want to control land, to one in which people in nations want to control how each worships. Revelation 12:10 says, "Then I heard a loud voice saying in heaven, 'Now salvation, and strength, and the kingdom of our God, and the power of His Christ have come, for the accuser of our brethren, who accused them before our God day and night, has been cast down.'" The accuser of the brethren must work with man. God designed man for His redemptive plan. The accuser must cause man to turn against man. When this happens and people come into agreement with the accuser, he can attempt to overcome people groups and dominate them to come under his thought process.

Once we use the name of Jesus and we rely upon the power of His blood, we can draw a bloodline that says to the enemy, "You have no right to cross!" We must learn this type of warfare in the days ahead. This protects our families and homes. This protects our bodies from diseases. Jesus drew a bloodline when He went to the cross and poured out His blood. The power of the blood should be as active in us today (Eph. 1–2) as the day that our Messiah shed His blood for us.

We have discussed the war within our bloodstream. We have touched on how the real war is over His Spirit flowing through our blood to cleanse our conscience so we can stand strong before the world and not allow the world to entice us to be conformed to its blueprint. We have talked about how our minds can be transformed so that we can do the will of God. The mind is transformed because of the Spirit flowing through the blood, the Word of God changing our belief system, and the Spirit of God bringing us into unity with the mind of Christ so we can do the Father's will. We must learn to draw a bloodline so the enemy cannot cross that line and entice us to do his will (2 Tim. 2:26).

Satan's goal is to break the circle of flow or cycle of life that the Father has to offer us from His throne. Jesus reconciled us back to Father and has given us access to go boldly into the throne room. Satan must break that cycle of life that has been offered to each one of us. When he does that, he creates his own cycle.

God always has a plan of *freedom*! Pass over from one season of bondage into a new place of multiplication. In the next few chapters, you will learn to break the power of vexation through the blood by the Spirit and develop a new testimony that overcomes.

Chapter 8

THE WORD KEY

I LOVE THE BOOK of Deuteronomy, which records where Moses reviewed all the Law, Torah, and the wilderness wanderings of a people. Through forty years of wilderness wanderings, the children of Israel had been vexed because of decisions they made that were influenced by unbelief and fear (Num. 14). However, now the time had come for the people to move forward past the confusion, uproar, and trouble of the last season.

In a later chapter I will explain *vexation* more fully, but let me give you a brief understanding now. The Hebrew word *mehuwmah* ("meh-hoo-maw") means "confusion or uproar leading to destruction, discomfiture, trouble, and tumult." When your spirit is vexed, your whole life seems confused.

Moses explained all the blessings that were available to the people in the future if they would obey the Lord and His commandments. Then he explained that the power of vexation would come upon them, spirit, soul, and body, if they did not follow after the Lord's way: "The Lord shall send you curses, confusion, and rebuke in every enterprise to which you set your hand, until you are destroyed, perishing quickly because of the evil of your doings by which you have forsaken me [Moses and God as one]" (Deut. 28:20, AMP). This is the concept of vexation that is linked with our disobedience to the Word of God. There comes a time to leave your wilderness and enter into the next level of prosperity for your life. However, if you review carefully every one of your wilderness times, you will see that during those times, the Word became much more powerful in your life.

In this chapter we will discuss wilderness and how we interact with the Lord in a place of desolation. The Word that we receive in our wilderness place can be a great key to help us to see past the wilderness and learn to overcome murmuring, complaining, and fear in the future.

A TIME TO BELIEVE

I powerfully came into relationship with the Lord when I was eighteen years old. Since that time, one of the things that I have always done is read the Bible. I can read as many as eight chapters per day or a complete book of the Bible. I can find myself lost in God's Word, because the Word is living and the Person of the Word is real. Every year I try to read through the Word based upon the times that we are living in. I guess this is what makes me known as an *Issachar prophet*. Issachar was the Torah tribe, and they knew how to use the Word in time to tell Israel what strategic moves to make to keep advancing.

Many times I will read the Word aloud back to the Lord. He inspired men to write it for us, so it's always good to read it back to Him. Once when I was in a trial to overcome, I had planned to read Romans 6–8. I began by reading Romans 6 and got to verse 14: "For sin shall not have dominion over you..." I stopped abruptly and asked the Lord a question: "Lord, is this a true statement?"

I heard a voice so loudly that I thought there was a person standing in the room with me. The voice said, "Yes!"

I said, "Lord, is this book completely true?"

He said, "Yes. Obey My Word." At that moment I knew that I did not have to submit to sin or allow it to be my master. I knew that nothing in my bloodline was against God, and His best for my life had to control my actions. I knew that I did not have to believe what a person said if it did not align with what God said.

I had never been taught this before in any of the church services that I had attended. A power that seemed to have an inherited control in my family broke at that moment in my life. The domination of something in my bloodline for generations had been exposed by the Spirit of God. The Word and the Spirit had addressed a power in my bloodline, rearranged my life, and then broke me into a new place of victory. My life took a drastic turn from that moment.

I knew I never had to submit to demonic temptations in the same way that my dad had submitted and been overcome. I knew I didn't have to fall to the same strategies and fears that Satan had used to entice my grandfather away from God's best. I knew that I could walk faithfully before the Lord and be in faithful covenant.

When I picked up the Word to read, the still, small voice of Father said, "Do not go to the next verse until you believe the verse you just read." Needless to say, that year it took me much longer to read through the Word.

THE WAR OF THE WORD, THE SPIRIT, AND OUR BONE MARROW

Upon this encounter with the Spirit of God that I just described to you, my daily devotional Bible readings and prayer took on new meaning. God was going to make me a man of faith just like those you read about in Hebrews 11. However, He was going to make sure His Word penetrated deep into me and changed all of my thought processes to align with His.

Hebrews 4:12 (AMP) says, "For the Word that God speaks is alive and full of power [making it active, operative, energizing, and effective]; it is sharper than any two-edged sword, penetrating to the dividing line of the breath of life (soul) and [the immortal] spirit, and of joints and marrow [of the deepest parts of our nature], exposing and sifting and analyzing and judging the very thoughts and purposes of the heart." This is one of the most incredible truths that I have ever encountered.

The Word of God is alive. This Word is full of power and is like a sword that can divide a person's soul and go down into their eternal part, the spirit. The Word is like a breath of life. The Word brings us life. Our bone marrow carries the Word through our body to nurture us with His life. The Word and the Spirit of truth flow through our blood and cleanse our conscience. This gives us clarity to see our way into the future.

The Word causes our heart to change. I believe this change is both a spiritual and physical change. Romans 10:17 says, "So then faith comes by hearing, and hearing by the word of God." Satan's greatest strategy is to stop you from hearing what God has to say to you. He knows that if the voice of God penetrates you, then it will go deep into your bone marrow and rearrange the production of the cell structures within your body, as well as the blood flow of your body. The Word is another key in the war with evil forces that try and stop spiritual life from entering into your physical being. I believe the enemy's greatest strategy is to separate you from the Word and love of God. If he can separate you from the Word of God, you lose the power of life working through your life-giving blood system.

As you read the Word of God and allow that Word to be stored in your heart and develop the way you think, your blood system begins to be purified. The Spirit of God will actually begin to invade blood structures. Then gifts of healing and unusual workings of miracles will manifest. Regarding the outflow of the heart, Matthew 12:34–35 says, "Brood of vipers! How can you, being evil, speak good things? For out of the abundance of the heart the mouth speaks. A good man out of the good treasure of his heart brings forth good things, and an evil man out of the evil treasure brings forth evil things." Romans 10:10 expands by saying, "For with the heart one believes unto righteousness, and with the mouth confession is made unto salvation."

I believe that each time we are ready to move across into our next dimension of promise, we must pass or cross over from one place of faith to our next dimension of glory. In this crossing-over time, there is always a wilderness through which we must journey. How we make this journey through our wilderness is a crucial key to our being established in the new place of promise and anointing.

The Wilderness: The Place Where Your Word Comes Forth

When the Lord began to impress me that His people were to move forward toward their promise, gain momentum, and not look back, the Spirit of God spoke to me and said, "It is time to come through fifty days of wilderness, receive instruction, and then move into power, war for the promise, and enter into rest." Let's see what happens at the end of fifty days in the wilderness. As long as the church is connected to the Head, we represent the Head on Earth and do not reflect the tail of society. We are not to fear the wilderness but confront our wilderness enemy and enter into a new level of relational power with the Father.

We all are destined for wilderness seasons. I would love to say that you will never experience a wilderness time, but that is not a biblical principle. *Wilderness* is a biblical principle. The wilderness is likened to our word for "desert." In reality, during biblical times, the wilderness was usually a rocky, dry wasteland.

We also find in the Bible that wildernesses included oases. Even though many times we find ourselves in a wilderness season, in the midst of our wilderness we can usually find a time of refreshing and a cool drink from the Lord. Biblically, the wilderness could also be a place of refuge. Remember, David fled Saul and entered a wilderness time. Even though his promise was not fulfilled during this time, the call of God on his life was protected.

The wilderness has a time frame.

We always find in the Bible that a wilderness season had a determined time. The wilderness period when God's covenant people left Canaan and went to Egypt was four hundred years. However, God had promised a release. God's covenant people wandered in the wilderness for forty years. Technically, they could have entered the Promised Land within seventy days. *However, God had a time of release.*

When God's people left His purposes to play the part of a harlot, they went into the Babylonian captivity or wilderness for seventy years. *However, God promised a release.*

Jesus was baptized to fulfill all righteousness and then entered into a forty-day wilderness period. *However, the Father had a release.*

I believe that we help determine the length of time we stay in our wilderness. If you want to do a interesting prophetic study, you can study the biblical wildernesses, which include Shur, Sin, Sinai, Paran, Zin, En Gedi, Judah, Moan, and Ziph, to name a few. We also need to remember that Jesus fed the four thousand in a desert wilderness place east of the Sea of Galilee. Therefore, He used the wilderness as the place to teach multiplication to His disciples.

Wilderness wanderings

Wilderness wanderings are complex. Many times people cannot understand what you are going through. However, if you will think of the wilderness as a departure from enslavement and an advancement toward your promise, you will stay focused to get to your next place.

In the wilderness there has to be a viable option for movement. There are usually several routes through your wilderness. The decision of the route determines the amount of warfare you will experience. Sometimes the best route is not what seems to our mind as the *best* or *shortest* route (Exod. 13:17). How we submit ourselves to God in the wilderness many times determines how long we will wander.

In the Old Testament, sins were transferred to a scapegoat, which was released into the wilderness. This is why Jesus had to enter into the wilderness to once and for all withstand all of our temptations. Therefore, Jesus is our best example of overcoming wilderness wanderings. Because of His resistance, He was able to withstand His wilderness time in forty days. I believe He resisted everything that we will ever have to encounter and resist. He entered the wilderness filled with the Spirit, but He came out with power. Any time you enter a wilderness season, have confidence you can resist and come into a new level of power.

Wilderness dangers

In the New Testament we find a warning to *wilderness Christians*. We are warned not to make the same mistakes as the Israelites (1 Cor. 10:1–13; Heb. 3:16–19). In biblical times we find that the wilderness was a place inhabited by beasts of prey, snakes, scorpions, and demons. These creatures were able to produce fear of destruction, but they could be overcome through power, authority, and submission. Our greatest snare in the wilderness is murmuring and complaining over our present position before we reach the place God has for us. Murmuring and complaining hold you in your wilderness longer than it should take to get to your next place. Wilderness complaining and murmuring are a form of unbelief. *Wildernesses are destined for the removal of unbelief.* However, many times when we enter into a desolate place, we forget God's goodness and find unbelief being created.

There is good news and bad news in the wilderness. We find the precedent of God sustaining His people in wilderness times. However, we find the danger of entering into dissatisfaction, remaining there the rest of our lives, and never experiencing the fullness God has for us.

Another key danger of a wilderness time is for *fear* to develop within as the result of the giants you see in your future. At Kadesh Barnea (Num. 20), the designated leaders of the tribes went in to spy out the promise. Numbers 14:34 (KJV) says, "After the number of the days in which ye searched the land, even forty days, each day for a year, shall ye bear your iniquities, even forty years, and ye shall know my breach of promise." Many times in your wilderness experience, God will begin to show you your promise. You will have an opportunity to mix the word of promise with faith or to choose to enter into fear over the resistant forces that you will have to face in your quest for God to manifest the promise. One of the greatest dangers of your wilderness season is that you may choose not to mount up with a mind to war over your promised inheritance. In the Israelites' wilderness wanderings, a whole generation was led astray by the leaders, who discouraged the people from entering into war over God's promise for their lives.

The journey

Life revolves around making your journey through the stops in your wildernesses and experiencing triumph—and then journeying again! For four hundred years, Israel lived as slaves in Egypt. They lived in fear, lack, bondage, and oppression by their enemy. Then God came to them with a promise. He said, "I have more for you than what you have known. I want to bring you out of bondage and take you into a rich land, *a land flowing with milk and honey.* This was a place of peace, prosperity, and blessing." The Book of Exodus describes the process of how, through the blood of the Passover lamb, God redeemed Israel out of Egypt.

However, when Israel left Egypt, they didn't find themselves in the Promised Land. They found themselves in the wilderness. That wilderness was not their destination, but it was a necessary part of the route to the promise. The wilderness was a place of testing. Nowhere did they see "milk and honey"—the picture that had been portrayed when God's promise had been reiterated.

The overall goal of the testing was to teach them to trust the One who was leading them. God had to become God to this people. He would have to become the object of their faith and worship. They would have to learn to respond to new situations by faith. Without faith, they would not be able to enter into the great blessings God wanted to give them. As you read through the Bible, you discover that those who learned to trust God in the wilderness finally did enter the Promised Land. God's goal for His people is always to bring them into the place of His blessing. Israel's journey is a picture of the journey all of us are on.

God has a personal promised land for each one of us! God has a goal, a call, a destiny for your life that includes the fulfillment of every promise. Your journey begins when you trust Jesus and are redeemed. That sets you free from bondage to sin and Satan, but it doesn't automatically bring you into the promise. Many times evangelists promise their hearers that *getting saved* will bring them into the wonderful experience of God's blessing. While these promises are true, many people don't understand the process. The result is that some people are surprised when they get saved, only to find themselves in the wilderness.

GOD'S JOURNEY *ALWAYS*
LEADS THROUGH WILDERNESS

You can't get to the Promised Land without going through the wilderness. God wants to bring you *through* wildernesses and into His promised blessing, but sometimes if you select the most direct route in an attempt to escape the wilderness, you miss your training for overcoming and end up being overcome.

Let's look at Israel's journey. As we read the Book of Exodus, the first thing we notice is that God didn't take them on a direct route. A direct route would have taken them from Egypt to the Promised Land in less than two weeks. But if they had gone the direct route, they would not have been prepared to enter when they got there. The enemies on the direct route were too strong for a people who were just following but not particularly understanding how to war.

God first took the children of Israel to Sinai to teach them to be His people. The journey to Sinai was a journey through wilderness. Now, the wilderness was not a pleasant place to journey through. The wilderness is not a place you would choose for a nice vacation. *Although the wilderness is not a comfortable place, the wilderness is a functional place.* Uncomfortable places make us feel insecure. Usually we can't see where our provision will come from. All we see is sand and dust, and we feel hot—and then more sand and dust and feeling hot. There may be a few rock clefts that we will need to climb while we are dusty and hot.

You can easily get lost in the wilderness, because you have few points of reference. The scorpions and snakes move quickly, and their abundance creates confusion. Sometimes your way seems blocked. How can sand block you? Well, you get so thirsty that you can't seem to get over the next sand dune. In the wilderness you can easily have fear and anxiety. In the wilderness, you'll be tempted to respond like Israel by murmuring and complaining.

UNDERSTANDING THE WILDERNESS— GOD'S PERSPECTIVE

It's not always a *negative* thing to be in the wilderness. There are times when God leads all of us into the wilderness. God doesn't want you to *live* in the wilderness. God doesn't want you to *wander* in the wilderness. God doesn't want you to *die* in the wilderness. But God has good purposes for taking you through the wilderness.

The wilderness is a place of transition. Israel had to go through the wilderness to get to the Promised Land. There are times you can't get to your destination without passing through the wilderness.

The most common Hebrew word for "wilderness" in the Bible is *midbar*. The NIV Bible usually translates *midbar* as "desert." As I stated earlier, when the Bible speaks of wilderness, it's not usually picturing a broad expanse of sand. There is more to the wilderness than sand, snakes, and scorpions. In the Bible, the word *wilderness* simply means "a desolate, uninhabited region." The wilderness areas described in the Bible were dry, but they were not without life. The wilderness had large areas of vegetation. In the ancient world, the wilderness fulfilled an important function. The Hebrew word *midbar* really means "pasture land"! It comes from a root word that means "to drive a flock of sheep."

The wilderness did not have enough vegetation for human settlement, but it was great for sheep. The wilderness was where shepherds tended their sheep. That's why the wilderness is often a picture of the Christian life.

Living in a fallen world, we are often in some kind of wilderness. God wants us to know He is there as our Shepherd to care for us in every wilderness. The wilderness is the primary place we learn God's love and protection.

When you find yourself in the wilderness, it doesn't mean you've missed God. In Luke 4, the Holy Spirit *led* Jesus into the wilderness. We read, "Jesus, being filled with the Holy Spirit, returned from the Jordan and was led by the Spirit into the wilderness" (Luke 4:1). God also led Israel into the wilderness. When Israel ended up in the wilderness, it didn't mean they had taken a wrong turn. They were following the cloud. God *wanted* them to be in the wilderness. There are times that God will lead *you* into the wilderness as well. It is important to know *why* He leads you into the wilderness and *what* He desires to accomplish there.

Let's use Israel as our example.

The Red Sea

Coming out of Egypt, the first thing the children of Israel encountered was the *Red Sea*. This was a traumatic experience. Israel made it out of Egypt, but when they got to the Red Sea, they looked behind and saw Pharaoh chasing after them to try to take them back. This is a picture of a brand-new Christian. When you give your life to Jesus, you are set free, but you quickly discover that your old life will follow after you and try to take you back. Old friends will come around and try to entice you back into the old lifestyle. Old habits will try to resurface.

For Israel, the key to freedom was to pass through the water, and God made a way for them to do that. As they passed through the waters, their old life was cut off behind them. That's a picture of baptism. Baptism cuts you off from your past. Baptismal waters make a declaration. They say, "You are a new creature." Baptism is a time of great joy. When Israel came through the water, they had a big praise celebration!

God will give you victory so that your faith builds for your next test on the road. To enter your destiny, your faith needs to grow. Faith grows when it is *tested*, so God will puts you in situations where your faith is tested, and that takes place in the wilderness.

Five Wilderness Tests

In their season of testing the Israelites encountered five key tests. This was not a pleasant part of their path to walk.

1. Marah: bitter water

When they left the shores of the Red Sea, Israel traveled through the desert for three days without finding water. When they came to Marah, they could not drink its water because it was bitter. So the people grumbled against Moses, saying, "What are we to drink?" Israel was in a bad situation. They were three days into their journey in the desert and were running out of water. This was a group of two million people—men, women, and children, along with all their livestock. If they found no water to drink, they would all die.

After three days in the desert, they came to a beautiful oasis. This appeared to be a miracle on their road. You can just picture them running toward the water and throwing themselves down at its edge, eager for a big drink of fresh water. But when they tasted it, they spit it out. The water was bitter! It was poisoned! Undrinkable! They *still* had no water to drink. Faced with this problem, they had a choice. Their first option was that they could choose to remember what God had done for them in the past. They could have chosen to believe He would provide. They could have said, "Lord, we will trust You to meet our needs."

Their other option was that they could focus on their problem and grumble in unbelief. Unfortunately, they did the same thing we often do—they grumbled and complained. Let me *camp out* here for a while since this is where we normally camp out. In the Christian life, many of us never get past this first wilderness stop. *Complaining, or murmuring, is dangerous.* Here are four dangers of murmuring:

> 1. *Murmuring cuts off our vision for the future.* Jesus did not murmur and complain on the cross, because His eyes were fixed on the outcome: "For the joy that was set before Him endured the cross, despising the shame" (Heb. 12:2). We don't complain in the wilderness if our eyes are on the promised land! Our problem is that Satan tells us there is no way out of the wilderness. Satan tells us, "You will die in the wilderness—there's no way out!" God says, "Follow Me! I have a promised land for you!" We get to choose who we're going to agree with. When we complain, we are agreeing with the devil that our future is cut off.

2. *Murmuring is dangerous because it causes us to doubt God's goodness for the present.* When we complain, we are saying, "God, I don't like the route You have mapped for my life."

3. *Murmuring causes unbelief to deepen and grow.* The Lord told me something awhile back. He said, "Unbelief is like a seed; if you water it, it will grow." Every time we complain, we are *watering* our unbelief. What happens when you are underwater and open your mouth wide? Water comes in! In the same way, when we open our mouth to complain, unbelief floods in.

4. *Murmuring invites greater adversity.* Some of us have gotten into a cycle that gets worse and worse! When we're having a problem with someone and we complain, what happens? We experience more adversity. Murmuring puts us under a curse. Let me prove this from Scripture. What was Israel's complaint in the wilderness? The Jewish people said, "We are going to die in the wilderness!" That was not God's plan. He had promised to get them to the Promised Land.

Then the Lord spoke to Moses and Aaron, saying, "How long shall I bear with this evil congregation who complain against Me? I have heard the complaints which the children of Israel make against Me. Say to them, 'As I live,' says the LORD, 'just as you have spoken in My hearing, so I will do to you: The carcasses of you who have complained against Me shall fall in this wilderness.'"

—NUMBERS 14:27–29

What was God was saying? "You have refused to come into agreement with My words over your life, so instead I will come into agreement with your words." We must be careful about what we say.[1]

Returning to the account of the bitter waters at Marah, we find that Moses cried out to the Lord, and God was gracious and provided. The Lord showed Moses a piece of wood. He said, in effect, "Moses, let Me tell you a secret. Bitter water is not a problem for Me! I can heal bitter water. See that piece of wood? Put it in the water and see what happens." Moses put the stick in the water, and the water was healed. And then God said something else: "And by the way, Moses...I not only heal water; I heal people! If you listen to My voice, I will keep you well, for I am the Lord who heals you." This is where God revealed Himself by the covenant name *Yahweh Rophe*. God was identifying Himself to His people as a God who would heal their physical infirmities. God wants us to know Him that way also. That is *always* part of who God is!

This was the precursor of our Healer hanging on a tree (the cross) to deliver us from all of our past murmuring and complaining and making a way for us to advance into the promise of eternal life. *We can learn to praise God in adversity. We can praise God for His goodness.* Even when God has us in the wilderness, there are blessings for which we can praise Him. When Israel was in the wilderness, they received manna (bread) from heaven. It came every day. Their shoes did not wear out for forty years. They saw the visible *Shekinah* glory of God leading them as a pillar of cloud by day and as a pillar of fire by night. God's goodness is not cut off from us in the wilderness. We need to take our eyes off the discomfort of our situation and look around us. We will surely find things for which we can offer praise. *We can praise God for His presence.* No matter what wilderness we are in, God is in it with us. His presence is there. *We can praise God for the outcome.* No matter what wilderness we are in, God has a plan for us through that wilderness, and it is a plan to take us into a place of promise.

2. Elim: abundant blessing

Their next stop was Elim. Exodus 15:27 reads, "Then they came to Elim, where there were twelve wells of water and seventy palm trees; so they camped there by the waters." Elim was a beautiful place, a place of rest and full provision. Usually when people teach about Israel's testing in the wilderness, they skip right over Elim. But Elim was a test also. This was a different kind of test. Elim wasn't a test based on lack but a test based on God's blessing. After the hot, dry desert and the disappointment at Marah, God brought them to a beautiful place. The test here was, *How would they respond to blessing?* When God blesses us, He's looking for a response of thankfulness. His goal is that we "serve the LORD your God with joy and gladness of heart, for the abundance of everything" (Deut. 28:47).

When things were bad, Israel was always quick to complain. Would they be just as quick to praise God with a thankful heart when He blessed them? Again, they failed the test. We read the account of their stay at Elim, and there is no mention of a thankful response.

3. The Wilderness of Sin: no food

Next they came to the *Wilderness of Sin*. The problem there was a lack of food. By this time, the people should have begun learning about the goodness of God. They should have concluded that they could trust Him to watch over them. But again, they only murmured and complained. Exodus 16 tells us that they came to the Desert of Sin and grumbled against Moses: "If only we had died in Egypt! There we ate all the food we wanted." When they got hungry, suddenly the place of bondage in Egypt didn't look so bad. They quickly forgot that their children had been murdered and they were worked to death! All they remembered was the *food*. Their problem was that they were looking backward to Egypt instead of looking forward to the promise. In a time of testing, it's important to keep your eyes on the promise. But even though they failed the test, God showed His willingness to provide. He brought them quail in the evening and manna in the morning.

4. Rephidim: no water

Then they came to Rephidim. The problem in Rephidim was that there was no water to drink. So they quarreled with Moses and said, "Give us water to drink." God was again testing them to see if they would trust Him.

They had already seen God's ability and power. They had seen that God handled *water problems* very easily. He turned the Nile to blood and then back to water. He opened the way through the water at the Red Sea then closed it back over the Egyptian armies. He healed the bitter water at Marah. In light of what they had seen, they could have chosen to trust God for water. But instead, they grumbled. But God was gracious and provided for them in spite of their unbelief. God gave water from the rock. In all of these situations, they had a clear choice. They could choose to focus on God's faithfulness and be filled with anticipation, or they could focus on their fear and be filled with anxiety. That kind of testing continued all the way through the wilderness.

5. Rephidim: Amalekites attack

Also at Rephidim, the Amalekites attacked. The Amalekites had been ambushing the stragglers and the weak. (That's still Satan's strategy. He tries to get people isolated. When you are isolated, you become vulnerable. You should always be *connected* somewhere.) But God again showed His goodness. Moses sent Joshua to lead the army against the Amalekites. As the battle raged, Moses went into intercession. He climbed to the top of the hill overlooking the battlefield, raised his hands, and prayed. As long as Moses held up his hands in prayer, the Israelites won. But when Moses grew weary and put his hands down, the Amalekites began to win.

Aaron and Hur saw that Moses was too weary to keep his hands up, so they got on either side of Moses and held his hands up so he could continue in prayer. Moses built an altar to the Lord. He proclaimed there the name of *Yahweh Nissi*—"the Lord, our Banner"—"for hands were lifted up to the throne of the Lord" (Exod. 17:16, NIV). Moses was setting an example for the people. He was saying, "You don't have to murmur and complain. You can lift up your hands to the Lord, and He will deliver. He will war with you. He will give you victory. He is a miraculous God and will be your rearguard as well as lead you forward."

LEARNING THE LESSON OF THE WILDERNESS

In all of these situations, it's important to see what God was doing. I believe there were several things He wanted to accomplish during this time. He was trying to teach Israel His faithfulness. They could count on Him to provide.

He was trying to build into them a response of faith. When a new situation arose, He wanted their first response to be one of faith in Him. He was testing them to see if they would reject fear and simply choose to trust Him. The problem was, they never learned. Because they didn't pass the test, they were ultimately not able to enter the land of promise. When you find yourself in the wilderness, you always have that same choice. You can trust in God's faithfulness and be filled with anticipation *or* you can give in to fear and be filled with anxiety. You can remember what God has done in the past and choose to believe He will provide again *or* you can focus on your problem and grumble in unbelief. You can *lift up your hands* in praise and commit your life to Him *or* you can *throw up your hands* in despair and try to find your own path. You always have a choice. And the choice you make determines your future.

CHAPTER 9

SINAI—GOD ESTABLISHES
A NEW ORDER

FINALLY THE PEOPLE arrive at *Sinai*. At Sinai, God established a new order for them. There are times God sits you down and says, "Here are some things you need to know!" Sinai represented a season of *instruction*. When God brings you into that kind of season, it's a very special time. Treasure it! What He teaches you in a season of instruction will equip you for all that lies ahead. At Sinai, God gave Israel two things: First, He gave them the *Torah*. *Torah* literally means "the teaching of God." In the Torah He revealed what He was like, what they could trust Him for, and how they could dwell in His presence. *He also gave them the tabernacle.* The tabernacle was a tent where God dwelt in their midst. Through the tabernacle, God revealed some very important things.

Here are some key, simple lessons from the tabernacle. At the tabernacle, God showed them that He wanted to dwell with His people. He wanted His *power and presence* to be the mark of a people who know Him.

For His presence to dwell with His people there must be *preparation*. He must have a holy (special) place set apart for His presence (Exod. 25:8). The Israelites were required to *honor* Him with their very best. Only our best is good enough for God. Finally, because the tabernacle and the presence were central to the movement of the tribes and the camps, they had to learn to *put Him at the center* of their lives. God had the people encamp in a very specific order—three tribes on each side of the ark of the covenant, which was in the tabernacle. Three tribes to the north, three to the south, three to the east, and three to the west, all with the ark, or His covenant, central. When they moved, the ark and the tabernacle had to move before them. Every time they stopped, they were to place the tabernacle in the exact center of all activity and people.

If we want to experience His blessing, God cannot be just a peripheral activity or interest in our lives. He must be the center around which all else is arranged.

In all of this journey, God was working to accomplish one thing: *to prepare a people for Himself.* He was teaching them that they could trust Him; from trust He would lead them into the fullness of His promise. He is the same today and is doing His will the same today. In every situation, God is working in your life to teach you and strengthen your faith so that you can enter into the blessing He has prepared for you. *To prepare* means "to erect a frame where a foundation is attached" and from where you can build your future. So let God take you on His journey. Learn the lessons of the wilderness. Receive His instruction. In every situation, commit your life to Him so you can be fully prepared to enter the promise.

Come Through Into Power

I see ten issues we need to understand as we come through this next wilderness season. Some of you have been in a wilderness season long enough. Others are entering in a season that should not be prolonged. And some are ready to come out of a wilderness and see their promise fulfilled.

1. *Look for your time of opening into the next season* (Gen. 8:6). At the end of forty days, Noah opened the window of the ark and sent out a raven and then a dove. He waited until he saw the sign of land that he needed. Declare an open window of heaven and look for the sign from the Lord that your wilderness is ending.

2. *Look for a shift from mourning to joy* (Gen. 50:3). Biblically, mourning has a set period of time. They mourned the loss of Joseph for forty days. Many of us are going through mourning seasons. However, let God break your mourning into dancing. Make a list of how death is

keeping you hostage, and declare that the power of loss and robbing must end at the end of this period.

3. *Get ready to receive revelation regarding God's covenant plan for your future* (Exod. 24:18; 34:28). Moses waited forty days, and God gave him the boundaries for the future generation.

4. *In your time of searching, do not let your perspective overtake God's reality* (Num. 13:25). A group of Israelites went out and spied on the land for forty days. During your searching time, let God reveal the intricacies of your promise. However, do not let the vision of war overtake you.

5. *Allow this time to be one of developing an inner responsibility so you can steward the riches that God has to release to you in the future.* This is a key time to look at the stewardship issues of your life. You may be linked into a wilderness issue of supply. Be willing to change and take what God has given you and invest in a new way (Num. 14:34; Luke 19).

6. *Use this as a time of repentance* (Deut. 9:18). One key reason for wilderness times is to use the time to change your mind and think the way God thinks. Allow the Lord to place His finger on what you must turn from so you can find your path out of the wilderness.

7. *Experience the wilderness as a time of mercy* (Deut. 10:10). Even though the people fell into idolatry when Moses went on Mount Sinai the first time, God let him go up again. Know that past mistakes can be rectified quickly. During this next forty days, look for your *second-chance* times.

8. *Do not agree with any atmosphere of unbelief.* This is not a time to fear the voice of the giant (1 Sam. 17:16). Goliath taunted God's covenant people forty days. The devil will try to convince you during your wilderness season that he will overcome you. He might speak, but do not receive his lies.

9. *Reconcile corporate vision* (Ezek. 4:9). Ezekiel interceded for Judah for forty days. Review corporate failures that you have experienced.

10. *Develop spiritual discipline* (Matt. 4:2). Jesus fasted during His wilderness time so He would stay alert to the enemy.

Move Into Multiplication

The triumphant release has begun. Keep counting until you move into multiplication! From the day they were released from the power of the Egyptians, God intended for the Israelites to escape and not look back. His intent was the same as when He placed man in the garden in the beginning. He wanted them to get to their garden or Promised Land and begin *to multiply.* For the children of Israel, He wanted them to count the days of the wilderness as a time to receive instruction. He did not want them entering a daily count that would add up to forty *years.* Rather, He wanted them to understand that if they kept their heart correct toward Him, they could count their way through the wilderness in a matter of *days.* They left at Passover, and fifty days later they received revelation for their future. From that time forward, this would become a pattern and way of life for the Israelites to learn harvest. Harvest would begin at Passover and shift fifty days later at Pentecost. If they learned to expect this shift of increase, they would know something was wrong if they did not see the harvest increase. They would know that they had hung in a place too long, and God's power of increase was not working in their life. They would know that they had remained in a wilderness transition too long.

Every year the Israelites enter into *the counting of the omer*. I believe this is a key to understand in our journey toward promise. Through this tradition, the people would always be reminded of their escape from Egypt from generation to generation throughout history. We discussed Passover in the last chapter. Passover was the day to remember deliverance and to begin *a counting* from one harvest entry point until harvest was moving into fullness. This was known as the *counting of the omer*.

So what is the *counting of the omer*? According to the Torah (Lev. 23:15), the period known as the *counting of the omer* is the period between the Passover and *Sahvu'ot*. This counting produces a time-sequenced guide that opens the way for new revelation (the time the Torah was given) and multiplication (the time between the barley harvest and the first wheat harvest). Some groups *count* different ways, but the real issue is the time and created anticipation of breakthrough produced. At the end of the fifty days after leaving Egypt, they received the Torah.

"The counting is intended to remind us of the link between Passover, which commemorates the Exodus, and Shavu'ot, which commemorates the giving of the Torah. It reminds us that the redemption from slavery was not complete until we received the Torah."[1] Thus the *counting of the omer* demonstrates how important it is for a Jew to accept the Torah in his own life. This is the counting of the days between Passover and Pentecost.

A passage that really speaks to me regarding the expectation associated with the counting of the omer is Joshua 5:11–12. The manna ceased on the day after the children of Israel entered into the land of Canaan: "And they ate of the produce of the land on the day after the Passover, unleavened bread and parched grain, on the very same day. Then the manna ceased on the day after they had eaten the produce of the land."

This counting season is a time to recognize that there is a host of heaven available to us even in the wilderness. Let the host of heaven aid you. Mark 1:13 says, "And He was there in the wilderness forty days, tempted by Satan, and was with the wild beasts; and the angels ministered to Him." This is a time to expect visitation (Acts 1:3). Fifty days from Passover, Jesus presented Himself to His disciples after He had suffered death. Let a new expectation rise in you. Count each day as a day that you will have a new level of faith arise, and you will enter a new power to overcome. Declare in every wilderness season that faces you, "*I will find my Pentecost!*"

FROM WILDERNESS TO POWER

Finally, receive power. Luke 4:13–15 says, "Now when the devil had ended every temptation, he departed from Him until an opportune time. Then Jesus returned in the power of the Spirit to Galilee, and news of Him went out through all the surrounding region. And He taught in their synagogues, being glorified by all." I believe the Lord is building a resistance within us at this time. This is a time of endurance. I also believe that Satan is looking for an opportune time to bring defeat and confusion on the body of Christ. However, the Lord is mounting us up with power. God is developing a new level of power within His people. The church must not continue hanging on to the last season of power, which is not enough for this new season.

Power is the ability to act or produce an effect. Power also signifies the possession of authority that an individual has over others. God revealed His act during Creation. We are about to see new creative acts of God occur. He is also raising up leadership new and fresh and developing people's gifting in a new way. This will give us dominion in the earth. We are about to see a new wave of power in relation to forgiveness of sin. The church is about to be cleaned up in such a way that we will have a pure conscience to advance. We are about to see a new release of power in the prophetic unction of God's people, which will come from prophetic accuracy. There is about to be a release of God's Spirit on the earth, and those who are willing to receive will receive power. When power is processed by faith properly, we see authority demonstrated (Matt. 8). Even though you might feel weak now, get ready to receive power. Let your wilderness time develop a new strength and power for you. He gives us power to tread on serpents and scorpions and over all the power of the enemy.

Who is this coming out of the wilderness?...Do not be afraid, you beasts of the field; for the open pastures are springing up, and the tree bears its fruit; the fig tree and the vine yield their strength.
—SONG OF SONGS 3:6; JOEL 2:22

Gain strength now so you can withstand the enemy when he comes at you at a more opportune time. I bless you as you stand and come through your wilderness time and into a new place of power and authority.

BITTER ROOTS PRODUCE SICKNESS AND DEFILEMENT

I am praying that we learn to make our journey through every wilderness season of our lives without murmuring and complaining. Sometimes complaining issues from *bitterness*. Bitterness has a definite progression. Perhaps you have prayed and are still struggling with a particular problem in your life. What do you do next? You tell someone (everyone who will listen) how upset you are about the situation. Most of us have done this at one time or another. When we do, we usually seek sympathy but often land in self-pity. Murmuring arises out of what I call *a heart of bitterness* and is a weapon in the arsenal of the enemy. Wherever there is complaining, you can be sure that faith is no longer present.

James 3:14 reads, "But if you have bitter envy and self-seeking in your hearts, do not boast and lie against the truth." The context of this passage is that of a teacher instructing with wisdom. Bitterness and envy go hand in hand. This combination produces confusion and every evil thing.

Hebrews 12:14–15 says, "Pursue peace with all people, and holiness, without which no one will see the Lord: looking carefully lest anyone fall short of the grace of God; lest any root of bitterness springing up cause trouble, and by this many become defiled." This verse is a warning that bitterness can cause us to leave the faith. Bitterness can become a root that not only defiles our whole body but also defiles God's corporate purpose, which we are a part of. Israel as a whole became infected with bitterness in the wilderness, and because of it a whole generation was unable to enter into the promise. When we are struggling in the area of murmuring or complaining, we must allow God to remove the bitterness and restore our pleasant fragrance.

Jeremiah 29:11 (NAS) says, "'For I know the plans that I have for you,' declares the LORD, 'plans for welfare and not for calamity to give you a future and a hope.'" God always has a promised outcome. When we are in the midst of the test, we can say, "Lord, I praise You! I thank You for this opportunity to trust You. Lord, I thank You for the outcome—for the blessings You will bring me through this test." When we choose to praise instead of complain, unbelief is cut off. At that very moment we are enabled to lift up our shield of faith and receive the promise.

Don't fear in the wilderness. Just keep going. The new waits for you. Isaiah 43:1–2, 18–19 says:

> But now, thus says the LORD, who created you, O Jacob,
> And He who formed you, O Israel:
> "Fear not, for I have redeemed you;
> I have called you by your name;
> You are Mine.
> When you pass through the waters, I will be with you;
> And through the rivers, they shall not overflow you.
> When you walk through the fire, you shall not be burned,
> Nor shall the flame scorch you....
>
> "Do not remember the former things,
> Nor consider the things of old.
> Behold, I will do a new thing,
> Now it shall spring forth;
> Shall you not know it?
> I will even make a road in the wilderness
> And rivers in the desert."

GO THROUGH TO OCCUPY

Every new season has a wilderness portion. That's a biblical principle I want you to understand to help you maneuver through your dry, rocky places. In every wilderness place there is an overall temptation. However, we also need to learn how the tempter operates.

We have to change our atmosphere and our sphere of authority so we can get to the place that God says, "This is where you occupy your land." In other words, the whole issue is this: *taking dominion*. How are we going to take dominion? How are we going to stay in communion with God so we never lose sight of His purpose? When do we reach our promised place? How do we take dominion in the promise He's given us?

You have a promise. You go through crossing out of one season so you can move toward that promise. Your ultimate goal is to rule in the promise you've been given. That was the issue of why the children of Israel left Egypt and came through the Red Sea: *God had a boundary for them to rule.* They were going to have to get to that boundary and learn to rule in that boundary. They were going to have to move little by little until they had fully taken dominion and established His authority in the area they had been given to rule.

In the Bible, *land* is often equated with your *mind*. How will you think? How will you submit your understanding to a holy God so you think like Father thinks? We will discuss the Lord as *the Father of your spirit* in a following chapter. *Yeshua*, the Messiah, during the forty days of wilderness He went through, could only do what the Father would do in that hard place. He had to recoup the failures of mankind in the past and resist their temptations in the future. To do this He needed to learn the voice of Father and resist the voice of the tempter; He had retake the *land* of fallen mankind.

If you lose sight of *occupying*, the wilderness will swallow you up. *Occupy* means "to take possession." You've been given something; how will you possess it? It's not just to take possession but also to keep possession. There is a great war to keep possession once you take possession. How will we keep worshiping so we keep possession of what God has given us? This is where I think most people don't understand dominion. It's not just *getting in your promise* and not just *getting the deed of your promise*, but *keeping* the deed to your promise.

Many of you have heard me share portions of my testimony. We had the deed to our promised land. My dad had gained the sections of his family land, twelve brothers and sisters of the Pierce clan. However, we did not retain the deed to that land, which created a great sense of loss. You can get the full deed and not keep the record and authority over the land where your deed was titled. *To occupy* means "to cover your field." Possession is, "The earth is the Lord's and the fullness thereof," so what you take possession of you have to cover with God's glory. That is what breaks the *wilderness* concept of your possession. Be sure your possession is filled with God's glory. Jesus did.

CHAPTER 10

JESUS—OUR BEST EXAMPLE IN THE WILDERNESS

I F WE MODEL after Jesus, we will always be victorious to come through and go into the next season. Jesus moved through His wilderness *stops*. To do so, He had to resist forty straight days. Never before had the enemy's tempting voice so bombarded anyone on Earth. All mankind hung in the balance over this forty-day confrontation and war in the wilderness.

The key to Yeshua's victory was that He submitted. When He entered into the wilderness, He immediately submitted Himself to Father God. From submission He was able to resist the enemy.

- He resisted presumption.

- He resisted pride.

- He resisted the lust of the eyes.

- He resisted the promise of grandeur.

We must submit in the midst of our testings. *To submit* means "to stand under." *To resist* means "to stand against." When we submit, we gain the power of what we are standing under. Then we can resist from that power and authority that are flowing from above into the very depth of our being. Our spirit man is filled by the spirit or Spirit to whom we are submitted. From the power and manifestation of that spirit, we resist. Jesus had entered the wilderness filled with the Spirit that had rested on Him when He submitted to be baptized by John the Baptist.

The moment we stop resisting, our spirit man is invaded with an atmosphere that leads to vexation. Satan will meet you on every front and use any tactic to take the deed that you have been given. The enemy's goal is to make sure you fall short in your ability to prosper. Not only are we to multiply, but we are also to expand the boundaries of our land, both spiritually and physically.

Each phase of expansion in your life has a wilderness front. Most of us think, "If I can just make it through one wilderness, I've won the whole war." Every phase of expansion has a wilderness front through which you must learn to war. You must always allow the Spirit of God to evaluate you in each of the phases.

Jesus Taught Us True
Humility in the Wilderness

The only way you can make it through the first stop on your path to destiny is to stay humble. Being humble does not mean you cower down to the enemy. To be humble means you *rely upon* someone other than yourself. You bend yourself over so you're not exalting yourself above everyone else. You submit your thoughts. You lay down your own human reasoning and listen for instruction. To be a disciple, you must be teachable. You must never believe that you *know it all*, or you will become apathetic to change. To be humble means that you're bending yourself over to get through a rocky, dry place with many dangers. In other words, if you stay *low*, your head will remain in a protected state so you can hear how to move. You will know when to go right or go left.

Anytime you are in a wilderness place, you must humble yourself until *the word that will lead out comes forth*. Revelation must meet you and lead you from destination to destination. All wilderness places have a release of the Word. When we embrace the exhortation or correction of the word we receive, we will experience victory and authority. That is a scriptural principle. The Word will come to you that will allow you to take possession of one wilderness place so you can move to the next and then the next until you have established your authority for the future.

REMEMBER THE PROPHETIC WORD

Always remember the prophetic Word while you move through the wilderness! John the Baptist transitioned his authority of one season over to the Messiah. The prophecy in Isaiah 40 defines this transition. A wilderness season was prophesied: "'Comfort, yes, comfort My people!' says your God. 'Speak comfort to Jerusalem, and cry out to her, that her warfare is ended'" (Isa. 40:1–2). Many times prophecy states the end and the beginning. In this wilderness place, Isaiah prophesied:

> "Her iniquity is pardoned;
> For she has received from the LORD's hand
> Double for all her sins."
> The voice of one crying in the wilderness:
>
> "Prepare the way of the LORD;
> Make straight in the desert
> A highway for our God.
> Every valley shall be exalted
> And every mountain and hill brought low;
> The crooked places shall be made straight
> And the rough places smooth;
> The glory of the LORD shall be revealed,
> And all flesh shall see it together;
> For the mouth of the LORD has spoken."
> The voice said, "Cry out!"
> And he said, "What shall I cry?"
>
> —ISAIAH 40:2–6

In your wilderness place, there is a prophecy working to bring God's plan of fulfillment into your life and the earth in which we walk.

Now look at another portion of that prophecy in Isaiah. Read all the way from Isaiah 40 through Isaiah 62, and you will understand the full concept of what will happen in the seasons ahead to fulfill the plan of Father in the earth. Good news is coming! These portions of Scripture say that we will press through our wilderness to get to the manifestation of the good news.

> The Spirit of the Lord God is upon Me,
> Because *the Lord has anointed Me*
> To preach good tidings to the poor;
> *He has sent Me* to heal the brokenhearted,
> To proclaim liberty to the captives,
> And the opening of the prison to those who are bound;
> To proclaim the acceptable year of the Lord,
> And the day of vengeance of our God;
> To comfort all who mourn,
> To console those who mourn in Zion,
> To give them beauty for ashes,
> The oil of joy for mourning,
> The garment of praise for the spirit of heaviness;
> That they may be called trees of righteousness,
> The planting of the Lord, that He may be glorified.
> And they shall rebuild the old ruins.
> —Isaiah 61:1–4, emphasis added

Repentance Has Three Dimensions

Look for those who are going before you with a message of change. Don't keep advancing through the wilderness without knowing why you're in that wilderness and what is being tested. John was preaching a certain message. That's why he's called *the Baptist*. He was preaching repentance. *To repent* means "to change your mind." If we change our mind, we can take new land.

Repentance has three dimensions. First, repentance takes an intellectual shift. Your brain has to shift. You have to say, "I believe this, but here is another paradigm that I'm having to choose." You see the theory presented, and you have to make the choice that *this is right*. You understand in your intellect that what you have heard is a correct direction for your life. We must remember that "the carnal mind is enmity against God" (Rom. 8:7).

The next level of repentance comes when all of a sudden your emotions have to let go of some old issues that would keep you from really grabbing hold of this new paradigm. This is usually where a lot of people never repent. Our emotions stay tied to the past, tied to the way we operate, whom we operate with, and why we had problems in a previous situation. Without allowing the Lord to touch and change our emotions, we really do not fully repent. Our spirit will remain in angst and annoyed. We always live with a measure of emotion that prevents us from seeing our future clearly. You have to be healed in your emotions of the past to shift into your future.

The third component of repentance is that there has to be a *will* action. The will action produces the reality of your repentance. John the Baptist was drawing people to the wilderness. Their status and upbringing didn't matter. Their wealth or poverty was not an issue. We find that publicans came out. Soldiers came out. The people had not forgotten that there was a Torah. Rather, they did not see a reality in the Torah; there was no reality in the operation of the Word. Most revivals take on this character of a wilderness-season repentance because we have gotten so far from the reality of the Word. We're acknowledging the Word in a new way by saying, "O my God, how did we drift so far from it?"

JESUS IS BAPTIZED

John the Baptist baptized people so they would actually recognize the shift in their thought processes. Certain denominations, like the Baptist denomination, follow the same method. John the Baptist helped people shift their way of thinking and move in a certain way. This was a valid baptism, and there was nothing wrong with his message. But unless the people also moved forward from this baptism, they would remain in a *wilderness* way of spiritual life. Today many moves of God remain in this place—left in the wilderness with this baptism. You're not out of the wilderness. You know you want to live a better life that has been presented to you. You want to have your conscience clean of the way you have been thinking and doing.

There's nothing wrong with John's baptism, and it is a wonderful method. People came by the droves to get into this form of change. Jesus Himself went there to get into and connect with that which paved the way for the next dimension that we must enter. Jesus went and got in this move. The only way we can be affirmed for the next move of Father is to connect with the last major move He was doing. The only way we will get to our next *there* is to come out to the wilderness, get dunked in what was, and then allow something new to happen.

When Jesus connected and was baptized, the heavens opened. Something Father had planned was completed in that wilderness season. This is important. You must watch for what was completed in your wilderness season. This is how *fullness* comes into reality. There are certain things that will produce a fullness in one wilderness season that release us into the Pentecost season ahead. Isaiah prophesied in one season. John the Baptist prophesied in the next. We're saying, "You can come out of that season. There is something coming!"

THE HEAVENS OPEN AND
A NEW SEASON BEGINS

Jesus came to the wilderness of the last season—a season that stretched hundreds of years back, to the point when time began. All of a sudden there was a fullness of time. All righteousness had been fulfilled. Jesus connected the last season of mankind to the season waiting in the future. The heavens opened and God spoke, and everyone there recognized that the season had ended. A new anointing came down upon Yeshua to lead us into the next season of repentance.

Jesus had to be affirmed as Messiah; He had to be affirmed as a different move of God. And that's what leads us up to the wilderness temptation. The wilderness temptation is not like other temptations. The wilderness temptation in your life is not the same as a normal temptation you go through. A lot of people don't think like this.

Jesus had been tempted since the day He was born. He wasn't *the boy in the bubble.* He was tempted when He was twelve years old when His parents wanted Him to pull out of what He was forming. He was tempted as a man. But this wilderness temptation when He was thirty years old was different from anything He'd experienced before because the wilderness temptation represented His new season that He was now leading in.

The wilderness temptation that Jesus went through was a greater type of confrontation than He had ever experienced, because a whole new season hinged on that temptation. That's why the warfare was different. He had to connect worlds. He needed to connect two worlds in this temptation. He was connecting a physical world with a spiritual world that was a new, divine connection. Heaven and Earth connected in a different way. In a wilderness temptation, we're not just prophesying to prophesy, and we're not teaching just to teach. Rather, we are in a different moment in a history of the manifestation of the word. There is this divine connecting of worlds, and that's why the temptation is greater.

Once Jesus made it through this temptation, He needed to return to last season's structure and look face-to-face at those who watched Him grow up. He had to go back to Nazareth, to the synagogue, and face off in the place He'd been going all those years. The very people who had been worshiping with Him in the last season needed to face off with who He was in the new season. Did you recognize this is what was happening? He had to go back to the same synagogue He grew up in and face them off in the *new* He came through. And in doing that, He cast a demon out of the synagogue leader! This is the reality of our wilderness temptation. In this wilderness temptation, certain things are so important for us to understand. First of all, these were not internal temptations Jesus faced. He'd been dealing with that for thirty years. We must get to a point where the enemy is not able to affect us with all our internal issues. These weren't internal issues that Jesus was facing.

The purpose of any temptation is to gain an advantage over you and to put an upper hand over your land; you are tempted so an upper hand can get over your land. But there's a level of temptation that is linked to your destiny. That is why the Lord has a certain grace for you when you're going through all your childish schemes, before you've put away your youthful desires. Some people grow old with some besetting sin still in operation that they should have gotten rid of by the time they were twenty-six. We must get past those internal issues, because there is a greater spiritual world out there that God wants to use us in. Jesus's temptation was linked with the original intent of Father for His life. Those temptations were coming to connect with the inward, original intent that He was to accomplish in His future.

Those temptations were not attacking Jesus the man but Jesus the Messiah, because seasons had shifted. There will be corporate temptations for a church, business, ministry, and family until that work reaches the true identity that God intended. The enemy intends these temptations to prevent a full identity from manifesting. You must get to a place of maturity where you display who you are and are used to change or influence the culture you are positioned in for your future.

There are levels and degrees of temptation. Unlike Peter, who went back to an old vocation after failing in his moment of trial, Jesus did not return to being a carpenter. With Jesus, the temptation was against His future destiny and identity as Messiah. He was no longer a carpenter; He was God as man, who would resist and redeem man. There are times that Satan will come against you to stop you from manifesting who you will be in the future. You have to recognize this plot every time you make a shift to a new place. You have to ask yourself, "Why am I going through this here?" It's because your destiny will now be seen in a new way in a new place.

Jesus's temptations were designed to tempt Him so He would not be the head of a new movement. He was not being tempted over the old, fallen race. He was being tempted in a whole new movement of a redeemed people who were going to take dominion in a new way. The temptations were to stop God's redemptive plan for mankind. They were to break the power of the anointing that had come from heaven when heaven opened. All of a sudden these wilderness temptations were contending with the voice that had entered the earth and commissioned the next level of redemption for mankind. These temptations were not contending with Jesus's last thirty years. Rather, there was contention because heaven had opened up and a new anointing had come down on Him like a dove. The Spirit was now leading a new movement, so hell had to attempt to keep an upper hand over mankind. Every time you get a new anointing, hell will contend against you.

Now let's look at the power of the tempter and how he works against us in a new season as opposed to an old season. First of all, he realized Jesus was in a famished condition. He was tired. He was hungry. He had pressed through one season, and now He was in the wilderness, led by the Spirit, with a new anointing that had come on Him—but without any sustenance. When this happened to the children of Israel, they murmured. Jesus withstood.

Satan must find the right moment to take advantage of you before your identity reflects your future. Jesus needed to redeem what the serpent did to entice Adam, the old man. The new man is already working, but Satan went back to Adam, the old man, and tried his oldest method on Him. He said, "Are You...?" He needed to put doubt in Jesus's mind, because when the heavens opened, the Word that came upon Him was, "You *are* My beloved Son."

Satan had to ask Him, "Are You really that? Are You really that which was said about You? Have you really shifted Your identity from the last season to this season? Are we really in a new dimension? Is heaven really connecting?" The tempter's oldest method was used first—but it failed.

He then attempted to incite Jesus to be dissatisfied. He does the same things with us and tries to make us dissatisfied with our new place. Some might say, "We were doing good. Why are you trying to change things?" In a new season, we must learn to be satisfied in our new place. We must see new manifestations of God's glory. We must move forward in a new way, but Satan will do whatever he can to stop us. One of his strategies is to say, "I have to make you dissatisfied with this new place you're in, and I have to make you impatient to try to get out of it sooner than God's going to get you out of it."

Satan said to Jesus, "I'm going to use Your self-will to try to tell You some good things that will get You out of this place sooner. Why should You be denying yourself? Why don't You go eat something? Why are You going through all this? You've already been called *Messiah*."

Jesus basically said, "I'm in a wilderness place because the Spirit put Me there. I'm going to deny Myself in this wilderness place until Father tells Me differently. I am going to stay here until I come forth with power. I am going to stay here until every temptation known to man has been resisted. Only Father knows when I have completed My time here. I can trust Him to keep Me here until I have fulfilled this assignment."

The tempter said, "Why don't You eat something? You'll be better off in here if You just eat." Jesus resisted by taking the Word of God. Satan also used the Word of God. It's the height of a religious force. Jesus had to use the Word of God to counteract the Word of God that Satan was using. That's how religion hangs on for dear life. Jesus resisted by going to Deuteronomy 8:3 and using that Word against the enemy.

The second temptation the enemy presents was based upon Jesus's call. Here's the subtlety of what the enemy does. Jesus came to redeem the kingdoms of the world, so Satan tried to take His call and offer it to Him out of time. "Let me give You this thing more quickly." In other words, "Let me show You a way to compromise for You to take dominion. You don't want to go through the process of all that warfare to take dominion in that thing God's promised You. I can show You some shortcuts!" What Yeshua does is to use Deuteronomy 6:13 (author's paraphrase): "Fear the Lord with all your heart and take your oaths in His name." The Word in the wilderness is an overcoming key to neutralize any strategy of vexation. I actually think this was the greatest of all His temptations, because the greatest of any temptation is going to be against your destined call. To accomplish your call, you will have to learn how to use the Word.

Remember when Jesus called Peter the name of *Satan*. Peter was attempting to divert the Lord from going to Jerusalem to meet His captors. When that voice of enticement is coming into your mind and heart, no matter the source, you must equate the voice to your adversary, Satan.

Here is another incredible temptation, and this is where your demise can come. Satan tempted Jesus to put God to a test. God tells us that we can test Him. In Malachi He said, "If you'll give, I'll prove Myself to you." God still says, "You can put Me to the test by giving, like I gave with My Son." But what Satan was attempting to do was produce the height of presumption. Everything being said was right, but it was not in God's timing. He was using the Word to justify this temptation. But Jesus used Deuteronomy 6:16 and rebuked the tempter. In your wilderness, the Lord will get you to a place where you rebuke your tempter.

These temptations were categories of temptations that will affect each one of us throughout our lives. However, there is nothing that we will face in any wilderness season that was not confronted by our Lord in His forty-day period of testing. He came through triumphantly. So can you!

Notice this: "Then Jesus returned in the power of the Spirit to Galilee, and news of Him went out through all the surrounding region" (Luke 4:14). One of the first places He returned to was Nazareth. There He displayed His new identity to those He loved and had grown with the longest. Nazareth rejected His new identity. They could recognize His goodness, perhaps even His prophetic ability, but because of familiarity, they could not *see* Him as Messiah. Many who are determined to stay in an old wineskin never embrace those who move into the new.

In this new season, you can be new, look new, and operate with new authority. Let every wilderness place work to empower you. Trust God to keep you there until you have heard the word clearly. Trust Him to empower you so that when you leave, you will overcome every obstacle in your path ahead.

CHAPTER 11

SEE PAST MAMMON

A T ONE TIME in history, the world thought that only America was controlled by greed and covetousness. However, as time has passed and resources have diminished, warfare has increased. Now nations are vying for the remaining resources in the earth. Most wars are controlled by the covetousness of man. James 4:1–2 (AMP) says: "What leads to strife (discord and feuds) and how do conflicts (quarrels and fightings) originate among you? Do they not arise from your sensual desires that are ever warring in your bodily members? You are jealous and covet [what others have] and your desires go unfulfilled; [so] you become murderers. [To hate is to murder as far as your hearts are concerned.] You burn with envy and anger and are not able to obtain [the gratification, the contentment, and the happiness that you seek], so you fight and war. You do not have, because you do not ask."

In earlier chapters of this book we discussed the Lord's call for us to succeed. Success and prosperity go hand in hand. In the next two chapters we discuss another handshake—but this is a hand-in-hand alliance with the enemy, and it results in an ungodly casualty covenant. A casualty covenant occurs when you come into agreement with a word structure or vow that will lead to destruction rather than blessing. This can be seen throughout the Word. This agreement vexes our spirit as it overcomes and controls us. When poverty and infirmity agree, a society suffers. When we make agreement with ungodly words, we grow weak and are enslaved to the enemy of this world. The ungodly confederacy of poverty, covetousness, and lust arises against God's kingdom people in an attempt to blind us from seeing our future. We need to break this covenant and overcome the vexation of poverty, fear, and infirmity.

In Deuteronomy 8:18–19, we read how the Lord spoke to His covenant people and prepared them to go into the land that He had promised. He told them that He would give them the power to get wealth, but He also warned them about the pitfalls of worshiping Mammon, which is wealth that has a debasing influence.

The whole Book of Joshua is about the *transfer of wealth* through covenant alignment. As the covenant people of God entered the boundaries that had been promised to their forefather Abraham 470 years prior, they could see abundance. However, they had to strategically move in unity by tribes to overcome the enemy who was holding their provision captive. They were required by God to keep their minds and hearts pure, follow the Law and rules of war as prescribed in Deuteronomy 20, and not be led astray to seek the gods that were worshiped by the people of the land, the Canaanites. One of those gods was Mammon.

God's assignment to Joshua and the tribes of Israel was to use their wealth for God's covenant kingdom plan. To fulfill this assignment, a spiritual battle had to be fought, Mammon had to be defeated, and all riches had to be transferred to God's rule and stewardship plan. Proverbs 28:22 sheds some light by declaring that a man with an evil eye will greedily pursue earthly treasures. Matthew 6:24 expands by explaining that no one can serve both God and Mammon.

This did not mean that the people of Israel could not take the spoils of war from the conquest of battle. But this did imply that their spoils had to be dedicated to the one God whom they served. In the battle of Jericho, they were forbidden to take anything. In the battle of Ai, they could take all.

MAMMON'S SNARE IS DANGEROUS

There is a great battle today over the transfer of wealth. I believe this battle is not just natural but also supernatural. Have you ever looked closely at a dollar bill from the United States? An *eye* is imbedded in the paper. While the origin and meaning of this *eye* are debated, it clearly resembles the traditional evil eye in occult structures. Moreover, in a wealth-driven world, people easily use their natural eyes to look at money (mammon) with covetousness.

Rebecca Wagner Sytsema and I wrote a book called *Protecting Your Home From Spiritual Darkness*. This book is about ridding your house of occult objects that could allow demonic spirits to control you. In this book we explain about burning occult objects, like Paul instructed the people to do in Acts 19 in the city of Ephesus. I have often jokingly told crowds to bring their dollars forward and place them on the altar so they will be protected. Obviously we can't burn and destroy every dollar bill we have, so we must ask God how to deal with the presence of the eye.

As any object, money is neither good nor bad in itself. The key issue for us is our relationship and dedication to the powers that lie behind and control the supply lines of the money we receive. We must guard ourselves against the *love of money* (1 Tim. 6:10). The Greek word for "the love of money," *philarguria,* refers to avarice, which is the insatiable greed for riches, or covetousness. It also means "to inordinately or wrongly desire the possessions of others." If we are not careful, this covetousness is the fruit that money will produce in our hearts. Moreover, the *deceitfulness of riches* is an issue in our lives that we must overcome.

Mark 4:19 (AMP) says, "Then the cares and anxieties of the world and distractions of the age, and the pleasure and delight and false glamour and deceitfulness of riches, and the craving and passionate desire for other things creep in and choke and suffocate the Word, and it becomes fruitless." My wife, Pam, and I wrote a book called *The Rewards of Simplicity*. This book teaches you practically how to rid yourself of clutter and confusion in your life so your vision becomes clearer. The book also reveals keys about overcoming anxiety, especially as related to money.

ALL KINDS OF EVIL

Deceit, anxiety, and covetousness seem to be powers strongly connected with the love of money. These produce an attitude of the heart that seeks to manipulate through false pretenses and appearances.

Envy is also linked with covetousness and the evil eye. When we look at something or someone else with an unholy desire, especially someone's riches, we fall under the power of its demonic grip. The power of envy is noted in Proverbs 27:4 (KJV): "Who is able to stand before envy?" To avoid this trap of the enemy, we must sanctify what God gives us and be satisfied with our portion. (See Psalm 16:5; Philippians 4:11; 1 Timothy 6:8.)

The term *mammon* predominantly signifies riches and wealth, but as Colin Brown, in *The New International Dictionary of New Testament Theology*, points out, "Material wealth can be personified as a demonic power, Mammon."[1] When our stewardship of wealth does not align with God's purpose and plan, we open ourselves to demonic activity. Covetousness can lead us away from God and encourage us to trust in our material possessions. When we turn our trust from God to money, we place ourselves in submission to a new master, Mammon.

Jack Hayford, in *Hayford's Bible Handbook*, refers to Luke 16:13 in the following manner: "Jesus said that no one can serve two masters— God and money—at the same time, and makes Mammon a potential 'master.'"[2] When we attempt to serve both God and Mammon, instability and double-mindedness are produced within us. Mammon should be recognized as a god when it leads us into worship of material possessions.

Money often has curses attached to it. If we don't break the curses before we get the money, we will get the curse that comes with it. The Bible lists some people who were cursed by wealth or were driven by impure motives to gain it: Judas, Esau, Gehazi, Ananias, Sapphira, Lot, and Achan are some examples. Each of these men and women was trapped by impure desires. One way we can break this curse is by tithing and giving offerings. (See Malachi 3.) These acts change our attitude about money. As we move forward against the enemy, we must renounce every issue of covetousness that is tied to Mammon, and we must break its curses.

Going back to the eye that is printed on the dollar bill, I do not believe that it has any power over God's children unless they are not stewarding their money correctly. God has given us a way to break every curse of "filthy lucre" that is put in our safekeeping. We can give Him the portion that belongs to Him. When we give Him the firstfruits of our spoils of the world, He can bless the whole lump that remains, and this evil eye is then representative of the *watching* demonic host that longs to trap God's people. Money is good when it is a servant to us and to God. However, we can become slaves to its dominion. That is when it truly becomes an evil eye. If we do not give and steward our resources properly, we become blinded by the deceitfulness of riches. The evil eye on the dollar bill becomes a demonic reality that blinds us, vexes our spirit, and causes us to lose our aligned benefits of God.

Cry out for an open heaven over your life, family, territory, business, and ministry. Ask the Lord to shine His light on all darkness so you can see. If the windows of heaven open, every dark spiritual force that has trapped us in the past will flee. When the heavens open, the earth comes into a divine realignment. When heavens open, man worships, and God renews covenant with man and the earth. Man's authority activates God's power. He then wars on our behalf! We need a wind of change from an open heaven to blow upon us and produce victory. *Victory* is the defeat of an enemy or opponent. Victory occurs when we gain success in a struggle against some difficulty or some obstacle that is impeding our path. It is the state of having triumphed.

See Past a Spirit of Poverty

The church is in an incredible season of change, and I believe we are all sensing those changes in us and around us. I can hear the Lord saying to us, "What you *seed* will begin to produce great fruit." There is a grace for our offerings to multiply—thirtyfold to a hundredfold—if we are obedient with what we have been given to steward. We can gain victory through giving in order to break the curse of robbing God in our generational bloodline. *This is a time to bud!* Our giving returns in multiplied form. Everything that we have seeded we can see multiply, blossom, and bud! Proverbs 11:24 says, "There is one who scatters, yet increases more; and there is one who withholds more than is right, but it leads to poverty."

One cycle that I feel we must break is linked to the *spirit of poverty*. In a materialistic society, this spirit tends to blind us from seeing the will of God. *We must declare victory over the spirit of poverty!* This spirit has violated God's perfect order and produced instability in many individuals. I feel that the Lord is saying that we need to take a violent and passionate stand on behalf of the body of Christ concerning this spirit—that we must press through difficulties and storms to force an atmospheric change.

Poverty creates an atmosphere. This spirit encircles you or your sphere of authority to create lack. No matter how much this spirit attempts to find a foothold in your life, this atmosphere can be invaded with the atmosphere of blessing and glory from heaven. *We can see His glory in our lives.* Noah found favor in His eyes. The heavens and earth realigned during his day. We can find favor, and heaven can come into our atmosphere and defeat poverty. Glory and wealth are synonymous.

The body of Christ needs to see restoration in our provision! Restoration is always linked with multiplication. Debt and past financial defeats in our lives need to reverse. A spirit of poverty that has held our generational bloodlines in captivity, keeping us from the fullness of the prosperity that God has for us, must be broken. The Lord is breaking begging off His people. He is making us a people of faith. He will change the identity of His people from beggars to kings! Ask Him to reveal *poverty* now. See how poverty works in your life.

In Joseph's life, in Genesis 45:11, we find that God said, "There I will provide for you, lest you and your household, and all that you have, come to poverty; for there are still five years of famine." Many individuals are afraid of leaving the familiar to receive their provision for the future. The famine in Canaan created a move to Egypt for all of God's covenant people. Egypt was not the promise but was the necessary place of provision for a season.

The War to *See* Poverty Break

If you are sent to war but lose the battle, you wear a reproach until you gain a subsequent victory. Many in the body are afraid to war, but war is necessary in order to conquer our enemies and take possession of what has been promised to us. War is receiving grace to fight. (See 1 Timothy 6:12; 2 Timothy 2:3–4.) War is receiving the necessary armor for victory (Eph. 6:11–17). War produces an opportunity for us to enter into victory (Rev. 3:21).

The Lord used armies to bring His people out of Egypt (Exod. 12:51) with a trumpet sound and a battle cry. Later He brought them out with the ark, the presence of God (1 Sam. 4:5–6). He used forces of nature when necessary to help them defeat their enemies (Josh. 10). God always releases strategies that enable us to plunder the enemy's holdings, to prosper, and to stand. (See Matthew 10; Ephesians 6.) He has a banner of victory over us. While Jehovah Nissi puts a banner over us to cover us, the Lord Sabaoth sends the hosts of heaven to help us. He is God of the armies of Earth (1 Sam. 17:45) and God of the unseen armies of angels (1 Kings 22:19). *He is the Lord of the armies* (Rom. 9:29). *He already has victory for you! See your victory over poverty.*

We must hear how poverty speaks and then operate in the opposite spirit. We are required to combat poverty by being kind and generous to others. Just as Boaz allowed Ruth to glean in field, we combat poverty by allowing people to glean in our vineyard and provide them with access to our excess (Ruth 2). We combat poverty by developing strategies to help those who have been ravaged by systemic poverty. In other words, we help others gain wisdom on how to break out of the system that Satan is using to hold them captive financially. We are also required to develop reaping strategies (Amos 9:13). When we do this, we overcome, and our increase will go from multiplication to multiplication.

Give your way out of poverty. See your path and cycle of prosperity. As children there were several Bible passages that many of us were taught. Psalm 23 was one that we memorized and used for comfort in distress and affliction. However, most of us never realized that this psalm really says, "I will lead you in your path of prosperity through paths of righteousness for *My* name's sake" (author's paraphrase).

In Hebrew, the word for "path" is `agol, which means "to be round or a cycle." The Lord guides us in the cycles of righteousness. The enemy hates the thought of us staying on a path of righteousness because he knows that we will *see* the fullness of God's plan for our lives. God already has our path of prosperity in place. This path or cycle is linked with the yearly return received from the feasts of Yahweh.

The Hebrew word *chag*, or "festival," means "to make a cycle." If we understand the feasts, then we understand cycles. We can be led properly, begin to prosper, move into abundance, and have no lack when we stay in the timing of God. "The Lord is my shepherd, I shall not want because He leads me in the cycle of prosperity. I will see my blessings wherever I walk. Even through the valley of the shadow of death, I can celebrate Him and not get out of time and see my blessings!" Robert Heidler's book *The Messianic Church Arising* explains God's feasts. By understanding the timing of the feasts, you go from harvest to harvest until increase becomes a way of life. The feasts are also prophetic in nature. You go from Passover to Pentecost to Tabernacles. This is the same cycle that the church is in from season to season.

Celebrating Firstfruits Keeps Us Seeking

Be lavish. Follow hard and gain momentum. Each feast celebration has a firstfruits dimension. There are great blessings that come from heaven when we participate each month in giving God our best. By understanding, celebrating, and giving at firstfruits, you gain momentum in the Spirit, and eventually God's blessings overtake you. This produces a kingdom mentality in you. You learn to give your *best* each month. This is different from tithing. This concept builds within you the call to *seek His kingdom first* and then *watch all else be added*.

When we quit seeking Him first, we lose momentum. This is a time to gain kingdom strength and momentum. Matthew 11:12 says, "And from the days of John the Baptist until now the kingdom of heaven suffers violence, and the violent take it by force." This was the statement that the Lord made to John the Baptist's disciples. John, who had chosen not to move with Jesus in his three-year ministry of revolution, was now imprisoned. During this time, he had begun to question the One for whom he had paved the way to produce the redemption of mankind. Jesus's ministry was gaining momentum, and John's ministry was coming to a close.

Jesus had just finished His charge to His twelve disciples and left to teach and to preach in some Galilean cities. Only Philip and Andrew had left John's wineskin to follow the Lord and seek the kingdom. When John heard about the activities of the Lord, he sent some of his remaining disciples to question Jesus by asking, "Are You the One Who was to come, or should we keep on expecting a different one? And Jesus replied to them, Go and report to John what you hear and see: The blind receive their sight and the lame walk, lepers are cleansed (by healing) and the deaf hear, the dead are raised up and the poor have good news (the Gospel) preached to them. And blessed (happy, fortunate, and to be envied) is he who takes no offense at Me and finds no cause for stumbling in or through Me and is not hindered from seeing the Truth" (Matt. 11:3–6, AMP). In other words, "John, at least remember, and believe and *see* what you prophesied in the past manifesting now. Follow hard! Do not get offended and stumble over something that I am doing differently."

It is the same with us. This is a time that many prophecies from the past season are manifesting. We must not look away and quit following because they are coming about in ways we did not expect. We must not get offended by the changes coming into our methods, messages, and worship structures. We must keep seeking first and not get shaken and lose momentum.

You are in a kingdom that cannot be shaken (Heb. 12:27–28). Unspiritual and carnal man cannot understand or see this kingdom. We become carnal when we lose the process of seeking Him first. Jesus taught and imparted an understanding of kingdom—kingdom manifestation has a perfect timing.

The issue of giving is probably one of the most controversial topics in the body of Christ. Giving does not mean bringing a check or dollar to the church. Rather, giving is built around a covenant relationship that is linked around an altar of worship. Giving occurs when we recognize that *our King* is *righteous* and *legitimate*. We bless the Lord so that He will take His stand righteously on our behalf. Giving occurs when we worship. Giving occurs when we respond to authority with generosity and blessing. Giving occurs when we realize the lesser is blessed by the greater—that God is the greater King, and we should want to give all to Him. Giving occurs when we do not hold back what we have been entrusted with by the Lord. Find a place to give. I awaken each day and ask the Lord to show me opportunities to give. He took our poverty by giving His Son.

The generation that came out of Egypt was filled with poverty resulting from slavery; therefore they resisted the war that would be necessary for them to be established in the abundance of God's promises. Their fear caused their perspective of God's purposes to be clouded and confused. They lost the ability to advance and enter into success. *They could only see their enemy and not their victory.* However, their enemy was in fear of the children of Israel because they knew God was backing the Israelites. Riches were waiting for the covenant people of God but had to be postponed to another generation that would develop a mentality of dominion.

I decree that you will succeed. May you be blessed and have success in all that you put your hands to. The Lord will give us the power to adapt to every circumstance so that we can have success and bring forth His covenant plan (Deut. 8:18). *To succeed* means "to follow after and dispossess the enemy and possess or occupy his territory." It means "to master the place or position that the Lord assigns to us." Success occurs when we accomplish God's redemptive plan for our lives. If we receive revelation, honor the prophets, and are at the right place at the right time doing the right thing, we will *succeed*. Let me remind you again of Joshua 1:8, which says:

This Book of the Law shall not depart from your mouth, but you shall meditate in it day and night, that you may observe to do according to all that is written in it. For then you will make your way prosperous, and then you will have good success.

Success occurs when we behave wisely and act prudently and when we study to develop skill and understanding. There is already help on our road to cause us to succeed.

See Your Way Into Wealth

We are in an era of seeing and establishing our future. During this time, the promises of God are extended from one generation to another. We are being called to worship in a new way and develop a memorial through our giving.

In Jacob's quest as he fled from Esau, he traveled three days to Bethel. That night he took one of the stones to rest against as he slept, and God gave him a vision of a ladder (or staircase, as some translate it) from heaven to Earth.

John 1 explains that the ladder symbolizes Jesus Christ. Jacob was unaware of God being near him. Many of us in our journey of life are unaware of how close the Lord is to us to save us from all of our messes and manipulations. He opens heaven for us and brings heaven's blessings to our lives. He alone can take us to heaven. We can then *see* our way into a new dimension of wealth. Jacob thought he was in a lonely wilderness but discovered that he had been at the very gate of heaven. Although Jacob still had some scheming about him, he offered God a tithe of everything he had if He would be with him on his journey ahead and bring him into the fullness of his destiny.

We have been given the power to get wealth and riches. Wealth is an abundance of possessions or resources. During the times of the patriarchs, wealth was measured largely in livestock—sheep, goats, cattle, donkeys, and camels. This was true of Abraham (Gen. 13:2), Isaac (Gen. 26:12–14), and Jacob (Gen. 30:43; 32:5). People of the ancient world also measured wealth in terms of land, houses, servants, slaves, and precious metals. The prime example was King Solomon, whose great wealth is described in 1 Kings 10:14–29. The power to get wealth is a key to our covenant advancement (Deut. 8).

Never forget wealth comes from God! The prophet Amos thundered against the rich and prosperous inhabitants of Israel, who sold "the righteous for silver, and the poor for a pair of sandals" (Amos 2:6). Their wealth was corrupt and under a curse because it was founded on exploitation of the poor. Wealth and money are two different things. Many times we look at how much money we have, and that determines our faith level. When we see the balance in our bank account, we experience anxiety or our faith rises up. Money can be a great tool for bartering and advancing, or the love for money can be the root of all evil.

By contrast, *riches* means "receiving the grace of the Holy Spirit to enable us to accomplish what we are called to accomplish." A person's gift is linked into the concept of wealth. Riches are linked with accumulation, or what we have amassed. A stewardship plan is devised from our riches. The more we steward our riches properly, the more we will receive. This is not just a money issue. God is looking for people who will shift in their stewardship so that He can release a transfer of wealth.

Look up! See your provision in a new way. See your wealth in a new way. See your money supply in new way. See how to take what you have and multiply it. See your increase in assignment.

CHAPTER 12

SEE YOUR PROMISE FROM GOD'S PERSPECTIVE

SEE PAST GREED, unbelief, and fear. See your promise from God's perspective! When the people of Israel decided to move by sight and not faith, the Lord allowed their leaders to go over and view the Promised Land that He had made covenant to give to Abraham's descendants. They saw the abundance, they saw the richness, they saw the development, but they also saw the warfare. The vision of the warfare in the form of giants caused one generation to reject the promise and postpone the manifestation of the blessings that had been offered.

In this season, *do not let fear win the battle!* Fear is a spirit that attaches to our emotions and clouds our thinking process. Fear causes us to withdraw into poverty and a mundane lifestyle. They saw the abundant crops that had been offered but rejected their moment of prosperity. One grapevine's yield was greater than an entire vineyard. Do not reject the *yield* and the *increase*.

The leaders' confessions, empowered by fear, bred unbelief in an entire nation. They were convinced that the giants were more powerful than they. They saw them from their perspective rather than through the eyes of the One who was giving them the land they would rule. They revealed a fear in their heart. They actually believed God was capable, but they did not believe they were worthy of His miracles and thus rejected their new identity and longed to be slaves again. They preferred returning to captivity. They passed their own sentence, that they would die in the wilderness (Num 14:2). They slandered the promise that God had offered and were therefore cursed in the process. They longed for their last season and rejected the new season ahead. This set the course of their undoing. It was forty years later before the window reopened for them to return (Num. 14:29). They refused to return to the *garden* that God had provided for them.

War for the promise! He has your garden of restoration and abundance. Don't be afraid to leave the past season behind. Remove any root of abandonment in you and strengthen your faith to go up against an enemy that appears stronger than you. Joshua and Caleb responded with a different spirit. Ask the Lord to break vexation from your spirit based upon wrong perception of the war ahead for your blessings.

Keith Pierce, my beloved brother and a wonderful prophet, recently sent me this:

> I saw a plate of cookies set before a group of children. POVERTY said, "Grab at least three and hurry back and take the last one, for soon they will be all gone." PROVISION said, "It does not matter; you can have the last one and not worry, because Mom will cook more because she loves you and wants you to be satisfied." Know that GOD is like Mom. There is always an ample supply to be cooked. The ingredients for our provisions in the future never run out. The Lord has many ways to create abundance. Plenty is there for the asking. HE will supply. Fear makes us grab. Greed makes us hoard![1]

Does it seem like God has forgotten you and the serious predicament you are in at the moment? Do you feel so surrounded by the enemy that you think there is no way out? God says, *"Look again!"* He is opening your spiritual eyes today to see what He sees. He is positioning you on the heavenly vantage point. He is empowering you with great faith to win every battle before you, without fear. *Lord, open our eyes that we may SEE.* Don't grab for your future—the provision is there for you to see.

Sabbath Is a Window Cleaner That Helps Vision

We have been declaring that poverty would no longer rule or blind us. Our *conscience* is the key to seeing. When Jesus is defining the conscience, He admonishes us that the antagonist of our seeing is *Mammon*. Matthew 6:19–24 (AMP, emphasis added) says:

> Do not gather, heap up and store up for yourselves treasures on earth, where moth and rust and worm consume and destroy, and where thieves break through and steal. But gather and heap up and store for yourselves treasures in heaven, where neither moth nor rust nor worm consume and destroy, and where thieves do not break through and steal; for where your treasure is, there will your heart be also.
>
> *The eye is the lamp of the body.* So if your eye is sound, your entire body will be full of light. But if your eye is unsound, your whole body will be full of darkness. If then the very light in you [your conscience] is darkened, how dense is that darkness! No one can serve two masters; for either he will hate the one and love the other, or he will stand by and be devoted to the one and despise and be against the other. You cannot serve God and mammon (deceitful riches, money, possessions, or whatever is trusted in).

There seems to be a key relationship between how we see, our heart's desire, and whom we serve. Bob Dylan's song "You Gotta Serve Somebody" is so true. God made us to serve Him and to set aside one day a week to rest and meditate on all that He is about in our lives. This is key to our seeing. "For in six days the LORD made the heavens and the earth, the sea, and all that is in them, but he rested on the seventh day. Therefore the LORD blessed the Sabbath day and made it holy" (Exod. 20:11, NIV).

By remembering the Sabbath we will see clearly. From the Mount, God told Israel to remember the Sabbath and sanctify that day. This meant to stop doing any creative work and break out of the cycle from the preceding week. God made all of creation in six days and rested on the seventh. To be a true son or daughter, we are commanded to rest on the Sabbath.

I was recently in Las Vegas, and I asked the Lord, "What is the real problem here?" I heard Him say, "Sabbath is not part of this culture!"

Until heaven and Earth pass away, we must recognize the Sabbath (Matt. 5:17–19). When we do, we acknowledge Him as Lord over creation and time. This is part of seeking Him first and seeing. There are blessings, vision, and rewards for those who seek Him first. Isaiah 58:13–14 (NIV) says: "If you keep your feet from breaking the Sabbath and from doing as you please on my holy day, if you call the Sabbath a delight and the LORD's holy day honorable, and if you honor it by not going your own way and not doing as you please or speaking idle words, then you will find your joy in the LORD, and I will cause you to ride on the heights of the land and to feast on the inheritance of your father Jacob."

Be intimate with Him today and seek Him. Break out of your old cycle of the week. See Him in a new way. Ask Him to cleanse your conscience from any infiltration of the world that invaded you the preceding week, and prepare yourself to see in the week ahead.

CYCLES OF INFIRMITY MUST GO

This is a time to break destructive cycles. A *cycle* is an interval during which a recurring sequence of events happens. A cycle can also be a periodically repeated sequence of events, something that happens over and over at a certain time. A cycle can be linked with a time or an event and orchestrated supernaturally so that a repeating wound or injustice occurs from generation to generation. Satan loves to keep us going around the same mountain or to hold us in a cyclical pattern. *But God* has a remedy for iniquity. By embracing the blood and redemptive sacrifice of the Lord Jesus Christ, we can break out of any old pattern.

As we prepare for a new level of freedom, we must deal with forces that wish to keep us captivated in an old season. We have looked at how poverty attempts to create a stronghold to keep us from seeing our prosperity. Now let's look at how infirmity tries to keep us from standing strong. *Infirmity* is a term that encompasses more than just *sickness and disease*. Infirmity is also related to *suffering and sorrow*. Matthew 8:16–17 states that Jesus "cast out the spirits with a word, and healed all who were sick, that it might be fulfilled which was spoken by Isaiah the prophet, saying: 'He Himself took our infirmities and bore our sicknesses.'" (See also Isaiah 53:4.) *Infirmity* can also refer to a disability of one kind or another. Infirmity can occur as a result of moral or spiritual defects that cause our will to stray from God. Infirmity can be related to the influence of an evil spirit. (See Luke 13:11.)

Infirmity can also be linked to an overall weakness in our bodies or with anything that created the weakness, such as grief. Romans 15:1 (NAS) states that those "who are strong ought to bear the weaknesses of those without strength." This weakness is infirmity. Not only did Christ bear our weaknesses and infirmities, but we are also called to bear the weaknesses and infirmities of our brothers and sisters in the Lord. This is called *intercession*. Romans 8:26 (KJV) says, "Likewise the Spirit also helpeth our infirmities: for we know not what we should pray for as we ought: but the Spirit itself maketh intercession for us with groanings which cannot be uttered." We have been called to intercede for the sick, which allows us to bring before the Lord someone weaker than ourselves. As we move into this season, we must start addressing those forces that have been sent by Satan to hinder us from seeing our destiny manifest.

A Generational Understanding

Infirmity can be a generational issue. I know in my life that the Lord had to show me this by His Spirit. People are often confused about how generational iniquity works. In *Possessing Your Inheritance* there is a great chapter on this. To fully understand generational iniquity, we need to first understand how DNA makes the blueprint of our body. DNA causes traits from one generation to be passed on to the next generation. As the cells in an embryo divide and multiply, they do so according to the structure of the base pairs in the DNA. The combination of these base pairs provides the hereditary instructions for how each cell will be coded in order to accomplish that cell's specific purpose. As cells continue to multiply, groups of cells come together to form tissues. Tissues, in turn, form organs. Blood cells are pumped through the body, providing oxygen to each organ to enable it to survive. The cells in our stomachs work together in digestion. The cells in our brains work together as we study and pursue knowledge.

When the sperm and egg unite and a new life is formed, already programmed into the makeup of that person is God's redemptive plan. However, we must remember that we are born in iniquity, so the iniquitous inherited traits that will resist that plan from coming into fullness are already programmed in us. But God!

Our blood begins to war with itself from the time of conception. Since cells are dynamic, an iniquitous pattern in a cell's DNA can affect our entire physical and mental makeup. If something is passed on in our DNA that has been *twisted* or linked with iniquity, that message is multiplied wrongly in our beings.

The Spirit of God can come into our lives so that we can become sons of God (Gal. 3:26). As we submit and yield our lives to the Spirit's work, He flows through our blood and cleanses our consciences from the thought processes linked with the iniquitous patterns in our bloodlines. Hebrews 9:14 (NIV) states, "How much more, then, will the blood of Christ, who through the eternal Spirit offered himself unblemished to God, cleanse our consciences from acts that lead to death, so that we may serve the living God!"

In my case, there was a generational weakness that had aligned itself with loss and trauma. But God! Once I began to see those weaknesses and define the losses that they were attached to, I could then pray and break a power that had me *bent over* and unable to stand fully. I confessed those patterns as sin. You might say, "Well, you had nothing to do with these sins." However, we must understand that repentance is a gift and grace of God that causes us to turn from one way of thinking and be transformed to think like Christ. Once you repent, you renounce the power of its effect. In my own life, this set me on a new road to health.

I have had trusted doctors and praying friends who have helped me greatly in developing a new order in my life. Each doctor played his role in diagnosing my condition. However, it was the Spirit of God that had begun to change me greatly from the inside. He is there now to start revealing things to you and cause you to *see* how weakness and loss are related.

Jesus Heals—Press Through and *See* His Power

I wish I could say that I have never been sick again since I started *seeing* how infirmity works with loss and trauma. However, since that time, a power to resist sickness has become resident within me. When the power of infirmity comes against me, I submit to God, resist the devil, and watch him flee.

Jesus healed sick people. This was one of His major ministries. He dealt with many organic causes of illness and with individuals affected by madness, birth defects, and infections. The blind, the deaf, the lame, and others who suffered approached Him for help. I especially love the story of the woman with the spirit of infirmity who "pressed through" in Mark 5:25–34. She is an incredible example of personal overcoming. She overcame the religious structure of the day, the reproach of being a woman, and the stigma of being unclean. She pressed through to touch the Lord. This caused the Lord to release "virtue" (KJV; "power" in the NKJV) from His own body that healed her condition.

In the Hebraic culture of the day, most people believed that illness was the direct consequence of sin. (See John 9:1–3.) However, Jesus shifted this concept by healing a blind man who had been sick since birth. When Jesus's disciples asked, "Who sinned, this man or his parents, that he was born blind?" (v. 2), Jesus answered that the sickness was not related to the man or his parents "but that the works of God should be revealed in him." Many wrong choices produce consequences that affect our body, but Jesus came to extend grace to bring us out from the bondage of the punishment of sin and into healing and wholeness. He had the power to both forgive sin and to heal. (See Matthew 9:1–8; compare Mark 2:1–12; Luke 5:17–26.)

On several occasions Jesus used His own saliva as an ointment or anointing (Mark 7:32–35; 8:22–25; John 9:6–7). I find this fascinating—one of the primary ways that DNA is collected for testing is through saliva samples. Jesus took His own saliva, placed it on the eyes of the blind, and watched their eyes form. He also healed those who suffered from mental illnesses and epilepsy, sicknesses usually associated with demonic powers (Mark 9:18). The Lord addressed issues of fever and dysentery (Matt. 8:14–15). Sterility and barrenness were also major issues in biblical times. Regardless of the cause of their distress, people found that Jesus could truly help.

He is there for you. Be like the woman in Mark 5 and "press through" all the structures stopping you from experiencing freedom and *seeing* a new wholeness and peace that are waiting for you.

GET OFF YOUR TREADMILL AND ENTER THE FIELD OF PREVENTION

One key to overcoming any strategy of the enemy is discipline and prevention. Prevention was the most important dynamic of combating disease in biblical times. Many of the laws that the Lord established in biblical times actually aid in preventing and combating various illnesses. Diet is one of the most important facets of health, which is why we find a number of laws relating to diet. (See Leviticus 11.) Wine was used to help stop problems and alleviate pain and discomfort (1 Tim. 5:23). We also find the use of ointments and salves in biblical times that were used for healing (Isa. 1:6). James instructed the combined use of oil, confession of faults, and spiritual authority to produce healing (James 5:14).

In a world of chemical stimulation and overwhelming stress, it is a wonder that any of us remains healthy. Stress has such impact on our bodies—both physically and spiritually—that without the Lord as our strength, it would be impossible for us to live in this world. Jesus told us to be *in* the world but not *of* it (John 17:11, 14). Do we need doctors? Yes, we need anyone who has developed specialty in understanding. Doctors are trained to understand dynamics *of* the world that can give us wisdom on how to be *in* the world.

Most doctors understand cycles. If medical doctors begin to take a biblical approach toward an individual—that of seeing the individual made whole—they will be able to find the root cause of that person's problem and not only help to heal that individual but also help to prevent disease in the future. With doctoral skill in prevention and advances in medicine, individuals can better reverse deficiencies that have created paths of decay. *Why do we need doctors?* Because they can validate what God is doing in a skeptical world.

One of my favorite books is *Dr. Gallagher's Guide to Twenty-First Century Medicine: How to Get Off the Illness Treadmill and Onto Optimum Health*. In this book, Dr. Gallagher says, "The body is a miraculous system equipped with an innate ability to achieve balance and health. We have, within each of us, the ability to work with, and nourish, this God-given gift."[2] Dr. Gallagher suggests a healthier diet, nutritional and herbal supplements, identifying and eliminating hidden food allergies and chemical sensitivities, a simple detoxification program to get rid of harmful toxins, chiropractic manipulation, and following sensible health rules.

He also gives instructions on how to break an old cycle, or *treadmill*, which he defines as "something that you run or walk on and get nowhere. An illness treadmill is something that snares you in an endless web of diagnoses, tests, prescriptions, and procedures and gets you nowhere, or even makes you sicker....Once you are on the treadmill, you may get some temporary relief from symptoms. But all too often the cause of your problem is ignored, so things just get worse. Meanwhile, the treatments used to suppress the symptoms often cause side effects and new symptoms."[3] Dr. Gallagher suggests finding the root of the illness and breaking the cycle.

My prayer for each of us is that we get off any treadmill holding us captive. If we are on a *treadmill*, we can only see from the perspective of the treadmill. I declare that we break old cycles and begin running and jumping in a wide, enlarged field of freedom.

Moving From Trauma or Failure to Healing and Success

After Jesus was crucified, His disciples were traumatized. The trauma caused them to lose sight of the prophetic words that He had given about His resurrection. You find this account when He is walking on the road to Emmaus, and the disciples walking with Him cannot see. Not until they commune are their eyes opened to see.

Trauma imprints in your memory system. Trauma is processed deep into the tissues of your brain (processor) and affects your thoughts (heart). Trauma becomes the flashbulb that creates what you see and how you define the world around you. Traumas can produce *lock-ins* of fear, failure complexities, emotional distresses, and anxieties. These locked-in emotions can cause your organs to overwork (spleen, kidneys, and pancreas) and create adrenal failure. Every situation in your life can be *seen* through your unhealed and reconciled trauma. Trauma, when not processed correctly, will shape your world from the point of view of the hurtful situation and circumstance that you experienced.

Tell fear and failure to go! Confusion and an unsound mind are results of a spirit of fear. The enemy does not play the game of life fairly. Trauma, when used by our enemy, will create a failure mentality and a confused perspective producing dullness, deadness, lost hope, apathy, and blocked emotions. Leave trauma behind and remove the dam on your blocked emotions.

The enemy's goal is to vex your spirit. You are created in the image of God. You are a whole person. He longs to sanctify your spirit, soul, and body. Your innermost part is your spirit. Your spirit is your eternal part. Your spirit has three functions: communion, intuition, and testimony.

Your conscience is the window between your spirit and soul. The conscience must be kept clean so you can see. During trauma, the enemy takes advantage of you so that you question God's goodness. If he can make you say, "God is not good, and He has withheld His promise and best from me," you will lose your power to see. When you go through a difficult or devastating time, ask the Lord to intervene for a miracle to happen.

See Miracles! Shout Today That *God Is Good!*

See the miracles that are pressing you into a greater glory! My wife recently made this incredible statement: "Expecting the miraculous is one of the childlike characteristics that has to be cultivated and protected in a world full of cynicism and disappointment." Miracles and faith must go hand in hand. Faith is related to every part of our Christian lives. By faith we receive salvation (Eph. 2:8–9). Faith is associated with our experiences of sanctification (Acts 26:18), purification (Acts 15:9), justification (Rom. 4:5; 5:1), and adoption (Gal. 3:26; Col. 3:24). All are dependent upon our faith. Faith comes by hearing and hearing by the word of God. There is a war of faith to hear and stand that we must enter into at times if we are to see our promises manifest. In the Book of Haggai, the people began strong to rebuild but got distracted and discouraged from the warfare.

The word *miracle* is linked with the principle of *wonder.* Wonderful events only God can conceive in heaven for us to see on the earth are really what a miracle is about. A miracle is a supernatural manifestation of divine power in this atmospheric world that we live in, in which special revelations of the presence and power of God are displayed. All natural events become subservient and aid His power from the throne room as released in and through us here in the earth realm. Once His power is released, He establishes and preserves His will and the life processes of human flesh in the world. A miracle, or His power, extends eternity into the atmosphere where we live and walk.

This power aligns with the "the Spirit of the Lord" so the "the finger of God" can have His work (Luke 4:18; 11:20; cf. Acts 3:12). Miracles are powers, mighty works, wonderful works, and manifestations of the power of God. He uses His finger to touch, paint, and work His will like the mighty molder of life that He is! He creates a new order out of a mess. He enters the natural laws of Earth and redirects their actions. The supernatural finger of God rearranges what seems to us as a natural world. The whole world is filled with wonders to those who have eyes to see. The natural world everywhere is full of marvels, but we must look for the finger that makes the natural wondrous and alive with God.

There is a *greater glory*! See and enter into the new. Shake off all discouragement, disillusionment, and disinterest from the last season that have caused you to shrink back. If the war from the last season turned you away from pushing back completion of any project, regroup and "go up again." Our worship team at Glory of Zion International actually recorded a CD entitled *Go Up Again*. (You can purchase this CD at www.gloryofzion.org.)

Tell your emotions not to hang on to past hurts. Do not be afraid that your last pain will recur again in the *new*. Believe that your latter can be greater than the former. *Come UP into a NEW spiritual realm!* GO BEYOND. A fresh anointing is being released as we cross over. Let go of trauma, and release forgiveness. Begin to worship in a new and fresh way, and interact with the angelic hosts. Decree that a new wave of the Holy Spirit will overtake you. Declare the *seeds* that you have sown in the past seasons will begin to multiply, and your storehouse will fill again. Recognize spiritual forces around you that have blocked the flow of the river of life.

SEE MIRACLES AS THEY HAPPEN

Miracles happen. I pray that you are seeing your miracles as they happen. A miracle is not only wonderful but also has the sense of being a *new thing*. This new thing awakens us to a divine power that our eyes were unable to see. His finger and working power have an appropriate place in the great plan and purpose of lives that have been knitted together in Him. Miracles produce revelation. What we could not normally see, we now see.

Faith sees when miracles happen! Faith was one of the main thrusts of Jesus's ministry. In the Gospels, we continually find statements such as, "Your *faith* has healed you." In Jesus's hometown, He could not do mighty miracles because the people there lacked faith. He wasn't powerless to do so, but the atmosphere in that place prevented our Lord from exhibiting the power of faith. However, when He found men and women of faith, He released His power, and miracles took place. God assures us that *if we believe,* then nothing is impossible, and He withholds nothing.

Move into the next season with a mentality of health and increase. Miracles happen! Expect visitation. Remove all distractions. Choose the *one* thing. Let the Lord *reorder* your day. Meditate day and night on His Word. Meditation produces success. Find your place in God's kingdom government plan. Ask Holy Spirit to reveal your *new* supply lines. War using prophetic words that will unlock your seeds sown in the kingdom.

CHAPTER 13

THE NEED FOR MENDING

W HAT WE DISCUSSED in the last two chapters will create an atmosphere of vexation in your life if you do not allow the Spirit of God to master your life. Mammon is linked with how we see. Actually, the *evil eye*, which we will discuss further in the next few chapters, works with the power of Mammon.

Other than Mammon, other probable spiritual wars we will battle in our lives are illness, infirmity, fear, and trauma. Illness and infirmity were a pattern in my life. Growing up with weakness and sickness was a way of life for me. Severe allergic reactions, bronchial asthma, stomach ulcers, and overwhelming migraines became the norm. Doctors tried many things. I was actually taking Valium by the time I was in the fourth grade. From the time I became filled with the Spirit, I had learned how to resist the power of sickness, yet I had never really overcome the power of infirmity in my life. In the early 1990s, I received some bad reports concerning my esophagus and colon—they were damaged and creating dangerous situations in my life. The Lord took me through a series of diagnoses from doctors that were not encouraging. (As a matter of fact, while writing this book, I went for an update and consultation. The gastrointestinal doctor I visited reiterated how severe my condition once was. Though I am still monitored every three months, I have transformed my health by the Spirit and submission to a change in lifestyle.)

Because of my internal situation, my body began to reject anything that entered my stomach and treated it as an allergen. I began to experience anaphylactic shock. I was miserable! At this point, I was very concerned about my future. At the National School of the Prophets that was being held in Baltimore, Maryland, Cindy Jacobs, a friend of mine, shared with me that she believed my sickness was related to the trauma I had experienced while growing up. She believed that my father's decaying leadership in our family and his premature death still held power over me. My first impression was, "How could this be? I have gone through so much deliverance. I have even written a book about overcoming the loss that had occurred in our family."

I came home from Baltimore very ill and unable to digest any food. My brother, Keith, was teaching Sunday school and gave me a call after his class. He said, "While I was teaching my class, the Lord told me that the sickness that you are experiencing is related to the loss of our dad."

I thought to myself, "Why isn't my brother ever sick? My dad was his dad also." So I asked him this question.

He responded, "You had a different emotional tie with Daddy than I. His loss wounded and affected you in a way that it did not affect me."

BROKEN SPIRITS CAN BE HEALED

This was an eye-opening statement for me. I knew that I still had a place of brokenness in my spirit that needed healing. I fell before the Lord and began to ask Him how to break this generational iniquity of infirmity that was linked with the trauma of loss that I had experienced. Since that time, the Lord has led me on a journey of understanding how trauma affects our DNA and weakens our spirit. One verse that has become a life verse for me is Proverbs 18:14: "The spirit of a man will sustain him in sickness, but who can bear a broken spirit?" *A broken spirit occurs when life's difficulties crush our abilities to resist.* Jesus came to heal our bodies. However, we find that His desire for us is that we become whole in body, soul, and spirit. When the Lord showed me the power of trauma, I could *see* how my past was continuing to hold this infirm spirit in place.

There are many ways to follow the Lord into healing. There are many methods and faith acts. However, I believe that to be whole, one must find the root cause of his/her infirmity and then press through into the process of *wholeness*. During my time of infirmity, I had to make a choice to follow the Lord to Nigeria. Dr. C. Peter Wagner was leading a gathering there with key apostolic leaders from the nation. I always serve Peter whenever he requests me to be somewhere, but the thought of traveling to Nigeria in my condition was difficult to reconcile. This would also require some yellow fever shots. With me reacting to everything, the thought of this was somewhat overwhelming. I went first to my wife and counseled with her. She reminded me that earlier in the year I had come to her and excitedly told her that the Lord was asking me to go to Nigeria. I said, "But what if I have a reaction in Nigeria?"

She asked, "But didn't the Lord say for you to go to Nigeria?"

I confirmed with a yes.

She said, "Then go."

I said, "What if I die from a reaction?"

She said, "If the Lord is telling you to go to Nigeria and you die, that would be where the Lord has planned for you to die!"

I thought to myself, "This woman is way too practical for me!"

Peter also encouraged me to go. He even said, "Because of how the power of God is moving in Nigeria, perhaps you will get healed." Pam was right. He was right. I overcame my fear of going to a foreign nation while I was ill. I went to Nigeria, and during a prayer meeting (of ten thousand people) the Spirit of God came. When Communion was served, those who were sick were invited to come forward. I was the first in line. When I participated, I felt a curse of infirmity leave my body.

With all disorders, we must seek the help of the Holy Spirit for wisdom. There are times when a person is in such a state of depression or agitation that he or she is unable to receive ministry until medication is administered. I have dealt with people who refused medication because they believed it meant they didn't have faith. I have talked with ministers who refused to minister deliverance to someone who was on medication because it was mind altering. If it is altering the mind to be able to think coherently and focus, then they should be allowed to receive ministry. The good news is that there is help for people with emotional and mental problems. Look for the cycles and be prepared to break them. God can break through any structure and start mending your broken spirit. Ask Him to show you how trauma is affecting your ability to *see* the future!

GOD HAS REDEEMED OUR LIFE AND PATH

Before we were ever conceived or knit together in our mothers' wombs, God had a distinct plan for each one of our lives. He destined us before the foundation of the earth. He knew the timing in which we would be born and the generation that we would be a part of. He had a purpose for us and knew what would be necessary to accomplish those purposes in the earth within that timeframe. Into that right time and season we are all born. Upon our conception, God's redemptive plan begins for our life.

Proverbs 4:18 says that the way or path of righteousness is like the first gleam of dawn or as a shining light that shines ever brighter until the full light of day. When thinking about our redemptive path, it is important to know that our Redeemer has already paid the price for us to walk victoriously through life. *To redeem* means "to pay the required price, to secure the release of a convicted criminal." Our Redeemer is the person making that payment. Therefore, Jesus has already redeemed us from the darkness in our path. Psalm 16:11 says, "You will show me the path of life; in Your presence is fullness of joy; at Your right hand are pleasures forevermore." Our life cycle, designed by God, begins at the point of conception and continues through birth, the age of accountability, our spiritual rebirth, maturing faith, and death, before entering eternity.

Padah is a Hebrew word that expresses the legal and commercial use of the redemptive concept in relation to the redemption of persons or other living beings. For example, if a person owned an ox that was known to be dangerous but did not keep the ox secured, and if the ox gored the son or daughter of a neighbor, both the ox and the owner would be stoned to death. If, however, the father of the slain person offered to accept an amount of money, the owner could pay the redemption price and live (Exod. 21:29–30; cf. v. 32). *Ga'al* is another Hebrew word that indicates a redemption price in relation to family members involving the responsibility of a next-of-kin. A kinsman was responsible to redeem the estate that his nearest relative might have sold because of poverty (Lev. 25:25; Ruth 4:4). It was the kinsman's responsibility also to ransom a kinsman who may have sold himself (Lev. 25:47–48). The Old Testament Book of Ruth is the most striking example of a kinsman who used his power and Jewish Law to redeem. Boaz demonstrated one of the duties of the kinsman—that of marrying the widow of a deceased kinsman. A correlation is sometimes made between the redemption of Ruth by Boaz and the redemption of sinners by Christ.

The Lord has *bought back*, or *paid in full*, your life. If we receive, trust, and believe in His ability, we can be successful on our path of life. Job knew that he had a living Redeemer (Job 19:25). Writers of the psalms prayed for redemption from distress (Ps. 26:11; 49:15) and testified to God's redeeming work (Ps. 31:5; 71:23; 107:2). The Old Testament witness is that God is "my strength and my Redeemer" (Ps. 19:14). The New Testament centers redemption in Jesus Christ. He purchased the church with His own blood (Acts 20:28), gave His flesh for the life of the world (John 6:51), as the Good Shepherd laid down His life for His sheep (John 10:11), and demonstrated the greatest love by laying down His life for His friends (John 15:13). The purpose of Jesus in the world was to make a deliberate sacrifice of Himself for human sin. He did something sinful people could not do for themselves. He brought hope to sinners, providing redemption from sin and fellowship with the eternal Father. As the suffering servant, He was a costly sacrifice, suffering the shameful and agonizing death on a Roman cross. New Testament redemption thus speaks of substitutionary sacrifice, which demonstrates divine love and righteousness. It points to a new relationship to God, the dynamic of a new life, God's leniency in the past, and the call for humility for the future.

God ordained us to be whole so that our created purpose could manifest fully. When we submit ourselves to Him and recognize that He has paid the price for our lives, we can enter into the success that He has on our path. This is really what redemption means. I defined *success* in an earlier chapter. By moving our lives forward so we are not constantly living in the pain and regret of the past, we walk in God's best daily. By prevailing over the enemy of our souls, we are able to resist temptation and reclaim our inheritance. This overcomes the vexing power of the enemy. Our relationship with the Lord should cause us to act wisely and strategically. This causes us to be favored and promoted to new levels at the right season. We will achieve our destined purposes when we cry out to Him along our paths.

Fragmentation attempts to keep us scattered. If we continue to carry within our souls the brokenness that can result from injustices and our mistakes, then we become fragmented. The scattered pieces of our soul must be gathered for us to be whole. This is simple to say but much more complex in reality, because we are made in the image of God. We are unique individuals. We do many acts that we are not even aware of that come very naturally to us because the complexity of our soul operates subconsciously. If we expand our perception of who we are, we become very aware of ourselves and others.

WHAT PRODUCES SOUL FRAGMENTATION?

Have you ever felt you were outside of your body? Have you had a feeling of floating or watching things happen? You were awake but felt in a dreamlike state. Usually this feeling is a result of *fragmentation of soul.* When trauma occurs, if you depend upon your own will to recover, you lose a portion of your soul or a portion of your soul is captured in the traumatic experience. When this occurs, your emotions are not enabled to express health, and your personality copes by compartmentalizing your thoughts relative to the emotional hurt.

As children of alcoholic parents, my wife and I knew that we needed healing. We are very open people with each other, so our communication of our feelings most likely helped save us from many destructive situations. I write much about anxiety and post-traumatic syndrome in *The Rewards of Simplicity* (Chosen, 2010).

The key to us overcoming was our belief system. In summary, we came to this agreement: "God knows best and has wisdom. His Word is perfect, and His thoughts are better than any human expression. When agreement is not in reach by either of us, we will submit our opinion and agree with His wisdom. When our thoughts are exalted above His, we will lay down our thoughts and agree with Him!" Not only were we open to press through our hurt and trust each other, but we also developed our thoughts around our communion with a holy God through His Spirit and Word. We knew that no matter what we had experienced in life, we were created to be in this earth at this time. We knew He had a plan, and we would seek His plan, which included healing and wholeness.

Most children who survive abusive, traumatic childhoods tend to *fade into the woodwork* or have such great separation anxiety that they contend with a lifetime of depression, suicidal urges, explosive anger, and most likely many demonic oppressions and possessions. These individuals can become very possessive of others, flock together, create gang mentalities, and produce harm to many around them. Many cults begin out of wounded, fragmented individuals who draw other wounded, fragmented individuals to themselves.

REASONS FOR FRAGMENTATION

The major reason for our personality or soul functions becoming fragmented is trauma. In traumatic events, many times a part of our soul splits to avoid excessive or continual suffering. This portion of our soul can be lost from us forever or enter a captive state within our overall personality. I usually explain this as a *submerged identity*. This spirit is reinforced by the traumatic memory that keeps replaying in our hearts and minds. The incident then becomes disruptive again at a certain key, opportune time when we should be progressing forward to our level of prosperity in life.

With this fragmentation, we can move on a scale of from being the *Incredible Hulk*—overly aggressive—to *Lilly Wallflower*, shy and retreating. We can go from "something is missing in my life" to "I have found my true inner self" all in one day's time. Many are diagnosed with a bipolar disorder, but in reality they need to be healed and reintegrated into wholeness. We can become so wounded that we lose a portion of our lives and are never the same again after the trauma occurs.

I also find that we consciously and unconsciously give portions of our soul and thoughts to be compartmentalized and put on a shelf or even give ourselves permission to take leave from the overall process of our life. This can be good or very bad, dependent on our denial of situations, relegating our authority to others to take control of us, or just plain not wanting responsibility for our actions. I see that many people who do not understand the fallen nature of man label portions of themselves that are crying for redemption as wrong and sinful and never develop the quality of uniqueness that God intended us to display. They condemn this area of self instead of submitting it for redemption through the cross, the blood, the Word, and the Spirit, and it becomes dark or is passed on in the bloodline for other generations to contend with.

RELIGION BINDS CREATIVE DEVELOPMENT

Religion—instead of spiritual life through the Son—tells us to just release our problems. Many think the manifestations of fragmentation (anger, bitterness, wounding, instability, addictions, depression, and so forth) will just go away if we are spiritually active enough to overcome the poor fruit of trauma. This will work only if we are moving by the Spirit of God and not in the flesh. We can begin by having a desire of "wanting to be better," but our end can only be greater if we allow the Spirit of God to redeem the portions of us that have been captured, fragmented, or submerged. We can't just run off what is bad in us and not unlock what was meant to be redemptive and expressive. Jesus said this:

> But when the unclean spirit has gone out of a man, it roams through dry [arid] places in search of rest, but it does not find any. Then it says, I will go back to my house from which I came out. And when

it arrives, it finds the place unoccupied, swept, put in order, and decorated. Then it goes and brings with it seven other spirits more wicked than itself, and they go in and make their home there. And the last condition of that man becomes worse than the first.

—MATTHEW 12:43–45, AMP

When children manifest evil tendencies, many parents, motivated by pride, tell that child to suppress the feeling and just do away with that portion of himself or herself. But if the child just sends that part of self away instead of seeing why the enemy has chosen to use that portion, he or she will never fully develop into who he or she was meant to be in Christ. Parents who do this are preventing their children from being totally redeemed. Does this mean that we should not correct our children? Of course not! However, we should explain why the child feels the way he does, and instead of just casting out that portion of the child's spirit, we must refill or liberate what the enemy has held captive. If we use legalism to deal with behavioral issues instead of spiritual liberation, later these children will feel they lost something in life and will resent the parent for not helping them *find themselves*. Spirit and life redeem (rather than oppress, captivate, and narrow) development of one's self.

TRAUMA FRAGMENTS AND STOPS MULTIPLICATION

During our fragmentation of soul, the enemy continues his attempts to gain access to us, vexing our spirits and affecting our bodies. We'll discuss more of this as we proceed through the remaining chapters. However, I find that the enemy generally targets the portions of our bodies that involve reproduction. We were called to multiply, so if the enemy can stop us from doing that by using our spiritual wombs, he senses he has succeeded by usurping God's ultimate plan for us. Many who have abortions never recover from fragmentation, and early promiscuity can lead to many later difficulties with reproductive organs, including men's prostates, where cancer is on the rise. We have some friends who desire to have children. They are a beautiful, virile-looking couple. However, they are unable to conceive. The man in the relationship lost a brother unexpectedly, and the effects of this seemed to deplete his life source. His sperm count actually dropped after the traumatic incident and has never fully recovered to this day.

In the Bible, barrenness is a curse. Many times barrenness comes from our sin or familial sin. However, trauma can affect us in such a way that we stop multiplying. Let's just take a moment and look at the male who was set in the garden to watch and to multiply.

What causes a male to multiply is his ability to fertilize the egg in a woman. Since my wife and I were barren for ten years, we had to learn many things about our lack of procreation, both spiritually and physically. We have written much about Pam's hostile womb, which the Spirit of God healed in January 1984. However, in the Word of God, the term translated "the river" is the same word used for sperm that is motile, fertilizes, and brings healing wherever it goes.

If a man experiences trauma, his ability to procreate can be stifled. Testicular trauma or torsion may affect fertility. Testicular torsion is a condition in which the testicle twists on the cord that attaches it to the body. Approximately 30–40 percent of men with a history of testicular torsion have an abnormal semen analysis. Environmental conditions, war, spiritual rejection, and many other issues can cause a man's "river" to lack health and motility.

The trauma in our lives affects us both spiritually and physically. Our enemy does not play the game of life fairly when we are traumatized. In other words, when we are down, he kicks us again. This affects us greatly. He loves to kick us in our area of procreation, wound us, and stop us from prospering. Satan has a goal—to stop life from occurring abundantly. He also wants to stop us from creating and multiplying. He hates the thought of freely flowing Christians who reproduce themselves physically and spiritually. You can use this scenario when you are looking at *revival* in the body of Christ. We get moving in God. We experience trauma. The move of God stops or eventually has no effect on multiplying. The river was flowing but then stagnates and has no power.

CHAPTER 14

GOD'S PLAN FOR WHOLENESS

W HEN WE EXPERIENCE the grace of God leading to salvation, that abundant grace permeates our entire being—body, soul, and spirit—with the ability to change every fiber of our makeup. As we yield to the ongoing, life-changing power of salvation, we can begin to understand wholeness. We are meant to be whole. When we came to the Lord, no matter what age we were, most of us were fragmented, with pieces of our lives scattered here and there. Why? Scattering is a curse that we come under as a result of sin. When we sin, pieces of the person God intends for us to be are left behind. We trade purity, blessing, health, and/ or a part of God's perfect plan for our lives for a sin we have committed. Therefore, parts of the whole person God intends for us to be lie scattered along the paths of our lives at each point where we have chosen sin.

Although we in the Western world tend to compartmentalize our lives into physical, mental, and spiritual categories (or body, soul, and spirit), the fact is that a proper biblical worldview is one of a unified, whole person in whom these parts are not separate entities but are interconnected. First Thessalonians 5:23 says, "Now may the God of peace Himself sanctify you completely; and may your whole spirit, soul, and body be preserved blameless at the coming of our Lord Jesus Christ." Here we see that God's interest in sanctifying is not limited to the spiritual being of a person but extends to the whole person. The concept of dealing with a person holistically did not originate in the Far East or in New Age thinking; it originated with God.

In fact, *Jesus's message was one of wholeness.* Many times He would respond to those whom He touched by saying, "Your faith has made you whole." Why? As previously mentioned, sin can leave us scattered. Sin also affects each part of us. Sin is not just a dark blot on the invisible realm of the soul; it can affect us physically, mentally, emotionally, or spiritually. Many people are facing illnesses today because of sin in their lives. For this reason, we must transcend our Western mind-set and realize that we need restoration and wholeness to be brought to every part of our being. E. Anthony Allen, in the book *Transforming Health*, edited by Eric Ram, states, "The ways people think, feel, relate and mange their lifestyles can maim and even kill. But divine healing and renewed hope can transcend normal healing processes. Divine forgiveness, reconciliation, deliverance, restoration and renewal bring healing. Where God reigns there is healing. Wholeness comes not by 'treating' but by healing."[1]

That is why Jesus said, "Your faith has made you whole." When He heals, He restores, and restoration is a holistic process. Only God has the power to gather the scattered pieces of our sin-ridden lives and bring them back into wholeness. That is part of what happened to me when I was eighteen. When the Lord said, "I will restore to you all that you have lost," I entered into a process of exchanging my early, fragmented life for a wholeness that gave me the power to obtain all the spiritual blessings that God had stored up for me in the heavenly places. My body, soul, and spirit all entered into that process.

A Divided Mind

He is a double-minded man, unstable in all his ways.

—James 1:8

But He gives more grace. Therefore He says: "God resists the proud, but gives grace to the humble." Therefore submit to God. Resist the devil and he will flee from you. Draw near to God and He will draw near to you. Cleanse your hands, you sinners; and purify your hearts, you double-minded. Lament and mourn and weep! Let your laughter be turned to mourning and your joy to gloom. Humble yourselves in the sight of the Lord, and He will lift you up.

—James 4:6–10

If we learn to seek God first and are able to prioritize properly in our lives, everything we need will be added to us. In order to do that, our mind is going to have to be renewed, transformed, and we will learn to think the way that God thinks. Romans 12:1–2 (NLT) says, "And so, dear brothers and sisters, I plead with you to give your bodies to God because of all he has done for you. Let them be a living and holy sacrifice—the kind he will find acceptable. This is truly the way to worship him. Don't copy the behavior and customs of this world, but let God transform you into a new person by changing the way you think. Then you will learn to know God's will for you, which is good and pleasing and perfect." However, hindering demons attempt to stop our mind from thinking the way God thinks. Demonic forces know that if our mind is operating with God's anointing, we will be able to prioritize and order our steps in the way God intends us to do on a daily basis. We will advance, and the kingdom advances. We will be useful tools in God's hands as well as prosperous in our lives.

One way the enemy builds strongholds in our minds is by forming blocks in our cognitive processes. A stronghold is a thought process that Satan has invaded to erect thought patterns against God's kingdom plan and purpose. What happens in cognitive processing is this: You gain information in a certain subject. You continue to gain and store information in your brain until you have a clear understanding on that subject. But if information that is coming to you cannot be categorized and processed, you get a blockage that forms in your brain, and the revelation that you're supposed to be getting cannot be connected properly. Therefore you're hindered in categorizing and aligning key knowledge that allows you to move forward. Think of a gas pipeline that flows through a network of connecting lines and systems and eventually reaches a processing station, where it is processed properly and then is sent for commercial use. If you can block that pipeline in the early stages, you can restrict the gas flow to an entire neighborhood and cause the neighborhood to remain completely without energy. This is what the enemy wants to do with our lives. Biblically that's called a *stronghold*. What the enemy does is form a blockage somewhere in your brain by releasing a bit of misinformation, a lie contrary to your destiny, resulting in a blockage. When new information or godly revelation starts trying to come into you, it cannot bypass the blockage and is not, therefore, processed at all.

> But seek first the kingdom of God and His righteousness, and all these things shall be added to you.
>
> —MATTHEW 6:33

FRAC-ED OUT OR WHOLE?

I want to explain a term that Allen Faubion, one of our ministers at Glory of Zion, used recently when teaching. He shared that a person has a choice to be "*frac-ed out* or whole." Let's look at how this phrase applies to overcoming fragmentation. Allen shared the following: "While ministering in Northeast Louisiana during the Feast of Tabernacles (2009), the Holy Spirit gave me a very clear picture. I saw five derricks surrounding the area. What flowed from those derricks flowed to the rest of the state. I heard the Spirit say: 'They will drill for one thing, but another will come forth.' As I ministered I observed something connected to this revelation. I saw that the reserve or deposit within people from the last season had dried up in them and great resources were held captive."[2]

How wells work

Like my family, Allen's grandfather had worked in the drilling business during its early days from the 1920s to the early 1960s. After his retirement he would periodically take Allen to visit some of his former colleagues still in the business. Allen tells this story:

> My grandfather would take me up on the drilling deck, where I would feel the powerful vibrations of all the equipment and the roar of the motors that were driving the drilling shafts deeper into the earth. It captivated me and scared me at the same time. It was an unusual place to be in. I could sense the danger and risk of the drilling task at hand. At the same time I somehow understood that

what came forth from the well was more valuable than the risk it took to get it there.

When a well is drilled and the bit reaches an underground reserve of oil or gas, there is an initial pressure in the hole that pushes the oil (the same is true for gas or water) to the surface. I remembered old pictures and film clips I had seen showing *gushers*. Gushers were wells whose pressure was so great it propelled the petroleum many feet in the air with an explosive velocity and a triumphal spray fan. My grandfather had worked in some of those fields where *gushers* were uncapped, places with names like Spindletop.[3]

Eventually, the tremendous pressure released from the initial breakthrough into the reserve declines. When the pressure declines, the well must be pumped to extract the reserve. Often after a period of pumping, the well goes dry. The word *dry* implies a time when all the reserve is extracted and there is no remaining reserve. Normal methods of oil extraction (drilling and pumping) successfully extract only 25 percent of the existing reserve. For every barrel of oil brought to the surface, there are three barrels of oil that remain in the earth. Many of our problems with petroleum have nothing to do with the lack of fossil fuels but with our inability to extract all the fuel that is there. A well goes dry at the point its remaining reserves still in the ground are captured in the fractures in the earth's strata and are unable to flow to the underground reservoir, where it can be pumped.

The reservoir in us

When Allen was sharing his story, he came up with three key points of great significance:

1. There is a reserve deposited in every believer and all the people of God. That reserve helped all of God's people (including us) to overcome certain things in the past season.

2. The outpouring of the Holy Spirit during that past season had a pressure that released a *gusher* of spiritual gifts, levels of intercession, and miracles for that season. Over time that gusher diminished to the point that we find ourselves needing something greater for the season we are now entering.

3. The enemy knows the status of our well(s). Satan knows that God has placed a valuable and powerful spiritual reservoir in us, of which only a fraction has been released. He also realizes that by fracturing the lives of God's people and our connections with one another, he can *trap* our gifts and resources.

I hope these insights help you better understand why incredibly traumatic circumstances at different times in our lives, especially after we become Christians, can fragment and hold us captive. The enemy does not play fair with trauma. He takes advantage of us at key times to trap the powerful and plentiful anointing that God has placed in every believer. Often, however, instead of realizing that there is a limitless reserve of creativity to be accessed by Holy Spirit, we submerge our identity and lose our true spiritual development. At this point in life, we become trapped and decline spiritually.

Releasing the reserve

The word Allen kept using was *frac*. He had made a spiritual connection because of his generational interest in various aspects of petroleum drilling. *Frac-ing* is an oilfield technology that is used to extract more oil (the 75 percent trapped in the fractures) from depleted reserves, or dry holes. Frac-ing is one aspect of what is called EOR, or *enhanced oil recovery*. After the initial reserve (the 25 percent) is depleted, a second hole is drilled into the reserve. Then a combination of carbon dioxide and water is injected under great pressure into the second hole. The pressure of the water opens up the fractures so that oil trapped by the fractures can flow freely into the reservoir and be pumped to the surface. Often the injection includes particles of sand or similar granular substances. When the pressure opens the fractures, the grains of sand wedge into the fractures so that they stay open once the pressure is gone. This ensures that a maximum release of the reserve can take place. The drilling industry has found that this technology allows them to extract two or three times more of the oil reserve than was previously possible.

The Spirit of God is saying this:

1. "Now is the time for the deposit, the reserve that I have put in My people, to come forth and come up." If you feel depleted or lack the reserve necessary to overcome your circumstances, know this: We have entered a time in which the Spirit of God is drawing forth from us more of that mighty reserve that He has placed in us. He is now moving on your behalf to bring forth your spiritual reserve. It is in you if the Spirit of God is in you. It is time for us to declare to the reserve in us to "come forth and come up."

2. "I am changing the way I do deliverance. In the past season I restored My people's fractured identities by closing up the fractures. In this season I am opening up the fractures to recover and release the reserve."

3. "What the enemy sought to capture, I am recovering. I am bringing forth the oil from the fractures."

We must realize that as God increases the pressure that will release our reserve, the enemy will try to convince us that God is allowing us to be traumatized again. It will be important that we see this lie for what it is. God is opening the fractures wrought by the enemy so that He can bring forth our spiritual reserves. This is a season when we must invite the Lord to turn up the pressure to *bring it forth.*

In the past season, the body of Christ utilized dimensions of pastoral counsel to help traumatized people understand their trauma and move to a greater level of comfort and restoration. Counseling and wisdom are good, but in this season God is activating a different strategy to bring forth our spiritual reserves. This is a new strategy. God is drilling new wells in us in which He will inject new pressures. At first glance that neither sounds comfortable nor easy. It isn't. However, He is a master driller who knows exactly how to draw forth a maximal amount of the reserve remaining in us. This is a time for us to realize that we are going to face some incredible pressure over the next season. If we allow the Lord to "frac" us, then He will use those pressures to release an even greater reserve of the strength and anointing in us.

How Long Will You Grieve?
Put on a *New Identity*

Leadership and wineskins change. In the midst of victory there is loss. Loss is part of life. We lose loved ones, relationships, financial strength, and influence. One of the most difficult losses to overcome is expectation. We have hope that something will happen in a certain way, and what we hoped for is deferred to another season. Hope deferred makes the heart sick. Another way of saying this is, *"Postponed manifestation causes us to be weakened and unable to stand firm."* We grieve when we lose.

There is a process connected with grief. We first experience shock then enter into denial over what we are experiencing. We try to determine if the event is really happening or if we are experiencing a bad dream. However, the pain of reality sets in, and we grow angry, depressed, manipulative, and even turn inward. "Why me?" becomes the identity we wear. The last phase of loss, and the most dangerous of all, is withdrawal and loneliness. To protect ourselves from more hurt and pain, we become our only focus.

When Samuel anointed Saul as king, there were expectations for him to accomplish much for Israel. Saul put on the *kingly robe* but never wore the identity of God's king. Eventually, the Lord determined that for the good of the whole of His covenant people, Saul must go. When the Lord communicated this with Samuel, he grieved over the loss. The Lord asked a question that rings through the ages in all losses: *"How long will you grieve?"*

This is a question that each of us must answer. *Will you wear grief and trauma from the last season as your future, or will you see that there is* new *waiting for you?* Stop, be still, and ask yourself, "What am I wearing?" If your answer is, "The residue from my last season, with all of the loss attached," the time for change is now!

Look Again

Get past your last traumatic experience and loss. He is there! I probably read the story of the Lord's life, death, and resurrection three times each year. Recently, I kept reading Luke 24:13–32. In this portion of Scripture, there are some disciples walking about six to eight miles outside of the trauma zone of inner-city Jerusalem, where they have seen their Master crucified on a cross. Let's read this story here:

> That same day two of them were walking to the village Emmaus, about seven miles out of Jerusalem. They were deep in conversation, going over all these things that had happened. In the middle of their talk and questions, Jesus came up and walked along with them. But they were not able to recognize who he was.
>
> He asked, "What's this you're discussing so intently as you walk along?"
>
> They just stood there, long-faced, like they had lost their best friend. Then one of them, his name was Cleopas, said, "Are you the only one in Jerusalem who hasn't heard what's happened during the last few days?"
>
> He said, "What has happened?"
>
> They said, "The things that happened to Jesus the Nazarene. He was a man of God, a prophet, dynamic in work and word, blessed by both God and all the people. Then our high priests and leaders

betrayed him, got him sentenced to death, and crucified him. And we had our hopes up that he was the One, the One about to deliver Israel. And it is now the third day since it happened. But now some of our women have completely confused us. Early this morning they were at the tomb and couldn't find his body. They came back with the story that they had seen a vision of angels who said he was alive. Some of our friends went off to the tomb to check and found it empty just as the women said, but they didn't see Jesus."

Then he said to them, "So thick-headed! So slow-hearted! Why can't you simply believe all that the prophets said? Don't you see that these things had to happen, that the Messiah had to suffer and only then enter into his glory?" Then he started at the beginning, with the Books of Moses, and went on through all the Prophets, pointing out everything in the Scriptures that referred to him.

They came to the edge of the village where they were headed. He acted as if he were going on but they pressed him: "Stay and have supper with us. It's nearly evening; the day is done." So he went in with them. And here is what happened: He sat down at the table with them. Taking the bread, he blessed and broke and gave it to them. At that moment, open-eyed, wide-eyed, they recognized him. And then he disappeared.

Back and forth they talked. "Didn't we feel on fire as he conversed with us on the road, as he opened up the Scriptures for us?"

—LUKE 24:13–32, THE MESSAGE

HIS WORD *DIVIDES,* AND *WE SEE*

In this account after the Resurrection, several things are revealed:

1. The disciples are in trauma.

2. Jesus asks them to explain the trauma from their perspective.

3. They had refused the women's report of resurrection but embraced the men who did not see.

4. Jesus rebukes then exhorts with the Word of God.

5. Jesus then communes with them. Upon communing, their eyes are opened and they can see the resurrected Christ in their midst. Their trauma is overcome, and their vision of the future is restored.

We are in a season in which we must divide to see and multiply. What do I mean? There have been walls built, veils formed, and curtains dropped that keep us from seeing. Walls have been built in relationships. Curtains have been developed to keep us from seeing the promises and blessings that await us. Veils and smokescreens have been released by the enemy, so we only see half of what we should be seeing. Therefore, the question "Behold I do a *new* thing—do you not perceive it?" may cause us to answer, "No, I don't see a thing!" We might say, "Everything looks the same as it last did... well, perhaps everything looks even a little blurrier than before."

What divides? The Word divides between the soul and spirit! Hebrews 4:12 says, "For the Word of God is living and powerful, and sharper than any two-edged sword, piercing even to the division of soul and spirit... and is a discerner of the thoughts and intents of the heart." This is one of my top ten favorite scriptures in the Word of God. Why? This statement defines the power, the energy, and the purpose of the Word of God. The Word *divides*! The Word is working to separate our soulish desires, inhibitions, and wounds. The Word cleanses the window of our conscience, the meeting place of soul and spirit. The Word gives us light to see through our own personality and see the *best* that God has to offer us. The Word allows us to see into eternity. The Word produces faith.

The Word divides the dichotomy between self and *spirit*. Faith works along this dividing line. We must choose trust over mistrust (Ps. 37:3; Prov. 3:5). We must have our belief system divided. We must make daily choices between belief and unbelief (Heb 3:12). We must choose between loyalty and betrayal (Luke 22). Our flesh will lean toward the latter, but His life can cause us to be loyal to those leading and the position of rule that He has placed us in. His Word is our covenant Book and divides us between fidelity and unfaithfulness (2 Sam. 11). His Word reveals our dependence or independence (1 Cor. 12). His Word makes us confident and divides our insecurity (1 John 5:14). His Word sets the standard for our obedience and makes our disobedience known to our conscience (1 John 2:5; 3:4). His Word divides our fragmentation (1 Thess. 5:23) and makes us *whole*. His Word creates our testimony so that we witness or keep silent and deny Him (1 John 5:11; Heb. 12:1). His Word is love, which causes our heart to dethrone hate (2 Thess. 3:5; Gal. 5:6; 1 John 2:9) and think of others more highly than ourselves.

His Word produces *faith*. Faith works from our *love*. Without our love for Him and others, our faith and vision suffer.

"I Will Surprise You as You Follow Me and Worship"

Here is a key prophetic word. No matter what has happened in your life, you can tap into a new level of creative power. You can gather all of what has been scattered. You can move your fragmented life into wholeness and power. In the midst of your tests, you can develop trust and walk in freedom.

> I will surprise you as I begin to manifest Myself in the month ahead. I will cause something that seems dead to begin to burn again. Turn and see. Turn away from your agreement with what you thought you were caught in, and TURN TO ME. I am burning again, and you will be *uncaught* and hear your next word from Me.
>
> You thought you were going to worship in one way, but I had to open a gate in heaven to create a different way of worship in you. There is a sound in you. Let the sound rise to Me on a daily basis as I begin a new movement around you. This sound will create movement, and you will SEE Me in a new way. If you had remained in last season's worship, you would have grown cold. Now, a new way of worship in heaven is opening up, and My people will worship Me in new ways with new sacrifices this month. You will shout, "Let me

GO that I might worship in a new way." Throw your hands out, for I AM going to fill them in a new way. You were tied up in one way, but I AM beginning to let you go free. Follow Me and you will SEE!

Listen carefully, for your ram is already positioned in the bush. Listen carefully, for you will sacrifice to Me differently. At your point of sacrifice is where you are held captive, but now you will sacrifice to Me in a new way. There is a trumpet blowing and announcing. Hear your ram in the bush. It will be the sound of your sacrifice. When you sacrifice the fat of a ram and you begin to sacrifice what I bring to you, it will open up the sound and give you the trumpet that you need to set your course in the heavens for the future. Get ready, for the fire gate is now opening.

As you take every assignment you've been given, you will begin to open up in a new way. Whatever I tell you to put your hand to, do that with all your heart. I will then add more and more for your hands to use.

The pupil of your eye is opening so it can receive more light. The way you were seeing is opening so you can see more light, rightly dividing and seeing what you did not see before. I AM opening your eyes so you see the doors and entry ways that were hidden in the last season. Your eyesight is adjusting now. What you need to see is already caught and waiting on you. Your eyesight is adjusting. Blinders have narrowed your vision, and you have not seen or ordered things to move the way I want to move. Because you are going to worship Me in a new way and bring the fat to the altar, I will allow you to hear the new sound that is waiting for you when you still your heart and emotions. I will allow you to see and hear the supply that is caught up in the bush. Bring the fat to the altar, and the supply in the bush will come alive and rattle. Bring the fat to the altar, and that which is in the bush will come alive.

Reordered for Victory

I have learned through the years that if I order my prayers, He will order my steps. *Order* is a mathematical, sequencing term as well as a military term. No matter what wilderness dimension is attempting to hold you,

you can *see* the order of your release and victory. What has been scattered can be restored. What has left can return.

Lift up your eyes and see (Ps. 121). You can see the victory ahead. Resist religion. God has promised that man is able to surpass himself by entering into a relationship with the One who created the world. Man, who is part of this world, can have relationship with the One who is greater than this world. He gave His Son to reveal relationship and restore access to us. We must have a sense of awe and mystery as we seek the Lord, to know Him and the power of resurrection that raised His Son from the dead and seated Him in heavenly places. All of our blessings dwell with Him. There is a new order to *see* in worship. This is a time to rebuild the altar. Many are being repositioned to find their new place of worship.

See victory over past structures that captivated your family. There is a new freedom coming in our lives. His *blood* can overcome the war in your blood. Ask the Spirit of God to penetrate and remove any deep, anti-Semitic root in your bloodline. *See* a divine recovery occur in your life. Break any power of scattering. If you have been uprooted from your inheritance, ask God to sovereignly set your course of return. If your thoughts are scattered, a curse is working. Reverse the curse and plant your feet like a tree by the waters of life and be healed. Remove and break any power from past words that have been linked with fear. If you have withdrawn from warring for your promise, repent. Do not slander the land you have been given or make light of the promise waiting for you (Num 13:32–14:5). If past generations in your bloodline were confronted by God and resisted advancing into the fullness of His destiny, repent and then move forward. You are the remnant that remains to pursue, overcome, and restore all.

> Show me the path of life. Let me feel Your presence. Let me experience the fullness of Your joy. I know that You are at the right hand of the Father and available to me. At Your right hand there are pleasures forevermore. Teach me Your way, and lead me in a very plain path. There are enemies all along my path, so You make my way

straight, that my enemies will not be able to attack me or distract me from the fullness You have for me. Even though I walk through narrow ways, You will give me a safe passage. You have already released commandments to instruct me along my path. I delight in these commands, since they keep my path straight. Your Word is a lamp unto my feet and a light unto my path. You are acquainted with all my ways along this path. You know when my spirit gets overwhelmed by the anxieties of the world around me. Even though the enemy has privately laid snares for me, You will make me sure-footed as I walk this path of life. Let all my ways be established as I ponder each step that I take before You.

—Excerpted and paraphrased from Psalms 16:11; 27:11; 119:35, 105; 139:3; 142:3; Proverbs 1:15; 2:9; 4:14

This is a time to enter into the fullness of our personality and destiny. Let's change garments. Let's remove what has been tattered and torn and put on the garment that has been mended. First put on a renewed mind. Leave the spirit of confusion behind, and call back all the scattered thoughts that have never joined into the necessary cognitive processes that will produce your vision for the future. Add revived expectations. Next, receive the garment of authority. Add boldness to your new garment. Remove and leave behind your last cycle of fear. Wear freedom! Daily walk in the Spirit, and declare that you are a servant of Christ and not a slave to the flesh or a host for darkness to dwell. Adorn yourself with faith. Counteract faith-destroyers of strife, procrastination, anxiety over the future, doubt, unbelief, anger, frustration, guilt, jealousy, and envy. Wear overcoming revelation that reflects the kingdom. To make your new garment radiate, let the Lord pour on favor. Wear glory. Let momentum and acceleration propel you into your future. We are in a new season. This is a season to *see*! This is not a time to grieve. His joy will be your strength. See yourself being reclothed for the future.

CHAPTER 15

BREAKING THE POWER
OF VEXATION

JOSEPH WAS A supernatural interruption or an intervention in our lives. Time would tell! He came to us at the age of thirteen when we were serving as administrators of an institute in Texas for children from dysfunctional homes. (Actually, he came to us as "Billy," nicknamed after one of the men that his natural mother had aligned herself with, but we discovered that his real name was Joseph.) Joseph did not know his natural father, and his mother was in prison. He was a street kid from Houston who had been in numerous foster homes and care group homes. As with many children who come from dysfunctional authority structures in the home, Joseph knew *the system* of how to lie and manipulate to gain favor. However, he did not know the Lord. He had been forced to be religious and to follow rules, but he had no reality of God in his life.

Our role was to lead Joseph to the Lord and fully establish him on the path that God had destined for him when He created him in the womb. We actually knew that we would have to go through a process to redevelop his identity and make him into the *Joseph* that God intended for him to be. He was a trial for us. Not only were we developing his character, but we were also undoing and unraveling many of the ungodly mind-sets of survival that he had developed. We were attempting to find pieces of his life that had been scattered all over Houston. Satan had grabbed hold of Joseph's destiny at an early age and was attempting to hold him on a path of destruction. *But God!*

The promise that God gave me for Joseph was that he would be an A- and B-grade student. Oh, my! This was neither a reality nor a desire in his heart. War after war proceeded. He did make enough C grades to keep him in sport programs that he enjoyed. But the several severe strongholds caused by the abuses from his past remained, and there was constant contention over these issues. Because Joseph knew the system, our discernment level had to rise so that we could distinguish the truth from the lies in what he told us.

I would love to say that this was an easy war, but that would not be true. I came home at the end of my rope one day after a discussion with one of his school teachers. I was ready to just let Joseph go down the path that he seemed to desire most. When I walked into the house, Pam turned from the kitchen window and said, "The Lord spoke to me and told me that He was going to fill Joseph with the Holy Spirit."

My weariness and unbelief took over, and I said, "Oh great. That means I have to endure this war longer."

Pam then said, "Well, you can agree with God or agree with what you see!" I chose to submit and trust the word that the Lord had spoken to my wife. When I did this, two things occurred. First of all, I began to see that Pam had a dimension of faith that I did not have because of her mother love for a son who had been given to her. Love and faith were working together to bring prophetic fulfillment. Second, I began to see how the enemy used weariness, turmoil, frustration, and circumstances to cause me to forget the word of promise and plan of heaven. Remember, the only thing that the Lord had ever spoken to me about Joseph was that he would make As and Bs in school.

I would like to say things turned around immediately, but they did not. After high school, Joseph went to a private college in East Texas and then attended a junior college in North Texas for two years. Yet he was still mediocre in school and was still filled with issues. Joseph decided to enter the air force, and Pam and I took assignments in New Mexico and Colorado Springs. Joseph married soon after, but his life continued to be up and down. I still wondered in my heart if he would ever really change. But Pam walked in faith and believed in God's promises.

When Joseph was thirty-two, Pam and I moved back to Denton. By this time, Joseph had four children, and he was now attending the University of North Texas and working part-time. When he and his family came for

Christmas at our home that year, he shared with me how they had little money because of his working part-time and attending school. However, he did have a special gift for me—it was his final grade report in college. He had gotten all As! He had made the dean's list and finished his schooling, just as the Lord had said in the beginning. He had finished strong! He had proven to the enemy, to himself, and to me that what God had said about him was a reality. Both Joseph and his wife now serve in pastoral ministry. The Lord had fulfilled the word He had spoken to my wife as well. I learned much through watching this orchid bloom!

Fragmentation Requires a Process of Recovery

I love to see people's lives redeemed, gathered, and made whole. Joseph has continued to progress through the grace of God. However, like most of us, he will have a month where things seem dark around him—mainly because in his life there were so many fragmented portions, hurts, pains, abandonments, and rejections. He was going through a very difficult month when he was thirty-eight. He was pressing into the Lord but struggling in his daily life. He knew the Lord wanted to do something, but he could not get in touch with his emotions for this to happen. So, like Joseph in the Bible, he had a dream.

> I was on a playground standing by an old metal merry-go-round. The place seemed familiar, yet I could not detect where I was. I saw a little boy standing on the playground with his back toward me. I walked up to him but was a little nervous that as a stranger I might scare him. Just when I got up to him, he turned and looked directly at me. The little boy was me. (I only have one picture from my childhood—of me when I was about seven years old. And that is the face I saw when this boy turned around. This time of my life was the most traumatic. My mother had been imprisoned, I had been abandoned and was living in an abusive situation with one of her relationships. I eventually was bouncing from foster home to foster home.)
> The little boy (me) looked directly at me and said, "Please help

me *find* my family." My emotions were stirred, and I wanted to help him. I started walking with him. But then I saw that the family he was leading me to was not my family. Where he was leading me was into one of the terrible, troubled relationships of that season of my life. Where he was leading was not a part of my today, the family of redemption that I have now, or anything that had to do with my future. I said, "I can't go with you there. My family is over there, and I must meet them." In my dream, sadness overwhelmed me, but I knew I was to walk away. As I walked away I kept looking back to make sure the boy was OK; he just stared at me. I felt myself leaving something behind as I walked farther and farther away.

I woke up from this dream, and I had been delivered. This dream came after a long nine-month deliverance process that had me at the end of myself, and it saved my marriage and my life.

This is the perfect picture of fragmentation. You must go through the process of sending away a portion of yourself that has been defiled by spiritual forces. Though you long for certain portions of your life to be *as it should have been*, you must be willing to cling to God's purpose today and walk in a new way. Other portions of your life you must call back into God's order and watch Him restore in multiplied form. Joseph had always longed for a family since he was abandoned and rejected. However, the Lord was showing him that he should send away the hurts from the season that would never be recovered and cling to the precious gift and family he had been given.

LEAVE *TRAUMA* BEHIND AND SEE

There were times when Joseph was being healed that he would just hold his head and say, "My head feels like it is splitting apart." The good thing about Joseph was that with every healing moment, he was getting freer and freer. The enemy of his soul was losing control.

The enemy's goal is to block a traumatized soul's emotions. The ultimate goal of the enemy is to vex your spirit. This means a blockage of your *communion* and *intuition*. The enemy desires to stop you from pressing through and developing an *overcoming testimony*. I want to encourage you to leave trauma behind and remove the dam on your *blocked* emotions. Trauma, when not processed correctly, will shape your world from the point of view of the incident. Trauma, when used by the enemy, will create these major areas in your life: a failure mentality, a confused perspective, dullness, deadness, lost hope, and apathy.

Who is the enemy? He is the same Satan that our Lord faced off with in the wilderness when He withstood every temptation and infiltration that would be known to man. He is not just your imagination but the *one who opposes you with a goal to block your way of freedom.*

A Blocked Spirit

When you have a blocked spirit, you are not just vexed *but stagnated*. A water source with no outlet becomes a cesspool for disease and decay. Each of us has a river of life within us. John 7:37–39 says, "On the last day, that great day of the feast, Jesus stood and cried out, saying, 'If anyone thirsts, let him come to Me and drink. He who believes in Me, as the Scripture has said, out of his heart will flow rivers of living water.' But this He spoke concerning the Spirit, whom those believing in Him would receive; for the Holy Spirit was not yet given, because Jesus was not yet glorified."

One dimension of man is spiritual. When the spirit of man finds the life-giving creative source from the originator of man, we can walk in the Spirit even though we are flesh. We must remember that the Spirit of Jesus *was* before He became flesh. Before the foundation of the world, He was! When He became flesh, He flowed, limited to a man's frame in the Spirit. We can do the same. Jesus in us is the hope of glory. Outside of Christ, our spirit is deadened and controlled by the world. In Christ, our spirit is alive and like a flowing river. The enemy loves to block this spirit flow. If the flow can be blocked, life becomes less livable. We become dull and stagnant. The soul is filled with joy and life as long as the Spirit is flowing through our spirit. The enemy must minimize our life in the

Spirit so we fall from supernaturally flowing to being naturally stagnated. You will learn more about this as you read this chapter.

Another picture of spiritual life is like a highway. Have you ever needed to get somewhere, but even though you are in a hurry, the road you are traveling is blocked? That is what happens to our spirit man when we are moving forward and our way gets blocked. We get frustrated, annoyed, and vexed. Instead of waiting and hearing clearly from heaven on how to proceed, we sometimes turn back to an old, familiar method. When your way is blocked, you must stop and say, "Lord, do I go through the blockade, over the blockade, under the blockade, or around the blockade?"

He might say, "Speak to the blockade and tell it to move!" However, most of the time, He says, "Wait, I will work out your way!"

You Can See

Anytime we have a blocked, fragmented spirit, our vision is skewed. I can still remember the eye doctor telling me years ago, "You have a blind spot." A blind spot? What could that mean? He showed me the test results, which indicated that a huge portion of my vision was being blocked. He called this *a blind spot*. A blind spot is that small area that is insensitive to *light* in the retina of the eye. Another definition of *a blind spot* is "a person's lack of sensitivity to a particular thing." A person may express prejudice or ignorance about a subject and still be unaware of this blind spot. When the eye doctor told me that I had a blind spot, more than a physical malady was present. I knew that the Lord was going to uncover whatever was hidden in me.

I was diagnosed as having a tumor on my optic nerve, or a blood clot that was pressing on the nerve and blocking my vision. In either case, this seemed to be serious enough for the doctors to want me to go quickly to the hospital for further testing. Little did I know that in addition to the doctor's tests, God had planned a week of deliverance. The week turned into a year. The year turned into a process of ten years. The ten years resulted in a testimony of freedom—and the Lord let in a lot of light.

Let's talk about the soul, our vision, and blind spots. In the remaining portions of this book, let's understand our spirit, soul, and body as three parts but expressing one overcoming reality: He came to give us life more abundantly! We can see and experience the best a holy God has for us. We can be like Him, and others can see Him in us!

God Breathed—Life Came

When God breathed into the earth, or humus-like dirt, He brought forth life. When life ceases, or the soul stops operation, death occurs, and our spirit departs. All through the Word of God we see this happening. The widow of Zarephath was barren. She conceived. The son died at an early age. Elijah prayed for the *soul,* or breath of life, to return to the dead son of the widow (1 Kings 17:21). He stretched himself upon the child and breathed into him, just as God breathed into the earth. The child sneezed seven times and came back to life. Life and breath are linked to produce a reality of who we are and what we are here for on the earth. Later, the testimony of this widow and child gave them the ability to overcome the drought of the region and see restoration in their natural lot in life.

Each spirit in man is unique. We will discuss this more in a later chapter. Because of having a unique spirit, each soul is a creation of God that is very unique from the moment of conception, or the time when given a body (Num. 27:16; Eccles. 12:7; Isa. 42:5).

Should we reject life because of some structure in our bloodline that can fragment us later in life? Absolutely not!

Recently a friend of ours seeking children went through the process of in vitro fertilization (IVF), which has proved to be a modern-day miracle for many families. Her eggs were harvested, and her husband's sperm was injected into the eggs. Those eggs that *took* were fertilized, and embryos began to form. Before these embryos were placed into the mother's uterus, the parents were able to view what was happening with each unique formation. The doctor said, "There is life, but there are some fragments in the formation process!" He had said the same thing to them three years earlier when their first child, now almost three years old, was *in process*. What was once known only to God before IVF can now be seen under the microscope, even from embryonic formation. God continued to knit together the child in her mother's womb, and their first child is now a beautiful, vibrant, wonderful creature on the earth. Many of us begin with fragmentation. We just do not have the opportunity to view those fragments while we are being formed in our mother's womb but learn of them later in life, in our striving to become whole.

Each soul is not only unique but also has its origin from the parents, along with each body. This helps us in understanding original sin through Adam and the true humanity of Jesus.

THREE AS ONE

In 1 Thessalonians 5:23, we find that all three—spirit, soul, and body—can be sanctified. The Greek mind-set would look at these three separately. However, from a Hebraic perspective of cognitively approaching things from a whole view, these three form a single human reality. So in Hebrews 4:12, the Word of God "piercing even to the division of soul and spirit," appears to mean simply that God's Word probes the inmost recesses of the total human being.[1]

The soul and the spirit are the two most important portions of a person's entire makeup. The spirit is eternal, and the soul expresses the type of spirit that we carry in life. When John and James wanted to call down fire on the people in a city, the Lord "turned and rebuked them, and said, 'You do not know what manner of spirit you are of. For the Son of Man did not come to destroy men's lives but to save them'" (Luke 9:55–56). This is why in Hebrews 4:12 we find the word: "For the word of God is living and powerful, and sharper than any two-edged sword, piercing even to the division of soul and spirit, and of joints and marrow, and is a discerner of the thoughts and intents of the heart." Because we don't know what spirit we are, the Word of God as an ultimate authority in our life must divide our soul and spirit. This type of division produces wholeness because it cuts away every impurity that is competing with the Spirit of God. This allows Holy Spirit to flow through us and stops any vexation from operating within us. The Word divides. This type of division is the only way to overcome a schism or division in you.

THE SOUL CAN BE DIVIDED

A schism is a division or separation within a body that keeps the reality of the person from being fully viewed. This can happen to us as individuals or as a collective group, corporately. First Corinthians 12:25 says, "That there should be no schism in the body." Paul tells us to resist any schism in the body so that the souls of believers may be strengthened through the ministry of others (Acts 14:22). Christian leaders have the responsibility of keeping watch over the souls of those in their charge (Heb. 13:17). "Unsteady souls" are especially vulnerable to being led into sin by false teachers (2 Pet. 2:14; cf. Acts 15:24 [RSV, "minds"]). But James 5:20 teaches that "he who turns a sinner from the error of his way will save a soul from death and cover a multitude of sins." Hope in God's covenant promises provides Christians with "an anchor of the soul, both sure and steadfast" (Heb. 6:19). First Peter 4:19 exhorts those who suffer according to God's will to "commit their souls to Him in doing good, as to a faithful Creator." Those who endure suffering without losing faith will save their souls (Heb. 10:39).

We must look at the body collectively as well as individually, as we see revealed in John 7:43 ("the people"), John 9:16 ("the Pharisees"), and John 10:19 ("the Jews"). When you go back and review how the Lord came to Earth to represent the Father, you find that all of the above areas were divided in their loyalty and conversion to Father's will. They divided over His identity, origin, and message. Jesus's presence, actions, and words caused people to take sides, to believe or not believe. The apostle Paul also caused a division among both Gentiles and Jews by preaching the gospel of Jesus and His resurrection (Acts 14:4; 23:7).[2]

The essence and expression of our being or life is the soul. The soul must be whole for the spirit to express the Spirit of God in His fullness. God "breathed" into man, thereby creating a "living soul." In Hebrew the word is *nepeš*. The soul denotes the *self*, complete with emotions, appetites, and volition. The soul represents our psyche. The soul encompasses what man was meant to be. This allows man to present the *glory* within him to the atmosphere surrounding him. Psalm 16:9–11 says, "Therefore my heart is glad, and my glory rejoices; my flesh also will rest in hope. For You will not leave my soul in Sheol, nor will You allow Your Holy One to see corruption. You will show me the path of life; in Your presence is fullness of joy; at Your right hand are pleasures forevermore."

When our soul and spirit are functioning as one, we are content on our path of life. Life might not be easy, but we can rest in His love and embrace every situation with confidence in Him. In the Word of God, *soul* is interchangeable with *bowels* (Isa. 16:11), *heart* (Ps. 73:21; Lam. 1:20; 2:11), and *reins* or *kidneys* (Prov. 23:16). Our body functions—heart, kidneys, and digestion—are dependent not just upon our healthy eating but upon the spiritual relationship and the type of communion that we have on a daily basis.

Soul can be used to refer to the seat of our cravings, desires, wants, and voice. However, this word can also be linked with the spiritual cravings of life as well as to the physical needs we desire. (Psalms 42 and 84 are key insights to this understanding.) Our experiences are linked to the memory of the soul. The soul can express a myriad of emotions:

- Sadness (Deut. 28:65; Ps. 42:6–7; 119:28)
- Grief (Job 30:25)
- Pain (Ps. 132)
- Weeping (Jer. 13:17)
- Distress (Gen. 42:21)

- Bitterness (Job 3:20; 7:11; Isa. 38:15)

- Anxiety or being troubled (Ps. 6:3–4)

- Trembling (Isa. 21:4)

- Hate (2 Sam. 5:8; Ps. 11:5)

- Rejoicing (Ps. 35:9; Isa. 61:10)

- Being cheered (Ps. 86:4; 94:19)

The soul was meant to bless the Lord (Ps. 103:1, 22; 104:1, 35) and love (1 Sam. 18:1, 3; Song of Sol. 1:7; 3:1–4) Him with all of our strength. A complete expression of needs, desires, and feelings flows through our soul. Our mind and emotions work together in thought and memory (Ps. 103:2; Lam. 3:20). The soul is *given life* by the blood. The blood is the life (*nepeš*, Deut. 12:23). As Abel's blood was shed in Genesis 4, his life was poured out on the ground. His voice continued to rise from the earth from which he had been made.

Life must be accountable to God, the Father, since He was the one who released life into the earth realm. We will discuss the "Father of spirits" in a later chapter. You can forfeit your life, as Judas did. Your life can be sought by others, as David's was sought by Saul. Your life is the object of salvation (Ps. 116:4) and redemption (2 Sam. 4:9; Ps. 34:22; 72:14). Yeshua the Messiah came to buy back life by giving His life. When our lives becomes fragmented and off course, we have access for deliverance (Ps. 55:18–19; 116:8), even from Sheol (Ps. 86:13).

In Luke 12:19, the rich man addresses his own soul. He speaks to himself. The term soul can also denote one's inner life or true personhood. Because God created the inner portion of man, He has the power to destroy it. But Jesus taught that whereas other human beings may succeed in killing the body, they cannot kill the soul (Matt. 10:28). However, the soul can be wounded and fragmented. The enemy's plan in doing this is to stop the spirit from functioning properly.

Jesus taught that the human soul is priceless (Matt. 16:26; Mark 8:37). Those who try to save their soul will lose it, but those who lose their soul for Christ's sake will find it (Matt. 16:25; Mark 8:36; Luke 9:25). Jesus Himself demonstrated this principle. In His death, which saved mankind, He gave His whole being—body, soul, and spirit—as a ransom for the many who were under penalty of death (Matt. 20:28; Mark 10:45).

In 1 Peter 1:22, we read that Christians' souls are purified by obedience to the truth. Jesus said, "If you love Me, obey Me!" John talks about Gaius obeying the truth (3 John). We have already mentioned that Paul prayed that his readers' "spirit, soul, and body be preserved blameless at the coming of our Lord Jesus Christ" (1 Thess. 5:23).

THE ENEMY'S GOAL—VEX YOUR SPIRIT AND OVERTAKE YOUR SOUL

The enemy's ultimate goal is to remove the vision of man. He must thwart who we are individually and corporately. He must block our vision. But God! You can see your way into your future victory. We must allow the Lord to open our eyes so we may *see*. Seeing is a prophetic dimension that allows you to gain the revelation you need to advance into your future. Without prophetic revelation, a people perish. *This is a season to see before we hear!* Get ready for your eyes to be opened.

The Bible defines *vexation*. King Solomon understood vexation and wrote about it in Ecclesiastes:

> I have see all the works that are done under the sun; and, behold, all is vanity and vexation of spirit.... And I gave my heart to know wisdom, and to know madness and folly: I perceived that this also is vexation of spirit.... Then I looked on all the works that my hands had wrought, and on the labour that I had laboured to do: and, behold, all was vanity and vexation of spirit, and there was no profit under the sun.... Therefore I hated life; because the work that is wrought under the sun is grievous unto me: for all is vanity and vexation of spirit.... For God giveth to a man that is good in his sight wisdom, and knowledge, and joy: but to the sinner he giveth travail, to gather and to heap up, that he may give to him that is good before God. This also is vanity and vexation of spirit....

Again, I considered all travail, and every right work, that for this a man is envied of his neighbour. This is also vanity and vexation of spirit.... Better is a handful with quietness, than both the hands full with travail and vexation of spirit.... There is no end of all the people, even of all that have been before them: they also that come after shall not rejoice in him. Surely this also is vanity and vexation of spirit.... Better is the sight of the eyes than the wandering of the desire: this is also vanity and vexation of spirit.

—Ecclesiastes 1:14, 17; 2:11, 17, 26; 4:4, 6, 16; 6:9, kjv

The spirit of man can be so vexed that we stop seeing our way in the world around us.

As we enter this season of *seeing*, let us be like Jeremiah. When the Lord asked him, "What do you see?" he answered, "I see an almond tree!" Start this season by seeing the almond tree and watching for the performance of His Word. The almond tree is the first tree that blossoms in Israel, representing the change in season. This tree also represents the power of watching.

The Lord instructed me to help us *see* better. In the process of seeing, we see our enemy in a new way. The Lord showed me a threefold spiritual force set against us. This evil structure consists of *poverty, infirmity,* and *self-pity*. These spirits work together in an attempt to blind and stop us from seeing the Lord's best in our lives. Let's begin to *see* and then to turn aside to *look* as the Lord manifests Himself to us in new ways.

The Lord is watching to perform His Word. We can *see* the performance of our promises. In the last chapter I gave you a brief, simple understanding about fragmentation. When we are fragmented in soul, our spirit man experiences vexation. One of the keys to our life is vision—not just physical vision but spiritual vision.

Where there is no vision, the people perish.

—Proverbs 29:18, kjv

THE EYE SEES

The eye is a major gate where information is perceived and channeled into the human soul and spirit. The Bible calls the eye "the lamp of the body." Matthew 6:22–23 reads, "The lamp of the body is the eye. If therefore your eye is good, your whole body will be full of light. But if your eye is bad, your whole body will be full of darkness. If therefore the light that is in you is darkness, how great is that darkness!" In the Bible, one method of punishment in war was to blind or put out the eyes of the captive (Judg. 16:21; 2 Kings 25:7; Jer. 52:11). If the eye is to be useful, it must see clearly. Biblically, the eye is of great importance for a person to prosper fully in God's plan. The eye also relates to the heart and mind, since the "eye of the heart" determines our spiritual perception. As we read in Matthew 6, if our spiritual eyes are open, we can receive enlightenment, and the Spirit of God can flow. If our eyes are darkened, our whole body becomes dark, and eventually we lose our way.

CHAPTER 16

GUARD AGAINST THE ENEMY'S TOOLS

Satan is also watching for that opportune time to vex and blind us from seeing the best that God has for us. The purpose of this chapter is to reveal Satan's hidden snares. We are called to see, but many times we must unveil the evil eye.

The term *evil eye* is found in the Bible. The New King James Version of the Old Testament usually uses a literal translation of the Hebrew words for "evil" and "eye" ("your eye be evil," Deut. 15:9; "an evil eye," Prov. 28:22), whereas the New International Version uses a figurative translation ("ill will" and "stingy"). These Bible versions translate the New Testament Greek words in a similar manner. The New King James Version uses "is your eye evil" in Matthew 20:15 and "an evil eye" in Mark 7:22, whereas the New International Version uses "envious" and "envy" in these verses.

The Bible warns that God will judge people who have an evil eye: "Woe to those who call evil good, and good evil; who put darkness for light, and light for darkness; who put bitter for sweet, and sweet for bitter!" (Isa. 5:20). From the Bible we also learn that our heart can be subverted by the evil eye. In Mark 7:20–23, Jesus explains, "What comes out of a man, that defiles a man. For from within, out of the heart of men, proceed evil thoughts, adulteries, fornications, murders, thefts, covetousness, wickedness, deceit, lewdness, an evil eye, blasphemy, pride, foolishness.... These evil things," Jesus says, "come from within and defile a man." In these verses, we see that covetousness is linked to an evil eye, as are evil thoughts.

The evil eye defined

As we have seen, having an evil eye can cloud our spiritual perception and cause us to look at things from a perverse, ungodly perspective. That leads us to the definition for *evil eye* that I will use: "the evil eye is a perverse perspective." *Merriam-Webster's Online Dictionary* defines the *evil eye* as "an eye or glance held capable of inflicting harm."[1] According to the *Columbia Encyclopedia,* the evil eye is principally "a Sicilian and Mesoamerican superstition, although it is known in other cultures."[2] According to the Native American version of the term, a person who stares fixedly at a pregnant woman or a child or who is too admiring or physically affectionate with children may produce a malicious effect on their lives, whether or not by intent. In rural Sicily, any person or animal was considered vulnerable to the evil eye, and many individuals wore protective amulets or charms to nullify its effects.

BLINDED BY THE ENEMY

The word *occult* means "to conceal or cause to disappear from view—to be secret, mysterious, supernatural." The Bible explains that we can be blinded by the deceptive ways of the enemy, but God gives us access to revelation that will uncover that which has been kept secret (2 Cor. 4:3–4, 6).

The enemy likes to hide. He plans strategies to divert us from accomplishing God's will and entering into our heavenly Father's blessings. Many of us have a hard time *seeing* the enemy's snares, which are strategically planted along our path. Thus we *step into* his tangled web and spend much of our time struggling to free ourselves.

There are several snares that the enemy lays: generational iniquity, covetousness, superstition, spiritism, magic and sorcery, and Freemasonry. At this chapter's end, I will suggest how to remove these snares and unveil the evil eye.

Blinded by Generational Iniquity:
The True Blind Spot

Occult practices were not unusual in the generations of my family. There was an inherited weakness toward sins of the occult and witchcraft that was passed down through our bloodline. A weakness like this is known as *iniquity*, and it forms a pattern in our lives that causes us to deviate from God's perfect path. Its root definition is linked to "unequal" or "twisted." In other words, we do something that is not equal to God's righteous standard, and we are unwilling to be reconciled to God's ways. This causes our path to be twisted.

In *Possessing Your Inheritance*, which I cowrote with Rebecca Wagner Sytsema, we share: "Have you ever noticed how such things as alcoholism, divorce, laziness or greed tend to run in families? These aren't just learned behaviors. They are manifestations of iniquity [or iniquitous patterns] passed down through the generations."[3] Occult iniquitous patterns work the same way, only they are more difficult to detect because they are hidden.

Soon after my doctor told me about my eye problems, I discovered that the blind spot I was experiencing was linked to many inherited occult influences in my life. When I entered the hospital, it was as if the Lord was pulling me aside so that He could go deep down and show me some things that had been hidden for a long time.

My family had all the potential in the world to prosper. My relatives were good, hard-working people. However, the enemy seemed to ravage and destroy all that God had planned. My dad was led astray and became involved in gambling and eventually in witchcraft. When I was a child, I watched certain family members operate in supernatural dimensions; therefore, the supernatural was easy for me to understand. My grandfather could speak words and bring about changes in the elements around him. I had cousins who would visit with an unknown source and then watch the table rise up off the floor. When I was ten years old, I thought nothing about buying my first Ouija board. I had never been told that it was not a harmless game, nor I had been warned that it might be dangerous; I just knew I could ask it questions, and it would speak back.

One side of my family was so steeped in superstition that all the rules became wearying to follow. Of course, I also had some family members who were totally devout, praying, godly saints. Talk about having your eyes unfocused and going in every direction. Mine sure were.

FAMILIAL AND FAMILIAR SPIRITS

My wife, Pam, used to tell me that at times there was something driving me to react. However, she could never put her finger on what it was. She would say, "It's linked to your family in some way. Every time we almost see what it is, like a bat it flies back into the cave. It never comes to the light enough so that we can detect it and pull it out of you—like the way certain members of your family operate!"

A family is defined as "a group of people living in the same house; one or more people, consisting of the same parents; or a group of people that have a common blood tie." When a member of a family sins, the door is opened for demonic forces to work in subsequent generations of that family because of the iniquity produced. Spirits assigned to a family are called *familial spirits*, and they can remain at work in the family for generations. They know the iniquitous patterns in a family bloodline. They know when the patterns began. They know that, unless dealt with through the blood of Jesus, these patterns will be passed on to someone else in the next generation.

Familiar spirits work the same way, only they do not have to be part of the family bloodline. *Familiar* is applied to that which is known through constant association. These spirits are linked with some sort of intimacy, such as sexual soul ties. The old saying "Birds of a feather flock together" does have some validity. The iniquitous pattern in one person is drawn to the iniquitous pattern in another. I call this a *cluster of iniquity*. If one member of the cluster dies or lets go of this iniquitous pattern, the pattern is strengthened in the other members.

The Revelation of Hidden Things

Once I knew about my spiritual blind spot, I went to a cell group and asked for prayer. One of the leaders, a very spiritual woman who at one time had been involved in the occult, laid hands on me and declared that anything hidden within me would be exposed. Oh my, did this stir up a nest! It was as if my blood curdled or the bottom of the lake came to the top. Over time, truths about my background began to expose themselves.

One day not long after I received prayer, I was trying to finish some tasks around our house before I went to the hospital. My wife has always kept a most beautiful yard, but she noticed a small brown spot in the grass. She asked if I could determine the cause of that spot. The brown spot reminded me of my spiritual blind spot. The more I dug, the larger the hole got in our front yard. I became frustrated because I had dug a hole three feet wide, although the spot looked to be only a couple of inches across. I found a huge piece of concrete underneath our luscious green yard. It was not evident until the heat of August had reached a certain level. But when things heat up, reactions occur.

So, when Pam walked out of the house and, of course, had a better way of digging so that the yard would not be ruined, I felt this strange feeling come over me. (Doris Wagner always says that this is one way to detect a demon—something *comes over you*.) I felt as if I were outside of my body. My natural self wanted to take the sledgehammer that I was using and throw it as hard as I could at my wife. Thank God for wisdom and self-control—and a measure of fear. I know my wife; she too can react!

I stopped where I stood and said, "Lord, I've had this familiar feeling before. Remind me of when and how this started." Immediately the Lord reminded me of times when I would have what my grandmother would call *a spell*. She would have me lie down in a bedroom, and then she would chant certain words until the spell subsided. Instead of throwing the hammer, I went inside my house, lay down on my bed, and remembered every word of the chant. Instead of chanting, I renounced those words and decreed that any power attached to them would no longer have the right to hold me captive. I prayed the blood of Jesus over my family and myself, and I asked God to fill me anew with His Holy Spirit. For me, this was the beginning of true freedom.

CURSES, LEGALISM, AND SUPERSTITION

Let's look at what stops us from seeing. Three tools the enemy uses to gain access to our mind so that truth cannot penetrate are curses, legalism, and superstition. A *curse* is a set of words uttered against someone to bring harm. Someone can speak a word toward you, and instead of it being liberating, that word begins to work in your mind to produce a stronghold. Before long, those words begin to penetrate your heart and then attach themselves to the issues of your life. Curses can alight through witchcraft, superstition, and legalism. Surprisingly, they all work the same way.

Legalism is an attempt to please God by erecting rules that we do not find within the Word of God. We then bind those rules to ourselves and our thought processes and make those rules as truth. These ungodly beliefs, which can seem good, narrow our path and sphere of life. Just as a curse binds us to an ungodly belief, so will legalism.

Legalism directs your behavior in a negative way. Legalism works through religious spirits. Paul told the church of Galatia:

> Oh, foolish Galatians! Who has cast an evil spell on you? For the meaning of Jesus Christ's death was made as clear to you as if you had seen a picture of his death on the cross. Let me ask you this one question: Did you receive the Holy Spirit by obeying the law of Moses? Of course not! You received the Spirit because you believed the message you heard about Christ. How foolish can you be? After starting your Christian lives in the Spirit, why are you now trying to become perfect by your own human effort? Have you experienced so much for nothing? Surely it was not in vain, was it?
> —GALATIANS 3:1–4, NLT

Have you ever had anyone take a scripture from the Word of God and use it as a whipping tool or a binding law? Many times this is how religious spirits work within the church in superstitious, legalistic form. They take what God takes for liberty and misuse the truth to bring bondage. Legalism, superstition, and curses all work to bind us into certain behaviors and keep us from liberation in God. Each of these works against your thinking processes. The minute you receive them as truth, even though they are a lie, you have been captured by a demon force. That is why Christians can be demonized. Even though they are saved through Christ, the lie they are receiving perverts their ability to think and receive truth into their minds. It calls good evil and evil good.

If the person ever begins to buy into a lie, the lie will go into the mind and end up in the heart. Proverbs 4:23 (NLT) says, "Guard your heart above all else, for it determines the course of your life" ("issues of life," KJV). A lie will go down into the issues of life that are in a person's heart and will try to thwart the life process that he or she has been sent into the earth realm to accomplish. Therefore, whenever you believe a lie, it actually interrupts the life cycle we discussed in the beginning of this chapter. Instead of life flowing through your blood, here comes the wrong word, which actually starts flowing through the veins of your body. As the effects of that lie start flowing in the blood pumping through your heart (which has accepted the lie), it begins to darken your conscience. Satan knows that if he can ever get your conscience darkened enough, he can trap you. As the effects of that lie flow through your body, it begins to build a stronghold and a wall to keep the truth from coming to you.

Every lie we receive in our minds works like a deadening anesthetic to us. In the Bible it is called "a spirit of slumber" (Rom. 11:8, KJV). It works by attaching to an unbelieving, mocking, blasphemous spirit so that you can't capture the truth and be liberated. It'll make you go to sleep at the right time to keep you from hearing truth. The enemy will try to bring false arguments and philosophy into your heart, which begin to exalt him in your mind above the knowledge of God. We are to cast down these things.

There is another dynamic at work: sin produces iniquity. Iniquity forms a pattern and a deviation from God's plan in a bloodline. Once that iniquity is there, it is passed on to the next generation. If you didn't guard your heart (according to Proverbs 4:23), that iniquity becomes part of the DNA structure that you pass on to your children.

Superstition works very much the same way. When I was growing up, my family had numerous superstitions. If certain things happened, then we had to do ten other things to neutralize that one happening. The Bible says that superstition is a sign of ignorance. Ignorance has nothing to do with not being educated. Ignorance has to do with not receiving present truth and life and aligning ourselves with the word of life. Superstition attaches to a generational curse of ignorance. Ignorance means that truth has been rejected at some point, and the truth is no longer operating. Superstition binds you to certain behaviors. Therefore, any time you embrace superstitious beliefs of any nature, they produce legalistic thought patterns. In *How to Minister Freedom* I wrote the following:

> Superstition is probably more closely linked with the evil eye than anything else. Superstition can actually mean "fearing demons." It is a belief, half-belief or practice for which there appears to be no rational substance, but which supposedly brings a person protection. Superstitions can fall into three categories: religious, cultural and personal. A religious superstition (against which Christians are not immune) may be something such as leaving an open Bible next to a bed to gain protection from demons. Cultural superstitions are folk traditions linked to irrational beliefs intended to ward off illness, bring about good results, foretell the future and prevent accidents. A personal superstition may include a perceived need to use a lucky pen or, when gambling, betting on a particular color of horse. Superstition develops a mind-binding fear within.[4]

My family was steeped in superstition. Several of these superstitions really affected my life as I was growing up. They kept me in bondage to fear.

SPIRITISM

The evil eye also works through spiritism. *The Catholic Encyclopedia* defines *spiritism* as "the belief that the living can communicate with the spirits of the departed, and to the various practices by which such communication is attempted."[5]

The Catholic Encyclopedia describes two types of phenomena that occur when spiritism is practiced: physical phenomena and psychical phenomena. The physical phenomena include:

- Production of raps and other sounds

- Movement of objects (tables, chairs) without contact or with contact insufficient to explain the movement

- "Apports," i.e., apparitions of [objects with no] visible agency to convey them

- Moulds, i.e., impressions made upon paraffin and similar substances

- Luminous appearances, i.e., vague glimmerings of light or faces more or less defined

- Levitation, i.e., raising of objects from the ground by supposed supernormal means

- Materialization or appearance of a spirit in visible human form

- Spirit photography, in which the feature or forms of deceased persons appear on the plate along with the likeness of a living photographed subject[6]

This encyclopedia describes *psychical phenomena* as those that "express ideas or contain messages." These include:

- Table-rapping in answer to questions

- Automatic writing, slate-writing

- Trance-speaking

- Clairvoyance

- Descriptions of the spirit-world

- Communications from the dead[7]

During spiritistic rituals and practices, such as séances, the dead do not actually communicate back; rather, evil spirits linked with familiar and familial spirits communicate to individuals to reinforce their fears and guide them on to twisted paths. In other words, the demon forces that were with the dead individuals during their lives know the answers to questions and pose as the dead people with whom the spiritists try to communicate.

This is a very dangerous and deceitful practice because it can seem real—after all, who but the real Aunt Nellie could have known that Rocky Road was her favorite flavor of ice cream? The problem is that those who are attempting to communicate with Aunt Nellie aren't reaching her at all, but they are contacting and inviting the presence and counsel of the demons who tormented Aunt Nellie during her life.

The only true outcome of these attempts to communicate with a dead person is opening wide a door to demonization by familial or familiar spirits. This practice can lead into delusion and even death. The torment caused by these spirits can bring great mental imbalance and vexation. Spiritism invites the evil eye and opens the soul to satanic influence and control.

MAGIC AND SORCERY

When we look at occult relationships that utilize an evil eye, we must also review how magic and sorcery attempt to influence people and events. Biblically we find that these two activities are linked with many aspects of the supernatural, including witchcraft, enchantment using charms, enchantment using spells, charmers, Chaldeans, divination, secret arts, snake charming, magi (or wise men), sorcery using drugs and potions, spiritual imposters, mind-binding spells, curious arts, and religious bewitchment. Magic itself may be associated with some forms of divination. Divination is the attempt to use supernatural means to uncover events or discover information.

Magic is universal and may be black or white. Black magic attempts to produce evil results through such methods as curses, spells, destruction of models of one's enemy, and alliance with evil spirits. It often appears as witchcraft. White magic tries to undo curses and spells and to use occult forces to advance the good of oneself and others. Of course, in reality there is no good magic. All magic is of Satan and leads to death and hell.

The magician tries to compel a god, demon, or spirit to work for him. He follows a pattern of occult practices to bend psychic forces to his will. Magic and sorcery are not mere superstitions; rather, they have a reality behind them. They must be resisted and overcome through the power of the Holy Spirit in the name of Jesus Christ.

FREEMASONRY

The evil eye is very attached to ritualistic practices and secret societies. One powerful secret society that uses the evil eye to influence its members is Freemasonry. In the short space here, a long explanation is not possible. I will give a brief description below, but for more information you can read Selwyn Stevens's *Unmasking Freemasonry: Removing the Hoodwink* and Ron G. Campbell's *Free From Freemasonry*.

There is much secrecy involved in this society. This often opens a person to fear and bondage. Interestingly, Wicca and Mormonism have rites similar to those found in Freemasonry. The initiations that bring a person into Freemasonry are humiliating. If a person is married, he has to remove his wedding ring, because he has to be totally married to, or in covenant with, the words that he speaks. Often unwittingly, this initiation also commits a person to the false god behind Freemasonry. There is a wall of secrecy between a Freemason and his wife. This is how the occult works.

In Freemasonry, there are thirty-three degrees of attainable power and authority. In the third degree, a mason swears that if he violates the Masonic brotherhood, his body will be cut in two, his bowels removed, and his body burned to ashes and scattered to the four winds. There are oaths taken in every degree. The oaths in Freemasonry are filled with curses that are attached to the generations. This is why it's so hard for anyone to get out of this false religion.

Those who are initiated live in constant turmoil, making blind contracts with the enemy by speaking things that can be very destructive in their lives and the lives of their descendants. Yet if a member tries to leave, he faces censure. Freemasons will not associate with someone who has left the fold. They believe that the sacred oaths have been broken. The person is then criticized and cursed and sometimes hounded, forever treated as untrustworthy.

Nevertheless, as Selwyn Stevens writes:

> God's Word requires a Christian to renounce a bad or sinful oath such as this. Leviticus 5:4–5 shows us that if a person is required to swear something which was hidden prior to the oath-taking, God says we should plead guilty to Him, confess it as sin and totally renounce and repudiate it, preferably publicly. When you have done this God says you are no longer bound by it. God wants us to know that repentance releases us from such a vow or oath. This is one of the major keys for removing the consequences of the curses invoked by Masonic oaths.[8]

How to Unveil the Evil Eye

I trust that through this chapter you have begun to understand that the enemy seeks to cloud our ability to discern. He hides himself. He plots and plans to divert us from accomplishing God's will and seeks to keep us from entering into God's blessings. Many of us have a hard time *seeing* the enemy's snare or diversion. As a result, we often *step into* the middle of this web and spend much of our time struggling to free ourselves. In response to the enemy's tactics, we must ask the Lord to help us look past the visible to see the invisible and to discern any supernatural force that would seek to ensnare us or keep us from accomplishing the Lord's will.

Here are fifteen ways we can remove the enemy's hidden snares in our life and unveil the evil eye:

1. The enemy has a voice to bring deception into our life. Ask God to reveal any deception or lie the enemy fosters.

2. Satan is the father of lies; however, he can only work with the resources that we give to him. We need to cut ties with anything in our soulish nature that holds us captive to the enemy.

3. We need to ask the Lord to fill us with His love so that we can break any sin strategy in our life and destroy the devil's work.

4. Jesus resisted the voice of the enemy. We can ask the Lord to fill us with the Holy Spirit in the midst of our wilderness so that we also can resist the devil.

5. We should not be ignorant. We must let God reveal to us the supernatural qualities that the enemy possesses—Lucifer's hidden characteristics.

6. We should be sure that we are operating our lives in humility and submission so that we can put up an effective resistance.

7. Satan manipulates us and wants us to believe that God is not directing us or that God is holding out on us. We can

ask God to break any manipulation that is aligned with our desires.

8. We need to be sure that our desires are correctly aligned with God's. Temptation is linked to selfish desires that are not within God's boundaries.

9. It is wise for us to ask the Lord to deliver us from temptation.

10. We should change our minds or redevelop our thought processes (repent). We can renounce acts linked with our wrong thinking. We also can forgive ourselves and other people who have seduced us and led us astray.

11. We can ask God to give us a mind-set for increase. We should ask Him to open our hearts to any prophetic word that will bring us success and cause us to be able to rake in the spoils that the enemy is holding.

12. We must declare deliverance from the hand of the wicked one who seeks to rob us of our provision and health.

13. We should declare that any generational curse that robs God of anything rightfully belonging to Him will be released from our bloodline. This is one of the four major generational curses, sometimes identified as "God-robbing" (see Mal. 3:9). We need to tear down mind-sets of poverty that might tell us, "God is not able." This is a lie to withhold everything that should be freely given.

14. We can dismantle unbelief over provision. "Prove Me *now*," says the Lord. Look up and see the windows of blessing that He wants to open. Watch Him overcome the devourer (see Mal. 3:10–11).

15. Rejoice that we are free from the enemy's plans and purposes.[9]

Let your eye be filled with light, and may the Holy Spirit direct every step of your path.

> The path of the righteous is like the first gleam of the dawn, shining ever brighter till the full light of day.
>
> —Proverbs 4:18, niv

Blind Spots in Leadership

One of the greatest problems in the body of Christ is when a leader becomes vexed, and those who are following get vexed as well. Blind spots bring down leaders and devastate the vision of the followers. In a recent account of a move of the Spirit of God, the predominant leader announced his moral failure. He then removed himself from what he was leading. Many who were following were devastated. In this move of God, a group of leaders had attempted to establish a new apostolic order. Why an apostolic order? First Corinthians 12:28 says, "…first apostles, second prophets." Many problems have occurred and many moves of God have become dysfunctional because God's order was never in place. Like other moves of the Spirit, the order that leaders attempted to establish seemed to come too late for this recent movement. If this could have occurred earlier, perhaps many who were influenced would not have been devastated and fragmented.

There are so many examples of leaders going astray. I've had dear friends chosen to lead incredible movements and influence entire nations go astray. I believe the enemy has an opportune time. When we allow fragmentation of soul and vexation of spirit to continue, the enemy finds a way to *hook* into our faults. He then uses that hook to pull down not just the individual but many of those who are being influenced from their leadership.

Many leaders are anointed, but the anointing and character

development are two (and sometimes opposing) dimensions. Many leaders who have never dealt with fragmentation of their soul bring only a piece of what God wants into a movement. Many even carry bipolar structures into the ministry. There is a side of that bipolar, fragmented soul that the anointing works through. Many in the religious world do not understand how the anointing can work in the bipolar realm. The anointing will flow through one portion of the redeemed personality of an individual, while the demonic subdues itself in a portion that is not sanctified. Then the demonic comes alive at an opportune time and works to rise up and create confusion.

We judge individuals based upon their wholeness as opposed to how God is working through their fragmentation. I think we must get a handle on this as we move forward in this next season. The next great move of God will be filled with fragmented individuals seeking wholeness, not whole individuals ready to advance.

Each move of God has an anointing that stirs up a hunger in the body. The Spirit of God is beginning to move greatly. Therefore a new apostolic authority must be established and set in place because of potential problems moving into this move of God. This will establish a structure and boundary for problems to be addressed. The thing we must remember is that God chooses to use donkeys in the body of Christ. We must learn the anointing and then discern our role in praying to bring wholeness into anything that God is doing corporately in the earth.

A good example is the life of Samson. He was a mystery. He had a Nazirite vow on his life and yet had many character flaws. His character flaws did not stop God from using him. In the end, he submitted all of his strength; he lost his life but overcame his enemy. I think this is the biggest misunderstanding that the body has when it comes to the anointing. That is why you see anointed men and women being used so mightily by the Lord and then falling into sexual sin or monetary impropriety.

When a new order is determined for a life, we can fully become accountable and break spiritual forces that could destroy our future. We must submit to apostolic authority and mature even while we express the anointing. Ministry should not be our only goal. But as we move in anointed ministry, we must all mature until we come to the unity of faith (Eph. 4:1–5).

There is a hunger in the body of Christ for miracles, healing, and just a touch from God. We must understand how God fathers our spirits until we are overcoming with Him on the earth. Many are called but few are chosen. There is a call being extended and a qualification being established in those who will lead the body in days ahead.

As the body of Christ, we must mature and grow through this public experience and also understand the dangers of the public season of ministry. Because of the world of communications systems, which control our lives daily, we must learn to operate in new ways. May we be purified as we move forward into the harvest fields that are beginning to whiten. The Spirit of God asked our ministry to start praying for the harvest of souls. That is a different form of praying. This type of praying is necessary as we advance into God's full kingdom expression in days ahead. I am taking teams around the world to decree a changing wineskin for the harvest.

We know that many different individuals and forms of ministries will be used as we enter this new realm. Yes, we must be very discerning and respect those who watch for the body. The fine line that must be walked is to receive wisdom while not quenching the moving of the Holy Spirit as He works out the salvation of many. We must gain wisdom as we move forward but not quench revelation as it is released.

We must stay on the edge of bringing forth revelation and demonstration for days ahead. Prophetically, I believe the Lord opened the next door of healing evangelism in April 2010, and we are learning of the many dangers that await this opportunity (1 Cor. 16:9). Lord, we ask for mercy as we enter this new realm!

CHAPTER 17

HE IS THE FATHER OF YOUR SPIRIT

SELF-HELP BOOKS, PSYCHIATRISTS, and counseling are excellent resources. However, I have found that no matter what method we are using to get *free*, we must have a touch of grace from the God who knit us together in our mother's womb! Psalm 139:11–14 (AMP) says: "If I say, Surely the darkness shall cover me and the night shall be [the only] light about me, even the darkness hides nothing from You, but the night shines as the day; the darkness and the light are both alike to You. For You did form my inward parts; You did knit me together in my mother's womb. I will confess and praise You for You are fearful and wonderful and for the awful wonder of my birth! Wonderful are Your works, and that my inner self knows right well."

His love searches out what He knit together. Previously we discussed how our spirit, soul, and body are all meant to be sanctified. We might have begun life with fragmentation of soul, but by His Spirit transforming our spirit man, our end can be greater than our beginning. Satan will do whatever is necessary to stop our *end* from being more prosperous than our beginning.

> I appeal to you therefore, brethren, and beg of you in view of [all] the mercies of God, to make a decisive dedication of your bodies [presenting all your members and faculties] as a living sacrifice, holy (devoted, consecrated) and well pleasing to God, which is your reasonable (rational, intelligent) service and spiritual worship. Do not be conformed to this world (this age), [fashioned after and adapted to its external, superficial customs], but be transformed (changed) by the [entire] renewal of your mind [by its new ideals and its new attitude], so that you may prove [for yourselves] what is the good and acceptable and perfect will of God, even the thing which is

good and acceptable and perfect [in His sight for you]. For by the grace (unmerited favor of God) given to me I warn everyone among you not to estimate and think of himself more highly than he ought [not to have an exaggerated opinion of his own importance], but to rate his ability with sober judgment, each according to the degree of faith apportioned by God to him. For as in one physical body we have many parts (organs, members) and all of these parts do not have the same function or use, so we, numerous as we are, are one body in Christ (the Messiah) and individually we are parts one of another [mutually dependent on one another].

—ROMANS 12:1–5, AMP

Faith works by love. Without faith we cannot please God. Faith overcomes. Our faith stops temptation from overtaking us. One of the most difficult understandings for many individuals to reconcile is the paradigm of *temptation*. We have talked about this in an earlier chapter. I believe many do not understand the enemy's power of temptation because they have never experienced the Father's love. I want to concentrate on Father's love since He is "the Father of spirits" (Heb. 12:9). Many bloodlines are vexed because of a dysfunctional family unit. But because He is Father of spirits, He can transform us into His image.

LOVE, TEMPTATION, AND BEING ADOPTED

I was sitting at breakfast with two of my sons, Joseph and John Mark, and I asked them, "Why does the Lord allow us to be tempted?"

John Mark answered, "To see if we are devoted or easily swayed." (Of course, he is the most disciplined kid in the world.)

Joseph, on the other hand (whom I wrote about earlier and who was adopted later in his life out of a horrid childhood), is a fun-loving, messy individual. He felt temptations were brought into our lives to exercise our inner man. He shared, "Temptation is to produce a resistant power in your life!" (I am so thankful for Joseph's wife, Cynthia, a true daughter in the Lord to Pam and me.)

I later asked Isaac, who is our emotional, six-foot-seven-inches giant, and he shared that temptations come to cause us to commit sins at crucial times in our lives. He exclaimed that he felt that the enemy knows when he is ready to break through and throws up a major blockade to keep him from accomplishing what he should. He recently went on a fifty-day fast to break out of an old generational iniquity.

Ethan, our youngest, just graduated from school and is experimenting in a *Torah* stage of his life. He is processing life from the perspective that if we will stay in covenant with God, we will be fine. He is not really a warrior at this time in his life and is forming his *theology of life* on a daily basis. I am just glad he has a *God awareness* that he is developing as he pursues college and life.

Why am I giving you a family synopsis? Daniel and Rebekah (two of my older children) and their spouses have learned to war along with Pam and me for the overall victory of our family. Each one of our children has the freedom to communicate their thoughts—right, wrong, or indifferent. As their father, I enjoy hearing their thoughts. A good father listens, then disciplines. In 1986, after three children, the Lord spoke to me and said, "I will make you a father!"

THE WAR OF FAMILY AND CORPORATE GATHERINGS

Dysfunction in our bloodline causes vexation in our spirit man. Entire generations can be vexed. Because I experienced the blessing of family and then the loss and destruction of family, the family unit is very precious in my heart and drive for freedom. I enjoy the uniqueness of each of my children. I love training them up in the way *they* should go. I watch and listen to their desires and then try to influence their choices as much as any dad would, without controlling them. I feel the same about the body of Christ. I long to see each member equipped and operating in his or her gift. My greatest role and service to both my family and God's people is teaching them how to war against their enemy. Not each one of us is warring against a shrewd foe, but we are warring collectively to overcome him.

Choose you this day! Understanding family, corporate spiritual gatherings, and gaining strategy for war are all important to our future. The greatest relationship in the ancient Mediterranean world was not just the husband-wife relationship but how all the siblings interrelated with each other. This is how the *tribe* concept was developed. The family or tribe concept produced the understanding of army. That eventually produced nations. That concept is still valid today. I believe a family's choice to be righteous in the earth can save a generation and prolong the Spirit of God in the earth realm. Noah gained favor and chose for his family. "As in the days of Noah" is now!

The mind-set of preservation and posterity was developed in the Hebraic culture. Families warred together, prospered together, and then their prosperity was passed on from one generation to another. In American society today, we do not have the same concern of the preservation of one generation's estate being passed on to another generation. In the New Testament, the concept of gathering was shifted from the tribe concept to the church, or *ecclesia*. Therefore, we find a relationship of church comparable to that of a family. Family, tribe, church gathering, and the body of Christ (a nation above all nations) have key relationships for us to understand as we go to war in the future. Therefore, the enemy strives to fragment this powerful organism to stay in control in any territorial region.

LEAVE FAMILY AND FOLLOW ME

All relationships get tested when covenant is in question. Abraham had to leave Ur of the Chaldees and then leave Haran after his father, Terah, died. When Jesus presented His call to discipleship, He seemed to attack the family unit. However, after looking at the original intent of family unit, you see why He could use the family unit as a point of discipleship. The family was the strongest of all units in the earth. In Matthew

10:34–36 (NIV) we find the most famous scriptures linked with war. The Lord said the following: "Do not suppose that I have come to bring peace to the earth. I did not come to bring peace, but a sword. For I have come to turn a man against his father, a daughter against her mother, a daughter-in-law against her mother-in-law—a man's enemies will be the members of his own household."

Matthew 12:46–50 (NIV) says, "While Jesus was still talking to the crowd, his mother and brothers stood outside, wanting to speak to him. Someone told him, 'Your mother and brothers are standing outside, wanting to speak to you.' He replied to him, 'Who is my mother, and who are my brothers?' Pointing to his disciples, he said, 'Here are my mother and my brothers. For whoever does the will of my Father in heaven is my brother and sister and mother.'" These statements seem hard, but the Lord is dealing with the emotions of those who will follow Him and creating a family unit that will survive the persecution and wars of the future.

"Jesus of Nazareth publicly dissociates himself from his natural family, professes loyalty to a new surrogate family, and apparently expects his followers to do the same. It is this resocialization—at the kinship level—that marks early Christianity as distinct among the voluntary associations of Greco-Roman antiquity. The social solidarity characteristic of the family model, in turn, goes a long way to explain both the intimacy and sense of community so often cited as unique to early Christianity, and the attractiveness of the early Christian movement to displaced and alienated urbanites in the Greco-Roman world."[1]

Consequently, if you were willing to leave your family unit to follow Him, you would be known for your ultimate devotion. The church was to become a surrogate kinship group. Jesus was never encouraging us to negate family responsibility. However, let me to paraphrase what He was saying in Luke 14. He seemed to be saying, "If you have any emotional tie that you are exalting above Me, I cannot teach you what you need to know as you enter the season that is ahead of you!" Family is a tremendous war unit, and nothing is as strong as a whole family bloodline that is submitted to the Lord.

He Is the Father of Spirits

"We have had fathers of our flesh.... The fathers of our flesh, i.e., our natural parents, were correctors; and we reverenced them, notwithstanding their corrections often arose from whim or caprice: but shall we not rather be in subjection to the *Father of spirits*; to him from whom we have received both body and soul; who is our Creator, Preserver, and Supporter; to whom both we and our parents owe our life and our blessings; and who corrects us only for our profit; that we may live and be partakers of his holiness? The apostle in asking, shall we not much rather be in subjection to *the Father of spirits, and live?* alludes to the punishment of the stubborn and rebellious son (Deut. 21:18–21)."[2]

We can overcome rebellion, break all fragmentation, and remove any vexing force from our spirit. "'If a man have a stubborn and rebellious son, who will not obey the voice of his father, or the voice of his mother, and that, when they have chastened him, will not hearken unto them; then shall his father and mother lay hold on him and bring him to the elders of the city, and they shalt say, This our son is stubborn and rebellious; he will not obey our voice: and all the men of the city shall stone him with stones that DIE.'"[3]

We must learn how to be subject to authority. Our earthly parents were meant to be protectors, nurturers. "Had he been subject to his earthly parents, he would have lived; because not subject, he dies. If we be subject to our heavenly Father, we shall LIVE, and be partakers of his holiness; if not, we shall LIVE, and be treated as bastards and not sons. This is the sum of the apostle's meaning; and the fact and the law to which he alludes."[4] However, because of grace, the "bastard curse" can be broken. The power of vexation linked with our spirits can be removed. He can become our Father.

He is the Father of spirits. This is an important revelation to understand our makeup. He allows us to develop our soul, but He is the Father of our spirit and knows how to transform us from the inside out. This is what makes us a child of God. This is why we can have an inheritance in Him.

ADOPTION IS A KEY

A person can be vexed from conception if he or she is rejected by those who were used in the act of creating that person. If a person is left abandoned, life is a constant, fragmented mess filled with vexation. However, the power of adoption can overcome the power of vexation!

The act of taking voluntarily a child of other parents as one's child is very important in understanding the grace of God. This is really an act of God's grace when a victim of sin, rejection, and abandonment is brought into his redeemed family. In the New Testament, the Greek word translated "adoption" literally means "placing as a son." It is a legal term that expresses the process by which a man brings another person into his family, endowing him with the status and privileges of a biological son or daughter.

Adoption was not common among the Israelites but did occur when Jews were influenced by foreign customs. However, we do find one of the most famous adoptions occurred by Pharaoh's daughter when she adopted Moses. When the pharaoh's daughter adopted Moses, we find this phrase: "And he became her son" (Exod. 2:10). By the time we get to Jesus's day and Paul's writings, we find Roman customs had great influence on Jewish family life. One custom is particularly significant in relation to adoption. In the eyes of the law, the adopted one became a new creature and was regarded as being born again into the new family. This is why in the Book of Romans we find adoption as an illustration of what happens to the believer at conversion (Rom. 8:15, 23; 9:4). Because God is the Father of spirits, He "predestined us to adoption as sons" (Eph. 1:5).

In Romans 9:4, Israel, as a nation, also found its place of honor in God's plan. Today, that is why if a nation blesses Israel and remains in relationship with it, they will have blessings. If a nation rejects Israel, they will eventually be vexed. Gentile believers have also been given the Spirit of adoption! This allows all of mankind to cry, "Abba, Father" (Gal. 4:6). This assures the Gentiles of eternal life and resurrection (Rom. 8:23). "For you did not receive the spirit of bondage again to fear, but you received the Spirit of adoption by whom we cry, 'Abba, Father'" (Rom. 8:15).

Knowing Father

He is the first person of the Trinity. God has revealed Himself as Father, Son, and Holy Spirit. He sent His Son into the earth to be the perfect and infinite object of His love. He is the "Father of our Lord Jesus Christ" (1 Pet. 1:3; 1 Cor. 8:6; Eph. 1:17). Yeshua taught His disciples to address God in prayer as "our Father." He did not use that form Himself.

He is the Father of the Jewish nation. Israel is not like other nations. Israel is "the nation." The chosen nation owed its origin and continued existence to His miraculous power and special care. Israel is a people and a land with the Torah. As their Father, He loved, pitied, and rebuked them. Also, He required obedience of His people. As a good Father, He disciplined them until they learned the joy of submission. *He has a fatherhood.* God is represented as the Father of various objects and orders of beings that He has created. He is "the Father of lights," the heavenly bodies (James 1:17). He is also "the Father of spirits" (Heb. 12:9). He is particularly the *Father of man.* We are created after His image (Acts 17:26; Luke 3:8).

Let the redeemed say so! He is Father of the redeemed. Those who receive Him as Father are actually saved through the Son, Jesus Christ, and admitted to the privileges of children in the divine household. This is how adoption works. Christ taught His disciples to pray, "Our Father..." He said to the unbelieving Jews, "You are of your father the devil" (John 8:44). Therefore, those who receive the Son have their spirit man activated and are brought under the subjection to the Father. Then the third person of the Trinity, the Spirit, fills the spirit of man. This breaks the power of the vexation that the fall of man has on any individual person. The spiritual and moral relationship that was destroyed by sin is restored by grace. A divine renewal of the soul and body then begins (Rom. 8:14–16).

This is how the adoption of man begins. Adoption simply means you receive the privileges of a natural son or daughter. We find examples in the Bible of both male and females experiencing this. Abraham even mentioned that he had adopted his slave, Eliezer, as one of his sons. In Roman culture, the adoption of a stranger into a bloodline caused that stranger to become a member of a family. This tie could not be broken. "Usually, the ceremony of adoption took place in front of at least seven witnesses with this statement: 'I claim this man (or daughter or slave) as my son (or daughter or slave).' That is why in the New Testament adoption was used as an important concept of our relationship with the Lord. Therefore, we are fully reinstated from a lost state of privileges into all the privileges of God the Father."[5]

Adoption is a positional word not just a relational word. I think many people do not understand their time or place since they don't understand the position of adoption they have with their Creator or Father. Many people really never experience God's love for them.

A FATHER'S LOVE

I have shared before about my earthly father. I loved him dearly, but I watched him stray from God, seek a life filled with lawlessness, get caught in a myriad of schemes, and end in destruction. However, one day when I was driving to work, the Lord's presence filled the car. His power was so tangible that I had to stop the car and pull to the side of the road. He poured His love into the car and into my heart. I said, "Lord, what have I done that You would manifest Your love to me like this?" The Lord said, "This is how much I loved your father." I immediately saw the love of God in a way that I have never seen His love for His children. No matter what my dad did, God's love was unchanging. My dad rejected that love, but the love was there and available. Once I saw the love of God for my earthly father, knowing how evil he was, I saw God's love as pure and holy. Matthew 7:7–11 (cjb) says, "Keep asking, and it will be given to you; keep seeking, and you will find; keep knocking, and the door will be opened to you. For everyone who keeps asking receives; he who keeps seeking finds; and to him who keeps knocking, the door will be opened. Is there anyone here who, if his son asks him for a loaf of bread, will give him a stone? or if he asks for a fish, will give him a snake? So if you, even though you are bad, know how to give your children gifts that are good, how much more will your Father in heaven keep giving good things to those who keep asking him!"

CHAPTER 18

A RENEWED SPIRIT

BECAUSE OF ADOPTION, we can break the power of vexation and have a renewed spirit. Everyone has been given a gift from God. Not only is life itself a gift, but we each have been built with a gift for God to display through us. When the life of God is flowing freely through us, the gift of God operates in abundance. The gift of God flows through our spirit. Not much is taught on the spirit of man. We talk much about the soul, the mind, the will, and the emotions. The Lord tells us by patience to possess our soul (Luke 21:19). However, like the war the people of Israel fought to possess their land, we have a war to fight to possess our soul. The real war concerns one thing: *life*. God places each of us in a specific time and space where we are meant to experience life to its fullest.

Acts 17:24–27 puts it this way: "God, who made the world and everything in it, since He is Lord of heaven and earth, does not dwell in temples made with hands. Nor is He worshiped with men's hands, as though He needed anything, since He gives to all life, breath, and all things. And He has made from one blood every nation of men to dwell on all the face of the earth, and has determined their preappointed times and the boundaries of their dwellings, so that they should seek the Lord, in the hope that they might grope for Him and find Him, though He is not far from each one of us."

In this age we must fight to keep those God-appointed times and boundaries. Each day we live is a life-or-death matter. I know that sounds dramatic, but it is true. Every day we fight against the forces that seek to steal pieces of our existence bit by bit. Some days the battle seems minor; on others we war for our very next breath. Our culture would have us believe that life can be compartmentalized and ordered—some areas are worth dying for, while others can fall by the wayside if they do not meet our moral criteria of importance. This is why people can fight for environmentalism, stem cell research, or human rights yet turn around and justify abortion. We value life—at least when it is convenient for us. But life involves the whole person. Therefore, if the enemy can vex one function of our spirit, the possession of our soul becomes fragmented.

Life is not just our physical surroundings or our emotional well-being; for every human being, it is a spiritual matter as well. Natural life has a beginning, but it really has no end. By that I mean that our Maker has established us as eternal beings. Yes, our natural bodies will pass away with the withering of the trees. But our spiritual beings will remain.

There are three aspects to our spiritual beings. The first and most important is *endless communion* with the God who created us and gave us His Son to redeem us from our self-imposed prison. "He who has the Son has life; he who does not have the Son of God does not have life" (1 John 5:12). Through Jesus we can enter boldly into God's dwelling place. We have direct access to His throne room. There is often, however, a war to get into this place, which we will discuss later.

The second dynamic of our spiritual being is our *testimony*. How we overcome our tests in life produces a testimony that has impact not only in the natural realm but even more so in the spiritual. As we rely on the mind of Christ rather than on our own understanding, we can testify to His truth. As we find strength in Him rather than our own abilities or fortitude, we bear witness to His power. Abundant life involves discovering the infinite attributes of God and aligning with them through our testimony. And each time we speak out our testimony, we overcome the enemy and seal our abundant life (Rev. 12:11).

Intuition is the third facet of our spiritual existence. We are shaped in the spiritual realm according to how we perceive or discern good and evil. When we intuitively display the mind of God, we walk in victory. As our intuition alerts us to the schemes of Satan before they come to pass, we have the opportunity to thwart the enemy and conquer territory in the heavens and on Earth. That is why there is such a war both over and around us. We are created to have endless union and fellowship with God. Satan wants to create eternal separation from God. Therefore he wars daily to separate us from God and cause our communion with our Maker to cease.

But to possess or occupy our soulish nature with the Spirit of God, our spirit man (where God inhabits us by the Holy Spirit) must not be blocked. Rather, Holy Spirit must be able to flow freely through our spirit, through our soul, out from our body, and into the world. This is what wholeness is all about. The spirit and the heart are interchangeable many times in Scripture. Therefore, to be whole our spirit must stay renewed and fresh.

A Clean Heart:
God's Remedy to Deception

Psalm 51:10 says, "Create in me a clean heart, O God, and renew a steadfast spirit within me." In this pasrticular psalm, David had made some big mistakes and was praying for God to get him back on the right path. His mistakes had caused his spirit to break alignment and communion with the holy God. He knew that unless his spirit was renewed, he would not have relationship with God, and everything else in his life would fall to ruin. Every one of us makes mistakes and receives lies at some point. Those lies will conform us to another image. This is called *deception*. The only way we can stay deceived is through pride. Once we humble ourselves, we break the devil's plan against our life. David humbled himself and asked for a renewed spirit. We must do the same. However, if we remain prideful, we remain in deception. This is Satan's plan. In some way, the enemy wants to take our lies and conform us to the way of the world.

Another way we stay in deception is by having an idol in our life that we are unwilling to give up. Idols are linked with worship. Therefore, if we are unwilling to change our form of worship and worship God, we will remain deceived and bound to a lie. This is how idolatry works. Eventually that lie brings you into a different form of worship so you are not worshiping the Holy God who fathered your spirit but rather an idol with a power to vex your spirit. Our Father can sanctify or make us holy as He is holy. However, when we fall to worshiping and being conformed in an idolatrous way to an image we place above God, our spiritual life is infiltrated by the spirit linked with that image.

Another way deception rules us is through self-idolatry. Therefore you have to understand how self speaks to you and how self wants attention and how self wants to be pitied. Several years ago I went through a very difficult time physically. One day I came home from an MRI and just felt terrible. As I was lying on the couch, my wife, Pam, walked by and said the trash had to be taken out. I looked at her and said, "Can't you see that I'm dying here?" My self wanted her to recognize what a mess I was in.

So she just said, "If you were dying, God would tell me. And He might do that—but not until after you get the trash out!" So, you see, when we rise up past that self-pity that's in our soul, and we keep moving, even to get the trash out, something happens in us. When you do that, your spirit breaks from passivity and becomes active toward God.

Remember, Satan's biggest strategy is to bring your spirit into *passivity*. If he can ever get your spirit passive so it's not communing and developing a testimony, and if your discernment of spirits is not working and you're just wandering through life, then he will just fill your mind with lies. He will build an entire fortress of communication with his demonic hordes so that they keep you in bondage and out of freedom. He'll develop strongholds in your mind. When your thoughts do not connect, you will lose vision and cannot see the full plan that God has for you. Think of a room where stacks and stacks and stacks of materials have accumulated. Those stacks have not been dusted in years. You really don't know what's in the stacks. Cobwebs have overtaken the room. That's what our mind looks like when the devil brings us into passivity. Shake those cobwebs out! Get them out of your brain. We need deliverance periodically in our life because we can so easily fall into places of passivity. It is at these times of passivity that the enemy can deceive us.

Once our minds are infested by evil spirits, or we have allowed a wrong belief system to come into our minds, our salvation might stay intact, but our spirit becomes affected, so it's not operating properly. The enemy begins to fragment the purposes of God within us. In John 1:12–13 we read: "But as many as received Him, to them He gave the right [or power] to become children of God, to those who believe in His name: who were born, not of blood, nor of the will of the flesh, nor of the will of man, but of God." This actually means He gave us the power and right, or legal entitlement, to position ourselves as His child. That power resides in the Holy Spirit, who lives within our spirit man. The enemy is in enmity with each one of us because he must find a way to block the flow of the Holy Spirit. To do that, he must cause our spirit to be unsettled. Second Peter 2:7–8 says, "[God] delivered righteous Lot, who was oppressed by the filthy conduct of the wicked (for that righteous man, dwelling among them, tormented his righteous soul from day to day by seeing and hearing their lawless deeds.)" If the functions of your spirit are not operating rightly, then the destiny of your life cannot be completed. These verses show us that our evil surroundings have influence on our spirit. Those evil surroundings and their influence upon us can actually cause our spirit man to be vexed. *To vex* means "to rage or be violent; to suppress, to maltreat; to destroy, oppress or do violence; to injure; to exasperate; to entreat evil, harm, or hurt."

THE FUNCTIONS OF THE HUMAN SPIRIT

The functions of the spirit are intuition, testimony, and communion. Our spirit is what becomes alive to God and must remain alive to God. Though the spirit is invisible and cannot be seen, it is the driving force of our life. That is why the enemy wants to vex our spirit so we cannot operate in freedom. Here are ten qualities of the spirit:

1. The spirit must be willing (Matt. 26:41).

2. The spirit can *know* or interpret something before it happens (Luke 1:4; Mark 2:8).

3. Our spirit worships and flows in exaltation to God (John 4:23).

4. Our spirit senses or can become troubled (John 13:21).

5. Our spirit can travail (Mark 8:12).

6. Our spirit can have the quality of fervency (Acts 18:25).

7. Your spirit must be determined but not stubborn (Luke 9:51; Acts 19:21).

8. Our spirit sings and blesses (1 Cor. 14:15–16).

9. Faith arises in our spirit and works through love (2 Cor. 4:13; Col. 1:8; Gal. 5:6).

10. Our spirit must be filled with wisdom and revelation (Eph. 1:17).

Without a renewed, vibrant spirit, our spirit doesn't operate in the above. And that's also why David, in Psalm 51, began to pray, "Make me have a right spirit." That means, "Bring me back into alignment with You so I'm communing, so I'm gaining testimony, so my intuition is working." We need to be renewing our spirits as well as our minds. Just as our mind has three parts, which make up the house of our personality—mind, will, and emotions—our spirit also has three functions that we need to understand to come into renewal. These functions are intuition, testimony, and communion.

The sense of our spirit is *intuition*. This is when you just know something *is*. Activated by the Holy Spirit within you, intuition includes wisdom, knowledge, discernment, and other such supernatural understandings of what is going on around you. Ordinary senses become aroused through soulish desire. However, the intuition of the spirit comes directly from an inner knowing. In Hebrews 4:12 the soul and spirit are very similar to each other, except the spirit has power and a supernatural ability. Intuition is where God's anointing arises within us and eventually brings us to spiritual breakthrough.

Communion is worshiping in Spirit and truth. "God is Spirit, and those who worship Him must worship in spirit and truth" (John 4:24). It takes both to produce reality. If a demon force blocks the power and strength that you have to worship, you cannot gain the daily revelation of who God is when you're worshiping Him. This causes you to be blocked from the strength and the renewal that your spirit needs on a daily basis. Worship and communion should be a daily occurrence because it keeps the flow of God's Spirit moving through us. Demons will block us from that. We need to pray and connect with God. The method isn't nearly as important as doing it on a daily basis.

Testimony occurs two ways. You can build a testament within you from the Word of God. That's where the commandment is written on your heart, as we see in Romans 2:15: "…who show the work of the law written in their hearts, their conscience also bearing witness, and between themselves their thoughts accusing or else excusing them." A testament also occurs when you prove God. The word *testing* is part of testimony. Therefore, when you go through a testing and come out on the other side victorious, He proves Himself to you. This proof of God is then recorded in the memory of your spirit. From that memory, when you come in contact with a situation that you know is contrary to God's ability, you speak that testimony forth.

What does a testimony do? It overcomes the devil. "And they over-came him by the blood of the Lamb and by the word of their testimony" (Rev. 12:11). A testimony comes out of your mouth by the Spirit of God and has the power to dismantle demons. That's why we must allow the testings we go through to become our testimony. If we *whine* through our testings, we lose any strength in the end to overcome. Whining is a part of the soul; it loves self-pity. When you're whining, it means that self is trying to draw attention to the circumstances that you're in. Self wants to capitalize upon our circumstances so attention is drawn to us as an individual and away from God's purpose. Satan surely doesn't want the circumstance we're in to become a testimony. If a testimony occurs, then the overcoming power of God's nature within us will displace the enemy and overthrow the devil's strategy within us from that day forward.

THE POWER OF RENEWAL

Once you are a child of God, you can be anointed by God. However, the enemy longs to keep your spirit encased. In Hebrews 4:12 we find: "For the Word of God is living and powerful, and sharper than any two-edged sword, piercing even to the division between soul and spirit, and of joints and marrow, and is a discerner of the thoughts and intents of the heart." By living in communion with God and knowing His Word, we can actually increase in discernment. Discernment is a function in the intuition of our spirit. This is a time when we must discern we are going to be victorious in the earth.

Psalm 103 is a favorite of mine. As we bless the Lord for His goodness, we find in verse 5 that He "satisfies your mouth with good things, so that your youth is renewed like the eagle's." When our spirit is renewed like the eagle's, it ascends into heaven. It's like a hot air balloon. It's filled up. We're soaring. We maintain vision. We have vitality. We have life. I try to find time to come before God so my spirit can remain in a renewed state. Several years ago I went through an experience where I had to seek God over my health. I asked the Lord if I had sinned in any way or done something wrong that He needed to remind me of.

He said, "Do you remember that gift that you gave at the beginning of the year that I asked you to give?"

And I said, "Yes, and I obeyed You."

He said, "Yes, you did obey Me. But you did not obey Me with joy. And because you didn't obey Me with joy, you have now lost your strength. For My joy is your strength. You can obey Me all day long, but if you're not doing it out of joy, you're not going to receive the strength to proceed into all that I have for you."

The lack of joy had caused my spirit not to be right. And because of that, it had given access to the enemy in my body as well. I immediately asked God to forgive me for obeying without joy, because that meant that I really wasn't respecting Him, and I really wasn't blessing through that gift. Therefore, the blessings of my obedience could not fully manifest because my spirit was not in right relationship with God.

THE WIND OF DELIVERANCE BRINGS RENEWAL

The spirit of man is the empowering perspective of human life. The Holy Spirit brings God's presence and power. The Hebrew word *ruach* and the Greek work *pneuma* can be translated as "wind," "breath," or "spirit." In both Testaments, *spirit* is used of both God and human beings. *Spirit,* whether used of God or of human beings, is difficult to define. The kinship of spirit, breath, and wind is a helpful clue in beginning to understand *spirit,* since the word *spirit* in the Bible is linked with wind. When you study demons, you find they are spirits. As demons inhabit our soul, they are like adverse winds within us that are set against the movement of the wind of the Holy Spirit. Confess any sin that you might have, and allow the Spirit of God to move freely in you. As He begins to move, declare that the Holy Spirit will blow the adverse winds of your soul completely out of your body.

RECEIVE THIS DELIVERING WIND OF RENEWAL, AND BE RENEWED

Israel had been scattered because of all their wrongdoing. However, God in all His love and mercy prophesied that they would be renewed. Ezekiel 36:25–27 says:

> Then I will sprinkle clean water on you, and you shall be clean; I will cleanse you from all your filthiness and from all your idols. I will give you a new heart and put a new spirit within you; I will take the heart of stone out of your flesh and give you a heart of

flesh. I will put My Spirit within you and cause you to walk in My statutes, and you will keep My judgments and do them.

Then in Ezekiel 37, we see Ezekiel prophesying to the wind to bring life. The wind of the Holy Spirit coming into our human spirit regenerates and empowers us. This wind has a restoring quality. Where we have grown desolate, the wind of the Holy Spirit breaks the power of desolation and brings life to us. This is how deliverance works. Even though we might be off our path, or our senses seem to be scattered and we feel confused, our Deliverer can come and bring a wind of refreshing. This wind will bring cleansing and restore us to the full walk God has intended for us.

CHAPTER 19

HIS PROMISE IS: "WE *WILL* OVERCOME"

SINCE GOD IS Father of our spirits, He can impart to us what is needed to overcome. He wants you, as His child, to overcome. I love Hebrews 12:9–11:

> Furthermore, we have been having indeed fathers of our flesh as those who disciplined, corrected, and guided us, and we have been in the habit of giving them reverence. Shall we not much rather put ourselves in subjection to the Father of spirits and live? For on the one hand, they disciplined, corrected, and guided us for a few days upon the basis of that which seemed good to them, but He disciplines, corrects, and guides us for our profit, to the end that we might partake of His holiness. In fact, all discipline, correction, and guidance for the time being does not seem to be joyous but grievous; yet afterward it yields a return of the peaceable fruit of righteousness to those who have been exercised by it.[1]

No matter where our life has gone astray, decreased, or experienced loss, we can profit again. In *Redeeming the Time*, I explain how our Lord has bought back time. You can overcome fragmentation and vexation. His promises are *yea* and *amen*. You can win in the end, and your end can be greater than your beginning. Revelation 12:10–11 states, "Then I heard a loud voice saying in heaven, 'Now salvation, and strength, and the kingdom of our God, and the power of His Christ have come, for the accuser of our brethren, who accused them before our God day and night, has been cast down. And they overcame him by the blood of the Lamb and by the word of their testimony, and they did not love their lives to the death.'" This book has been about having vision for your future and overcoming every process the enemy uses in attempting to stop you from seeing your future.

You may have been in a vexing situation, but I want the final chapters of this book to clearly say, *"You can overcome."*

GIDEON'S ARMY

When we remember the importance of the concept of family, we can see why the visitation that Gideon had from the Lord, giving him instructions to change the course of the nation, was so drastically revolutionary. Gideon had to overthrow his father's altar to Baal. With the understanding of family that I just presented, you see why this was such a major shift in the thought process of the time. The iniquities of the father must first be overturned for the next generation to advance. If we go to war without recognizing our father's iniquity, we will be weakened in the heat of battle.

If you will remember, for seven years the people of Israel were raided each year at harvest time. After Deborah had led the nation into a season of righteous prosperity, the people had returned to do evil. When we agree with evil, our spirit becomes vexed. But we must remember that an entire nation of people can be vexed if they turn from God. This opens a door of iniquity that gives any enemy access to enter and bring decrease. In this case, the enemy would rob the harvest. Midian had reduced the Israelites to a grinding halt and had them captured in poverty. The people cried out, and God came.

> The angel of the Lord came and sat down under the oak in Ophrah that belonged to Joash the Abiezrite, where his son Gideon was threshing wheat in a winepress to keep it from the Midianites. When the angel of the Lord appeared to Gideon, he said, "The Lord is with you, mighty warrior."
>
> "But sir," Gideon replied, "if the Lord is with us, why has all this happened to us? Where are all his wonders that our fathers told us about when they said, 'Did not the Lord bring us up out of Egypt?'

But now the LORD has abandoned us and put us into the hand of Midian."

The LORD turned to him and said, "Go in the strength you have and save Israel out of Midian's hand. Am I not sending you?"

"But Lord," Gideon asked, "how can I save Israel? My clan is the weakest in Manasseh, and I am the least in my family."

The LORD answered, "I will be with you, and you will strike down all the Midianites together."

—JUDGES 6:11–16, NIV

Most who have read the story of Gideon remember him as a mighty deliverer in Israel's early days in the land of promise. Indeed, Gideon became a mighty deliverer, but as these verses point out, he didn't start out that way. When the angel of the Lord came to him, he found Gideon threshing wheat in a winepress. Normally wheat was threshed on a large, exposed area of bedrock. Gideon was afraid to thresh in the open because he lived during a season when God's people were dominated by the Midianites. The Midianites were a well-equipped and greatly numbered marauding army from the east that would descend on Israel at harvest time in order to raid their harvest and carry it back to Midian. By concealing himself in a winepress, Gideon hoped to avoid the plundering horde.

I am sure Gideon was both frustrated and humiliated by his circumstances and those of his countrymen. In the midst of those circumstances the Angel of the Lord greeted Gideon with an incredible statement: "The LORD is with you, mighty warrior" (v. 12, NIV). Apparently the Angel of the Lord recognized something in Gideon that Gideon could not recognize in himself. Rather than agreeing with the Angel (remember, the Angel of the Lord was how God the Son revealed Himself to men before He became a man, Jesus), Gideon regurgitated all the questions that were stirring in him due to the trauma wrought by the Midianites. Gideon's response clearly reveals that he was trapped by fear from the trauma of his encounters. As far as he was concerned, it took all his might just to conceal his harvest from his enemies.

Gideon answered the Angel of the Lord with three questions and his personal opinion about the circumstances facing him and his people. The Angel addressed none of Gideon's complaints. Instead, He unlocked the mighty reserve in Gideon when He commanded: "Go in this might of yours, and you shall save Israel from the hand of the Midianites. Have I not sent you?" (v. 14). When Gideon questioned this "might," the Angel brought an end to his questions by decreeing: "I will be with you, and you will strike down all the Midianites together" (v. 16, NIV).

Now is the time for you to let God unlock the might that is in you! The Lord is saying, "I have put My might within you. Though the fractures from your trauma have concealed and captured that might—it is in you and in the midst of you. Behold, I have sent My 'mighty One' to release a sound within you. The pressure of that sound will unlock the might within you. Leave behind your fractures, and go forth in My might. Let the might I have put in you rise up, rise up, rise up. See it bring forth the reserve that I have deposited in you."

There is always a false altar in our lives that holds vexation in place. We must determine what that demonic hold is and overturn its power. Usually that spiritual structure is linked with an actual object of empowerment. Gideon had to overturn his father's altar. Many times we have a small household idol tucked safely away in our care. However, this object gives a horde of demonic structures influence in our lives. Once again the Lord of hosts is unlocking and activating the mighty reserve He has put in us. There is no formula for this. As with Gideon, He is meeting you at your points of greatest struggle. He is coming in this way to activate the might that is in you if you will let go of the questions. (As with Gideon, God may not even address those questions, let alone answer them.)

LOT: RIGHTEOUS AND VEXED, BUT RESCUED

Lot was an interesting character. The Bible says that he was righteous, yet he was wayward. Lot experienced such loss because he was unable to see what was really taking place around him. He had sight but lacked insight. Lot's lack of insight was caused by two things. First, Lot was covered by a shroud of darkness. Lot's name reflected this. The Hebrew word *lot* means "a covering, shroud, or a blanket." It refers to a covering that blocks things out. In Lot's case there was a shroud over him that prevented him from seeing where God had placed blessing for him. Thus, he found himself in a succession of circumstances that diminished his portion rather than expanded it.

When Lot journeyed with his uncle Abram from Ur of the Chaldees, they both came out of their homeland with the identities forged by their family and homeland. After Abram entered fully into his covenant relationship with God (Gen. 15), God enlarged his name from Abram ("father") to Abraham ("father of many nations"). Though Lot was right with God, there is never any indication that he aligned himself fully with the promise coming through Abraham. Unlike his uncle's, Lot's name remained unchanged. His perception of things remained unchanged as well.

Lot's lens for seeing

Lot's insight and foresight were also greatly affected (and impaired) by the fact that at critical moments he viewed his circumstances and decisions through a lens of vexation rather than revelation. Vexation takes place when circumstances make one feel hurried, alarmed, dismayed, terrified, terrorized, trapped, captured, confused, worn out, run over, or desperate. When one is vexed, he/she feels pressed and pulled and worn to the point of being unable to endure anymore. At this point, vexation provokes a person to make a decision or take a decisive step that is off the path of God's blessing and actually moves that person in the direction of disaster.

When a person is vexed, that person's vision is distorted so he cannot clearly perceive God's revelation for the next step and path. He is driven by vexation, and those who see the vexation may consider taking advantage of that person. Car salesmen are sometimes known for their technique of pressing a person to sign on the dotted line before they have taken the time to really consider the deal. Politicians can be purveyors of fear, because they realize it is easier to control people when they are afraid.

Fear clouds our vision. Some ministers use desperate times to solicit contributions, promising contributors a way out of their desperation. The ultimate mastermind behind vexation is the devil himself. He looks for those occasions in which there is little or no time, money, opportunity, or help to move forward. He promotes fear and provokes rash responses. He vexes our emotions to distort vision so that we step out of time and place to make the wrong choice at the wrong time.

When Lot separated from Abram, his problems seem to escalate.

> So Abram said to Lot, "Let's not have any quarreling between you and me, or between your herdsmen and mine, for we are brothers. Is not the whole land before you? Let's part company. If you go to the left, I'll go to the right; if you go to the right, I'll go to the left." Lot looked up and saw that the whole plain of the Jordan was well watered, like the garden of the LORD, like the land of Egypt, toward Zoar. (This was before the LORD destroyed Sodom and Gomorrah.) So Lot chose for himself the whole plain of the Jordan and set out toward the east. The two men parted company: Abram lived in the land of Canaan, while Lot lived among the cities of the plain and pitched his tents near Sodom. Now the men of Sodom were wicked and were sinning greatly against the LORD.
>
> —GENESIS 13:8–13, NIV

Vexation was working in the camps of both Lot and Abram. Abram graciously gave Lot the opportunity to choose first the place where he would relocate. What gave Abram the freedom to graciously grant this choice to Lot was that he walked by the revelation that God would lead him to the land prepared for him. He had cut ties with his past, the idol-making, Mammon-controlled world of Ur of the Chaldees. Abraham was able to overcome the vexation operating in his camp. Several things enabled him to do this.

Abraham confronted his vexing circumstances. Abraham refused to let the quarrels in the camp cloud his vision or his direction. He confronted the circumstance by releasing control of his circumstances rather than taking control of them.

Abraham was not afraid of losing his promise. Because Abraham had revelation from God regarding his promise, he knew that God was responsible for that promise's fulfillment. Because he had no fear for his promise, Abraham was able to live free from vexation. He did not feel the need to protect his promise because he trusted God was able to do so.

Abraham chose to move by revelation rather than imagination. When one's soul is vexed, revelation is replaced by imagination, and vision is distorted. Lot chose Sodom without seeing the real truth of Sodom and the unrighteous root of that territory. Sodom had yet to come under its destruction, so Lot was unable to see beyond the appearance of things.

Revelation from God is the only effective antidote against vexation. When the Holy Spirit releases revelation, He literally uncovers what needs to be revealed. Look again at Lot and Abraham and compare their responses. As you do, look at your own decision-making process in the midst of vexing times.

Abram looked where God told him to look (revelation). Lot, however, made his choice based on sight. The *plush* of the world drew him. So, Lot chose Sodom! This moved him into an environment that released him on a path of destruction for his inheritance. Lot chose what looked best to him. Lot made his choice and, instead of being delivered from the past of vexation, was vexed in the future. At the beginning, both had prospered greatly. Lot's livestock and Abraham's livestock increased so much that the land could no longer support the increase. In the end, instead of prospering as Abraham prospered, Lot eventually lost all.

Lot's tragic circumstances in Sodom (the destruction of the city, loss of possessions, and the untimely death of his wife) were simply the result of a big and bad choice. Peter's summary evaluation of Lot's life in 2 Peter 2:6–9 (NIV, emphasis added) was, "If he condemned the cities of Sodom and Gomorrah by burning them to ashes, and made them an example of what is going to happen to the ungodly; *and if he rescued Lot, a righteous man*, who was distressed by the filthy lives of lawless men (for that righteous man, living among them day after day, was tormented *in his righteous soul* by the lawless deeds he saw and heard)—if this is so, then the Lord knows how to rescue *godly men* from trials and to hold the unrighteous for the day of judgment, while continuing their punishment."

Lot was righteous, which proves that the righteous can be vexed.

Lot was distressed. Lot's life became a great mess because He lived in a time and a place that was profoundly messy. This mess stretched Lot's life to the limits of his righteousness. In spite of this unbearable tension, Lot never snapped or broke. Yet he was tormented. Lot's distress penetrated beyond the physical level into the depths of his soul. The relentless morass and chaos of Sodom traumatized Lot's mind, will, and emotions. He could hardly think a thought, make a decision, or experience an emotion without some kind of torment from the things going on around him. *However, Lot was righteous.* In Peter's revelation, God deemed Lot a righteous man. When He decided to judge Sodom, He had a way of escape for Lot and his family. In the only biblical revelation in which God assessed the life and choices of Lot, God breathed the word *righteous* as His epithet for Lot. Lot was right with God because he left his vexing environment. In spite of him living in the midst of the greatest moral mess the world may have ever known, God rescued Lot.

GOD KNOWS HOW TO RESCUE

At times it seems like the boiling cauldron of unrighteousness that was once limited to Sodom and its surrounding area has reappeared globally. There is hardly a person or family on the face of the earth who is untouched or unscathed by what is now taking place. However, one foundational reality remains the same: *God knows how to rescue those who are right with Him!* If you are right with God, know this: God knows how to rescue you. If your circumstances are exceptionally messy, take hold of what God is speaking into you today. Shout it so your soul can hear it: "God knows how to rescue me, and He will do it!" *He* sent angels. *He* saved Lot from a dangerous crowd. *He* struck the crowd with blindness. *He* gave advance warning of danger. *He* took Lot and family by the hand. *He* instructed Lot. *He* released favor on Lot. *He* withheld judgment until Lot was in the clear.

As you read the biblical account, you will see that Lot understood very little of what God did on His behalf. God knew how to rescue Lot. Lot knew God. Knowing God was all the know-how Lot needed. God knows how to rescue YOU, and He will do so!

Lot was rescued but nearly lost everything that was important to him. In the midst of all the turmoil, Lot's wife and sons-in-law lost their lives. Lot's provision was destroyed. Remember, Lot was a successful rancher when he departed from Abraham. Lot was rescued, but not his herd. In the end, Lot's inheritance was corrupted. Scripture recalls the sordid details of the impact of Sodom and its demise on Lot's heirs. (See Genesis 10:30–38.)

God will rescue us, but we may experience great loss in regard to our inheritance on Earth. Lot experienced great loss, and his inheritance in the earth turned in a destructive direction. All of us face great difficulties at various times in our lives. Those who were not rescued looked back. Do not look back. Look forward, even if you must leave much behind to enter into freedom.

MOVING FROM TRAUMA OR FAILURE TO HEALING AND SUCCESS

You may have made decisions that produced a traumatic situation in your life, but you can be rescued and move forward. We have already discussed how trauma fragments us. Your blood system has a memory. When we experience trauma, the memory of the hurt gets imprinted in your memory system. Trauma is processed deep into the tissues of your brain (processor) and affects your thoughts (heart). Trauma becomes the *flashbulb* that creates what you see and how you define the world around you. Traumas can produce lock-ins of fear, failure complexities, emotional distresses, and anxieties. Traumas can cause your organs to overwork (spleen, kidneys, liver, and pancreas), affecting the way your body efficiently works. However, you can overcome and restore all.

God can restore and redeem our times when we listen. In the last few years, many of us have experienced a greater measure of trauma from loss than ever before. Jobs, homes, retirement funds, investments, and just about every material asset linked with the word *security* have been stripped from millions of Americans like you and me. During this time, the fear of the world's economic uncertainty has created a proverbial prison for many sons and daughters of the Most High. We have frequently been scattered in our vision, *willingness* to hear, and in the trusting of the Lord's battle plan for our victory. But no more. All of creation is eagerly waiting for God's glory to be revealed. When it is revealed, the kingdom will exponentially multiply where the soles of your feet tread.

See, turn, and hear your way out of captivity and into the new! When Isaiah heard the Lord make the statement and ask the question, "See, I am doing a new thing!…Do you not perceive it?" (Isa. 43:19, NIV), the people were in danger of not shifting their sight to *see* their way into their future. They were a people going into captivity, but He was promising them that He would show them their way out at the perfect time. However, they would have to *see* the opening and opportunity to change their identity for the future. In this season, we must see our way out of our past captivities.

We are shifting from hearing to seeing. In the past we have heard a "word from behind us telling us which way to go," but now He will manifest in a way that we have to notice Him, turn, look, and then hear His word telling us which way to go. We have a great example of the time to shift and the pattern for the season ahead when we look at Exodus 3:1–4 (THE MESSAGE):

> Moses was shepherding the flock of Jethro, his father-in-law, the priest of Midian. He led the flock to the west end of the wilderness and came to the mountain of God, Horeb. The angel of GOD appeared to him in flames of fire blazing out of the middle of a bush. He looked. The bush was blazing away but it didn't burn up. Moses said, "What's going on here? I can't believe this! Amazing!

Why doesn't the bush burn up?" GOD saw that he had stopped to look. God called to him from out of the bush, "Moses! Moses!" He said, "Yes? I'm right here!"

The heavens had changed because the cry of the people of Israel in their slavery had reached God's throne room. He responded and remembered His covenant that He had made four hundred years earlier. His response came in the form of a new manifestation. Moses recognized the new manifestation, which caused him to stop his normal daily activities. He did not just see the manifestation. The Word above says that "he had stopped to look." He turned from his past and present to *see* his future. When Moses saw, he then heard his calling to advance. *The key is letting go of the old duties, routines, thought patterns, emotions, relationships, and ambitions.* When we see, then turn (the same word for "change"), we will hear the transition and be repositioned out of last season's captivities and into *next* season's freedom. Be willing to see and then say, "Here I am."

THE VOICE OF GOD IS LIKE A GPS NAVIGATOR

In most new cars there are devices that help us to navigate. One of my friends sent me the following: "I used my new GPS to get to downtown Houston for jury duty. I was struck by how much God is like this GPS system in my car. First of all, the GPS tells you what to do when you are a short distance from your shifting turn. The voice of the GPS then grows more urgent as you get closer to your needed turn. However, the voice does not give you too much information too far in advance. If you miss the turn to your destination, the GPS recalculates and gives you another way to the destination. Isn't that like God? He forewarns us of how to get to where we need to go. The Spirit then gets stronger when we get close to the perfect timing to shift. Then, even if we *miss it*, He is longsuffering and recalculates our path into victory."[2]

May you see and hear every turn on your path as you press forward. If you miss a turn, may you find grace and find your way. Proverbs 4:18

(AMP) says, "But the path of the [uncompromisingly] just and righteous is like the light of dawn, that shines more and more (brighter and clearer) until [it reaches its full strength and glory in] the perfect day [to be prepared]."

WE OVERCOME BY THE
WORD OF OUR TESTIMONY

All of the testings you are going through are linked with the word of your testimony, which is produced at the end of the testings. Your spirit man is like the ark of the covenant, where the testaments were placed to be secured for the future of all mankind. When you endure the enemy's temptations and your own soulish carnal ways, your spirit man develops an overcoming power. When you speak from your spirit man, you overcome.

First, let's make sure we share the same definition of the word *testimony* as it relates to the life of faith. I recently asked a few people what they think of when they hear the word *testimony*. All of them said pretty much the same thing: the story of a person's spiritual journey. Basically, they defined *testimony* as someone's personal spiritual narrative. And while our testimony includes parts of our biography, that isn't the heart of it. We'll set aside the definitions dealing with legal or courtroom testimony and focus on the spiritual dimension.

The verb *to testify* is defined like this:

- To express or declare a strong belief, especially to make a declaration of faith

- To make a statement based on personal knowledge in support of an asserted fact

- To declare publicly; make known

- To bear witness to; provide evidence for

The noun *testimony* is defined this way:

- Evidence in support of a fact or assertion; proof

- A public declaration regarding a religious experience

The Word of God is full of people who testified to the power, majesty, and mercy of God:

- Joseph testified to his brothers when he said, "Do not be afraid, for am I in the place of God? But as for you, you meant evil against me; but God meant it for good, in order to bring it about as it is this day, to save many people alive. Now therefore, do not be afraid" (Gen. 50:19–21).

- Job said to the Lord, "I know that You can do everything, and that no purpose of Yours can be withheld from You" (Job 42:2).

- David said, "I sought the LORD, and He heard me, and delivered me from all my fears" (Ps. 34:4).

- Mary declared, "For He who is mighty has done great things for me, and holy is His name" (Luke 1:49).

- Stephen, moments before he was stoned, said, "Look! I see the heavens opened and the Son of Man standing at the right hand of God!" (Acts 7:56).

- And Paul told the Philippians, "Everywhere and in all things I have learned both to be full and to be hungry, both to abound and to suffer need. I can do all things through Christ who strengthens me" (Phil. 4:12–13).

One thing all of these testimonies have in common is that all the speakers direct our attention to the Lord. Our testimony, like our worship, is meant to magnify the Lord, not our own ego. Only when Jesus is exalted will our testimony bear the witness of the Holy Spirit.

CHAPTER 20

NOURISHING YOUR SPIRIT

O NE OF THE hardest things to deal with is vexation of spirit. Vexation of spirit occurs when circumstances make you feel pressed or pulled to the point that you can't take another problem. Vexation of spirit causes you to act in haste, alarm, or even terror. You feel that you have no other choice; there is no other time or any other way out of your present circumstance. You act in vexation rather than revelation.

OVERCOME VEXATION OF SPIRIT

There are many reasons we become vexed in spirit. As we discussed, Lot was vexed as a righteous man living among unrighteous people. He had moved his family into Sodom when he and Abram parted company. He had become one of the leading men in the city, an "elder at the gate." But even in that place of influence, his righteousness did not bring any change in the city. Second Peter 2:7 (KJV) says that he was "vexed" by what he saw going on around him. Even though he was a righteous man, his vexation skewed his judgment and perception. The result was that when God offered him a way out of his vexation, he could not move in faith, and his inheritance was corrupted by the same sin that had vexed him. Failure to overcome vexation of spirit can have serious consequences for us and for our generations after us.

David experienced many times when his soul was vexed, when situations turned bad, or the enemy surrounded him. David knew what to do. He did not get discouraged or feel sorry for himself or sit and pout. He cried out to God. Psalm 70 says:

Make haste, O God, to deliver me!
Make haste to help me, O LORD!
Let them be ashamed and confounded
Who seek my life;
Let them be turned back and confused
Who desire my hurt.
Let them be turned back because of their shame,
Who say, "Aha, aha!"
Let all those who seek You rejoice and be glad in You;
And let those who love Your salvation say continually,
"Let God be magnified!"
But I am poor and needy;
Make haste to me, O God!
You are my help and my deliverer;
O LORD, do not delay.

If your soul is vexed, if you are surrounded by your enemies, return to God. Rejoice and praise Him. Call out to Him, and watch Him come.

When we read a psalm like this about being in great distress with many against us, we need to realize that the Lord wants us to know that we will be in vexing situations. One of the ways we overcome vexation is by rehearsing the revelation that God brings to us. It is not going to just soak in. We have to be deliberate about meditating on it, going back over it, and taking note of it.

Recently on a Sunday morning, LeAnn Squier gave a testimony about revelation she received during her daughter Abbie's volleyball game. Abbie's team was getting beaten badly. It seemed that nothing they did worked, and the other team was taunting them. They were vexed! As LeAnn watched the game, the Lord spoke to her and told her to move up in the stands so that she would see the game from a higher vantage point. As she did, she gained a whole new perspective on the game. She saw that the other team had a strategy. They knew the strengths of Abbie's team and how to avoid them. They knew their weaknesses and how to target them. Even when positions changed, they knew how to target the weaknesses and avoid the strengths. When LeAnn got up to a place where she could see not just what was in her face but what they were doing overall as a team, she could see the way to change the team's strategy and remove the vexation. One key revelation for overcoming vexation is to gain a higher perspective on the problem or circumstance.

In the United States, when a football team is playing, they have people called *spotters* up high. They have headphones and microphones so they can communicate with the coaches on the field to tell them what it looks like from up there. The coaches can then send in the plays and coach the players from the higher perspective. We have to put on our headsets and hear what the Lord is saying in spite of what is going on around us. We must listen to the voice of the coach telling us what play to run, what direction to move, and what position to get into. He says, "Look up, look again! I will show you another thing that is happening on the field. It is not what you have been seeing. I will coach you from up here. Still your soul so you can hear what I am saying to you. Trust in the voice that is speaking to you. Move with it instead of what you are hearing on the ground."

When our spirit gets vexed, we need to check and see why. We need to know if we are vexed because we have moved into Sodom or if we are vexed because we are fighting as best we can, but we don't yet have the strategy we need for victory. The Tuesday after LeAnn shared, we began to pray about breaking the vexation of our spirit during early morning prayer. LeAnn had this prophetic song:

> We're going to come up just a little bit higher, higher, higher,
> To the place of holy fire, fire
> You will purify our desire when we come up just a little bit higher.
> We're not going to stay in the fray and be tossed around one more day.
> I'm gonna take some steps, and when I see that ladder going up to heaven,
> I'm not going to stay where I have been, in the reasoning of men.
> I'm gonna come up, I'm gonna climb up a little bit higher.

When LeAnn finished singing, someone else shared this observation: "Recently I watched the movie *UP*. The little man had to leave his past behind to go up. He wanted to take the past with him because that's what he thought he was supposed to do, but he had to leave his past behind to fulfill his destiny." *UP* is a good movie about overcoming vexation and fulfilling your destiny. As we saw earlier, going up higher—ascending— is one of the keys to gaining revelation for overcoming vexation. In the psalms of ascent, the Lord shows all the things necessary to "go up." Think about LeAnn climbing the stairs in the volleyball arena to get a better view of what was happening in the game. Most people do not like to climb stairs, especially in stadiums, and yet she had to exert the effort to get up there. In the psalms of ascent, the writer first had to get a vision for where he was headed. He had to have vision for the reward that awaited him. He had to know that the reward was greater than the effort of the climb. In Psalm 122 he gains vision for where he is going. He is set on getting through the gates of Jerusalem to praise God.

The next thing he says in Psalm 123 is, "If You don't help me, I won't make it. I am lifting my hands to You. Have mercy!" In whatever vexing situation you find yourself, put your eyes on the goal and call out for the Lord to have mercy. When you do not know how you will overcome the situation, when you do not know what He will do to bring you up and over the situation, call out to Him. In Psalm 124, David sees that there are snares on the path. We are like birds. If we get caught in a snare, then we cannot go up. Psalm 126 talks about remembering the grief of the past. In order to ascend, we have to make a break with the mourning from the past.

As you ascend, you must be aware of the obstacles you will have to overcome on the way. In Psalms 127 and 128, the psalmist is about halfway up the ascent when he suddenly remembers his family, which he has left behind. He has left his children and his wife and his home. He wonders what is going on with his family, and then he says, "Unless the Lord builds the house, those who build it labor in vain. Unless the Lord guards the city, the watchman stays awake in vain." Unless the

Lord is watching over my family, I can stay awake all night, and it will not do any good.

You must come to a new perspective about the things you have to leave behind in order to go where God is calling you to go, even if it involves your family, your kids, your home, or your inheritance. Unless you know that the Lord is watching over them, you will get halfway up the mountain and turn back because you are so worried about them. You will have to resolve the issue of your family and your home and your livelihood. These worries will vex your spirit and block your progress.

As the psalmist continues his ascent, Psalm 129 says that he is so afflicted that it feels like someone is running a plow over his back. It feels like he is being flayed alive. You are going to have to let God expose some things in you if you are going to keep going. Linda Heidler, another ministerial leader here at Glory of Zion International, shared an experience like the one the psalmist describes. She said, "One of the best ministry times I have ever had was when I went to Keith Pierce, and it felt I was being flayed. It exposed some things so that I could see what was really going on inside of me. It was one of the best things that ever happened!"

The psalmist says, "I feel like they are tearing me apart, but I have the vision of Mt. Zion, and I don't think I can stop, even if I am leaving a trail of blood as I go. I have got to get up and over." Persecution and discomfort can be vexations that stop you, or they can be used to reveal things that you would have never seen, had you not suffered the discomfort. You can turn vexation into revelation.

In Psalm 131, the psalmist gets to the place where he says, "I cannot figure any of this out. It is beyond me. Everything I thought has not worked, and what I did not expect has happened. All I can do is lean back on You, Lord, and be at peace in my heart. This is the path I am supposed to be on, and I will trust you to get me there." Trying to figure everything out will wear you out and will bring vexation to your spirit. Trusting the Lord with what you cannot figure out and resting in Him will quench the power of vexation and will bring you to peace.

In Psalm 133 and 134, we find David has made it up to Zion and says, "How good and pleasant it is for brothers to dwell together in unity. It is like the oil poured on the head that runs down over the beard. Bless the Lord, you servants of the Lord, who minister to Him by night!" He makes it the whole way up, and then the Lord commands the blessing! He had been down in the place where the enemy was picking him off; now the Lord is about to command His blessing, and there is nothing that can stop the blessing of the Lord. When you reach this place, His blessing will overtake you. It is a battle to ascend, but when our hearts are set on ascending to Zion, we will overcome everything to get up into the place where we bless and worship and praise the Lord. His blessing is commanded down into the vexing situation we have come out of.

Daniel could have been vexed when he was in the lion's den. Joseph could have been vexed when he was in the pit. However, they never lost contact with God. God came through for them. He can come through for us. Their way out of the vexing was through submission to the Spirit of the living God. He is full of power. His eyes see, so when we are in that vexing situation, we can come up and look for God. Guess who's going to be vexed when we come out?

The biggest change in the history of Israel in the Old Testament, from their lowest point their highest point, came because God allowed a woman to become miserable. Hannah was vexed because of her barrenness. If our spirit is vexed, we need to realize that God might change the whole earth when we press through and overcome. The Hebrew word for "vexation" means "miserable"! When she pressed in at the altar and interceded, the Lord met her need. She brought forth Samuel!

The enemy is able to vex our spirits when we shrink back and do not lay hold of the promises we have been given. God's promises are yes and amen. We must apprehend our promises and keep moving forward. In a time of vexing circumstances, hold up your hands and say, "Lord, I need every strategy I can get. I need every revelation and bit of wisdom I can get. I need to hear every testimony that releases faith. I need You to breathe on Your Word so that it is alive in me as I try to find my way through vexing circumstances."

God wants us to come out of a season of vexation with a testimony that releases inheritance. God will make a way for the testimony of His ascending, resurrection power to be released. We cannot be naive about what we will have to overcome and press through. On the way, we will rejoice and declare the goodness of God. We will dance as we ascend. We will hold up our hands in praise, and we will hold up our hands for help, but vexation will not overcome us. We will not be captured. We will not be stopped. We will not be hindered. We will not let God's purposes be thwarted or perverted by our vexation. We must cut ties with sentimentality and emotions. Hannah made a choice not to be held by those two things. Ask the Lord to bathe you in a strategic anointing. It is separate from emotions or memories from the past or what we set our desires on. There is a new mantle of authority God will give you that enables you to set the agenda. We must make a choice and move in a new way in the earth. That is how divine recovery is going to come—through a strategic people. In order to break away from the normal way things go, you will need to have a new anointing of resurrection life in you. Choose to come up! You will have to purpose to come up to a higher place to do that. Thank the Lord for the anointing of resurrection life that can lead you up. Thank God for His plumb line, so we can know that our way is ordered right through a season of vexation. Jesus has already overcome and will release that spirit into us as we overcome every vexation of spirit.

Nourishing Your Spirit

Gaining an understanding of the spiritual dimension of your life is one of the most important things you can do. While this is one of the most important things to understand, it is also one of the least understood. Much of our thinking about the spirit comes from the Greeks, who divided everything according to *spiritual* or *physical*. The physical was human and earthly, and the spiritual was divine and heavenly, and "never the two shall meet." It was inconceivable to think of a human spirit. Yet this is precisely the concept we find in the Bible. We are spiritual beings. In fact, when you read the Bible, you discover that this spiritual dimension of our lives is the whole basis for any relationship with God. Not only that, but this spiritual dimension forms the essence of our true identity. Without an understanding of our spirit, we do not really know who we are, nor do we comprehend our true worth.

Let's look at what the Bible has to say so that we can have a true foundation of the spirit. Genesis 2:7 says, "And the LORD God formed man of the dust of the ground, and breathed into his nostrils the breath of life; and man became a living being." In other words, all of the physical components can be present without the life and breath of God being present. The source of our life is our spirit. It was that way in Genesis, and it is still that way today.

One of my favorite verses is in Ecclesiastes 12:6–7 (AMP). "[Remember your Creator earnestly now] before the silver cord [of life] is snapped apart, or the golden bowl is broken, or the pitcher is broken at the fountain, or the wheel broken at the cistern [and the whole circulatory system of the blood ceases to function]; then shall the dust [out of which God made man's body] return to the earth as it was, and the spirit shall return to God Who gave it." The body will return to dust, where it came from, and the spirit will return to God, where it came from. This means that before God breathed our spirit into us, it existed with Him. Isn't that an amazing thought? It really sheds light on verses like Ephesians 1:3–4, which say that before the foundation of the world, God knew us. Jeremiah 1:5 says (author's paraphrase), "Before I formed you in your mother's womb, I knew you." Before we ever existed in physical form, God knew us, chose us, wrote a plan for our lives, and died for us.

Your spirit is the part of your being that first knows God. Since your spirit existed in eternity past with God, your spirit somehow knows that there is more to life than just the physical universe. Ecclesiastes 3:11 (AMP) says, "He has made everything beautiful in its time. He also has planted eternity in men's hearts and minds [a divinely implanted sense of a purpose working through the ages which nothing under the sun but God alone can satisfy], yet so that men cannot find out what God has done from the beginning to the end." We have some sense of eternity because our spirit existed there with God. This is why we feel so complete when we are saved. We are reconnected to what we had become separated from.

Because of the foundation that most of us have in Greek thinking, we tend to overlook, or neglect, our spirits. We will often try to relate to God through our soul or our physical body. We will try to find our worth and identity through our mind or emotions or looks. Unless we understand our true spiritual nature, we cannot function as a whole person. Very often we have spiritual needs, but we try to fill them with things that do not satisfy the spirit. We now want to look at how we can nourish our spirit.

Ephesians 5:18 says, "Do not be drunk with wine…but be filled with the Spirit." I have always taken this to mean to be filled with the Holy Spirit, which I'm sure it does, but the Word here does not specify that this is the Holy Spirit. The spirit is the vital portion of life, the principle of life residing in man. This is the breath breathed by God into man and again returning to God, the spiritual entity in man. In other words, the verse is saying to let your human spirit be full. This word *full* literally means "to cram full, to satisfy." I love that! Let your spirit be crammed full, fully satisfied.

How can we do this? We do this by nourishing our spirit with things that satisfy it. Paul lists some of the things. He says we should be filled with songs, hymns, and spiritual songs. Our spirits like it when we sing! Have you ever wondered why music has such an effect on us? John Dickson and I have two books on worship, *The Worship Warrior* and *Worship as It Is in Heaven.* We explain the connection between heaven and Earth: man's worship! Our spirit loves it. Paul goes on to include giving thanks to God. Our spirits know God, and they love to thank Him for who He is and what He has done. Our spirits get full and satisfied when we give thanks to God.

First Corinthians 14 tells another way to nourish your spirit. Praying in tongues edifies your spirit. In fact, Ephesians 3:16 says that our inner man (the Greek word is *eso,* which is also used for the human spirit) is strengthened by the Holy Spirit. In other words, the more active the Holy Spirit is in our lives, the stronger our spirit becomes. When we minister, prophesy, or exercise any ministry of the Holy Spirit, our spirit is strengthened.

We must never stop Holy Spirit from moving. The Holy Spirit can be quenched, grieved, provoked, and resisted. If the Holy Spirit strengthens our human spirit, then it stands to reason that if the Holy Spirit is quenched, grieved, provoked, and resisted, then our spirits will not reflect the power and liberty of Holy Spirit. The quenching of Holy Spirit can even affect an entire territory. I used to walk around saying, "My spirit is going crazy." Many of those around me and those I ministered with would have no clue what I was talking about. Gradually, some have come to understand that my spirit was sensing that the Holy Spirit was disturbed about something, and He would not rest until He got it settled.

Finally, our spirit is nourished when we see things in God's reality. Second Corinthians 4:16–18 says that our inner man, our spirit, is renewed day by day as we look not at earthly, temporal things but at eternal things. If we only look at things from a physical perspective, we can get pretty distressed. In this passage Paul says that when he looks at his earthly body, it is perishing! If all we had to look forward to was a weakening body and a deteriorating mind, that would be depressing. Paul says that when we look at things from the perspective of eternity, our spirits are nourished. Our spirits say, "Oh yeah, I remember where I came from. Things here may be hard; I may be experiencing affliction, but I have an eternal weight of glory waiting for me." That is very nourishing, strengthening to our spirits.

A strong spirit is God's desire for us. Ephesians 3:14–21 says:

> For this reason I bow my knees to the Father of our Lord Jesus Christ, from whom the whole family in heaven and earth is named, that He would grant you, according to the riches of His glory, to be strengthened with might through His Spirit in the inner man, that Christ may dwell in your hearts through faith; that you, being rooted and grounded in love, may be able to comprehend with all the saints what is the width and length and depth and height—to know the love of Christ which passes knowledge; that you may be filled with all the fullness of God. Now to Him who is able to do

exceedingly abundantly above all that we ask or think, according to the power that works in us, to Him be glory in the church by Christ Jesus to all generations, forever and ever. Amen.

Exercising Your Spirit

Exercise is defined as "activity for training or developing the body or mind; movement to strengthen some part of the body." In thinking of how we exercise our spirits, there are several kinds of exercise I want to look at.

Resistance training

The first kind of exercise is *resistance training*. This kind of exercise is also called *strength training*. Resistance training increases muscle strength by putting more than the usual amount of strain on a muscle. So how does this translate to the spirit realm? What does it look like for our spirit to go through resistance training?

The two main places we find this described are in James 4:7 and 1 Peter 5:8–9. Both of these passages say we are to resist the devil. While we are always to be resisting his plans and purposes in our lives and in the earth, there are some times when we feel that we are in a special battle. These are the times when we find ourselves in God's strength training exercise program.

So how do we resist the devil? The dictionary definition of the word *resist* is very enlightening. It is:

- To defy; say, "No, you are not going to do that."

- To stand up to or offer resistance; physically block what he wants to do.

- To protest or express opposition through actions or words; declare, "That is not the truth."

- To withstand the force of something, stand your ground, refuse to go the way he is trying to push you.

- To refuse the introduction of a foreign body; say, "That is not coming in here."

- To refuse to comply; say, "I am just not going to do that."

Now, none of this is easy. In fact, 1 Peter 5:9 says that we may suffer, but in our suffering, our spirit can be strengthened. "Resist him, steadfast in the faith, knowing that the same sufferings are experienced by your brotherhood in the world." One of the results of resistance training is that it stimulates muscle growth. So as you are resisting the devil, envision your spiritual muscles getting stronger.

Endurance training

Another kind of exercise is *endurance training.* Endurance enables you to keep going for the distance. You are able to finish the race, finish the course. Endurance is not so much a matter of strength as it is of stamina. *Endurance* is defined as "the power to withstand hardship or distress." Paul describes his life this way in 2 Corinthians 6:4–10. It is a state of survival, remaining alive. The perfect description of this is in Ephesians 6 when Paul describes all the spiritual armor but concludes by saying, "And having done everything, stand firm." Robert Heidler says it this way: "Don't give up, and you will win!" Endurance is *the act of sustaining prolonged stressful effort.* This is the way the Book of Hebrews describes Jesus. Hebrews 12:2–3 says that Jesus endured the cross and that He endured hostility of sinners against Him. I don't know of anything that would be harder than that—to be suffering for someone and then to have that person be hostile toward you. To finish your assignment under distressing circumstances takes endurance.

In Hebrews 12:1 the writer challenges us to run the race set before us with endurance. It is interesting that he uses the analogy of running, because this is one of the best endurance exercises. This passage says that two things will block endurance. The first is *weight* that you are not supposed to be carrying, and the second is *sin,* which entangles you. A weight will sap your strength so that you do not have what you need to finish the race. In order to finish the race, you cannot carry excess baggage. You cannot carry someone else's load and still finish your race. You also cannot carry something that God has said to lay down and still finish your race. The other obstacle is sin. The passage says that it is easy to get entangled in sin. In other words, it takes effort not to get entangled in sin. It takes resistance.

How do we get endurance? Hebrews 12:2 tells us to look to Jesus. Since He did finish His race, He can tell us how to finish ours. First Corinthians 13:13 says that three things endure: faith, hope, and love. If we have these, we will also endure.

Toning exercise

A third kind of exercise is *toning* exercise. This is not to build strength or stamina but just to keeps things in good working order. While you will find yourself in seasons of resistance or of endurance, toning is ongoing. Walking is one of the best toning exercises. Almost every area of your body, including your muscles, bones, heart, and lungs, benefit from walking.

Walking is defined as "the manner in which one lives one's life." It has to do with regular habits or personal characteristics. Walking has to do with being consistent on a daily basis in seemingly small things, which, over time, promote good health. Walking has to do with faithfulness. It is about making good choices because you see the long-term benefits.

How do we walk? Galatians 5:16 says to walk in the Spirit. Colossians 3 describes the things we used to walk in and instructs us not to walk in these anymore. Ephesians 5:15–16 says to walk in wisdom with regard to time. Colossians 4:5 says to walk with wisdom toward outsiders. It is interesting that *wisdom* is one of the words connected with walking. The Hebrew word for "wisdom" means "to have skill in living." It means "the ability to take something ordinary and make it a work of art." To walk in wisdom means to take your life and make it a work of art. I'd really like for my life to look that way. Whether we are in a season of endurance, strengthening, or walking, we need the spiritual exercise.

Fellowship of the Spirit

One of the essentials for life is personal contact with others. In Genesis, the only thing God said was that it was not good for Adam to be alone. We were made to fellowship. *Fellowship* is defined as the companionship of persons on friendly or equal terms; the state of being together with joint interests." As with everything else we have been looking at, this goes beyond our physical and soulish dimensions. This also includes our spirits.

Communion is the fellowship function of our spirits. The primary way that we fellowship in the spirit is by fellowshiping with the Holy Spirit. The first place this is mentioned is in Philippians 2. The passage describes what happens in our lives through the fellowship of the Holy Spirit.

- We all become likeminded (v. 2).

- We all become humble (v. 3).

- We watch out for one another (v. 4).

- We develop a servant's heart (v. 7).

- We *are obedient* to God (v. 8).

The end result is that we become like Jesus through fellowshiping with the Holy Spirit. As we are on friendly terms with the Holy Spirit, as we enjoy the company of the Holy Spirit and work together for joint interests, we become more like Jesus. This is one of the aspects of covenant. What He has becomes ours.

Another way that we fellowship in the Spirit is when we take communion with each other. Acts 2:42 describes the four basic elements of the early church—teaching, fellowship, communion, and prayer. From this I would say that fellowship with each other is high on the list of things that make a healthy church. How does this look spiritually?

The first way we fellowship with each other in the spirit is through Communion. When we take Communion, we are affirming our companionship, our connectedness with each other. Another way we fellowship by the spirit is through finding our place in the church. In 1 Peter 2 where Peter is describing the church, he says that we are all being fitted together as living stones. In Ephesians 4 where Paul is talking about the church, he describes us as being joined and knit together as a body. We are made to be connected to others. If we are not in fellowship, we cannot get connected. When we are connected, we begin to enjoy success in accomplishing our common purpose.

Now, if we are not fellowshiping with the Holy Spirit, we cannot fellowship with each other on a spiritual level. If you try to find your place in the church without letting the Holy Spirit make you like Jesus, it will just not happen. There is no way we can be built into a spiritual house or become knit together into one body unless we are likeminded, humble, watching out for one another, servants, and obedient to God. First John 1:7 says that if we walk in the light as He is in the light, we have fellowship with one another. There is no other way for this to happen.

Now you can come into fellowship and work together for a common purpose and be very successful without the Holy Spirit. This is what happened at the Tower of Babel. We just need to decide if we want to build a Tower of Babel or the church of the living God! I would choose the church of the living God, because we all know what happened to the Tower of Babel.

The last way I want to talk about fellowshiping in the spirit is through fellowshiping with your own soul. This may sound schizophrenic, but it is biblical. There are times when your spirit needs to fellowship with your own soul. Let's look at a few verses that convey this concept.

- Psalm 4:4 says, "Commune with your own heart...and be still" (KJV).

- Psalm 77:6 says, "I commune with mine own heart: and my spirit made diligent search" (KJV).

- Ecclesiastes 1:16 says, "I communed with mine own heart, saying, Lo, I am come to great estate, and have gotten more wisdom than all they that have been before me in Jerusalem" (KJV).

There are some times when your soul needs to hear what your spirit has to say. In 1 Samuel 30:6, when David and his men found that Ziklag had been burned and their wives and children had been captured, it says that David "strengthened himself in the LORD." In 1 Samuel 23:16 we are told that Jonathan came to David and strengthened David in God. He reminded David of the promises of God to him, but Jonathan was not at Ziklag. In fact, the ones who were with David wanted to stone him. They obviously had not been fellowshiping with the Holy Spirit. David had to strengthen himself. His soul really needed to hear what his spirit had to say.

Have you ever had to encourage yourself? At times like that you want to be sure that you have a well-nourished, strong, healthy spirit that has been fellowshiping with the Holy Spirit, because there may not be anyone else around. If you had to encourage yourself, if your spirit had to encourage your soul, how would you do? Let me encourage you to nourish your spirit, worship, and minister in the power of the Holy Spirit. Exercise your spirit, resist the devil, run with endurance, and walk in the Spirit. And keep your spirit in fellowship with the Holy Spirit so that you are becoming more like Jesus and are connected to others who are doing the same.

GOING BEYOND

I HOPE YOU ARE now seeing in a new way. Recently Tiffany Smith (one of the psalmists at Glory of Zion International) came forward and prophesied, "There is power in sonship. I won't relent until you get to the place I've destined for you. I won't relent. I am committed to you." Until the day Jesus returns, He is committed to you—every day, every step, and every purpose. There is a place called *"beyond"* that the Lord is calling you to. See your place called Beyond and start pressing toward that place!

I hear the Lord saying to us, "Know Me as the Voice who creates order from chaos. I have called you to dominion. Man's call is to watch, multiply, and worship. The serpent's voice is subtle. Abraham was tested on Mount Moriah but overcame by faith. Your covenant rights can be extended to another generation. I can cleanse the heavens, rend them, and come down. There is a power in My Passover. The blood of My Son will overcome. You can see abundance. I have a journey planned for your promised land. I will restore David's tabernacle from generation to generation. The celebration of my feasts are important, each one—Passover, Pentecost, and the Feast of Tabernacles (Rosh Hashanah, Yom Kippur, the Feast of Trumpets) release a prophetic piece of your puzzle of life. Let the redeemed say, 'So!' The virgin birth of Jesus, your Redeemer, secures eternity. The Word became flesh. Allow this word to change your flesh. My Son's sacrifice and surprise of the cross created the enemy's defeat. The same power that raised Jesus from the dead is in you. Demonstrate this power to a dying world. Colabor with angels. Walk under an open heaven. The Lion of Judah will have a triumphant remnant. 'Follow *Me!*' These two words will cause you to see. Do not be afraid to come and see your future. Surrender to the Lord, receive My Spirit, and follow."

Understand these key principles so you can see your promises manifest. You are made to be an overcomer! Overcome sin, the flesh, the world, and the devil. Your last battle in life is death. Because God fathered your spirit, if you will allow your spirit to fellowship, be nourished, and exercised, you will remain strong. Though the enemy attempts to vex you, you will remain in right standing with the One who knit you together. Take every trial as a project. Know that you can be creative to overcome. The blood and the word of your testimony will overcome. Fear not death or the loss of your life. Your spirit is eternal. You can overcome the last sting of death. You win in the end! Your end can be greater than your beginning.

NOTES

CHAPTER 7—THE BLOOD KEY

1. Marty Cassady, personal communication with the author, March 15, 2010.

2. H. A. Maxwell Whyte, *The Power of the Blood* (Springdale, PA: Whitaker House, 1973), 12–13.

3. Ibid., 12–17.

4. Ibid., 21–36.

CHAPTER 8—THE WORD KEY

1. Chuck D. Pierce and Robert Heidler, *Restoring Your Shield of Faith* (Ventura, CA: Regal Books, 2003), 71–73.

CHAPTER 9—SINAI: GOD ESTABLISHES A NEW ORDER

1. "The Counting of the Omer," *Judaism 101*, http://www.jewfaq.org/holidayb .htm (accessed August 9, 2010).

CHAPTER 11—SEE PAST MAMMON

1. *New International Dictionary of New Testament Theology,* vol. 2, ed. Colin Brown (Grand Rapids, MI: Regency Reference Library, 1986), 829.

2. *Hayford's Bible Handbook,* ed. Jack W. Hayford (Nashville, TN: Thomas Nelson Publishers, 1995), 962.

CHAPTER 12—SEE YOUR PROMISE FROM GOD'S PERSPECTIVE

1. Keith Pierce, personal communication with the author, February 3, 2010.

2. Martin P. Gallagher, *Dr. Gallagher's Guide to Twenty-First Century Medicine: How to Get Off the Illness Treadmill and Onto Optimum Health* (Greensburg, PA: Atlas Publishing Company, 1997), 7.

3. Ibid., 2.

CHAPTER 14—GOD'S PLAN FOR WHOLENESS

1. E. Anthony Allen, *Transforming Health*, ed. Eric Ram (Monrovia, CA: Marc and World Vision International, n.d.), 7.

2. Allen Faubion, personal communication with the author, October 18, 2009.

3. Ibid.

Chapter 15—Breaking the Power of Vexation

1. Adapted from F. F. Bruce, *Epistle to the Hebrews* (Grand Rapids, MI: Wm. B. Eerdmans, 1964), 81–83.

2. Adapted from *International Standard Bible Encyclopedia*, revised edition (Grand Rapids, MI: Wm. B. Eerdmans Publishing Co., 1979).

Chapter 16—Guard Against the Enemy's Tools

1. Merriam-Webster's Online Dictionary, s.v. "evil eye," accessed January 12, 2011.

2. *The Columbia Encyclopedia,* sixth ed., s.v. "evil eye," quoted at Bartleby. com, http://www.bartleby.com/65/ev/evileye.html (accessed February 16, 2005).

3. Chuck D. Pierce and Rebecca Wagner Sytsema, *Possessing Your Inheritance* (Ventura, CA: Renew Books, 1999), 172–173.

4. Doris M. Wagner, ed., *How to Minister Freedom* (Ventura, CA: Regal Books, 2005), 262–263.

5. *The Catholic Encyclopedia,* volume XIV, ed. Edward A. Pace, s.v. "spiritism," quoted at *New Advent,* http://www.newadvent.org/cathen/14221a.htm (accessed March 2, 2005).

6. Ibid.

7. Ibid.

8. Selwyn Stevens, *Unmasking Freemasonry: Removing the Hoodwink* (Wellington, New Zealand: Jubilee Resources, 1999), 19.

9. Wagner, ed., *How to Minister Freedom,* 262–271.

Chapter 17—He Is the Father of Your Spirit

1. Joseph H. Hillerman, *The Ancient Church as Family* (Minneapolis, MN: Fortress Press, 2001), 25.

2. *Adam Clarke's Commentary,* Electronic Database, copyright 1996, 2003, 2005, 2006 by Biblesoft, Inc., s.v. "Hebrews 12:9."

3. Ibid.

4. Ibid.

5. *Nelson's Illustrated Bible Dictionary* (Nashville, TN: Thomas Nelson Publishers, 1986).

Chapter 19—His Promise Is: "We *Will* Overcome"

1. *The New Testament: An Expanded Trsanslation,* trans. Kenneth S. Wuest (Grand Rapids, MI: Wm. B. Eerdmans Publishing Co., 1969).

2. Personal communication with the author, August 22, 2009.

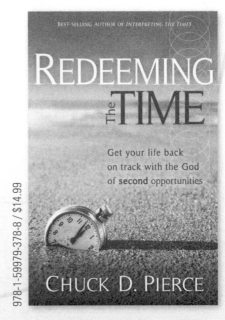

FREE NEWSLETTERS
TO HELP EMPOWER YOUR LIFE

Why subscribe today?

- ❑ **DELIVERED DIRECTLY TO YOU.** All you have to do is open your inbox and read.

- ❑ **EXCLUSIVE CONTENT.** We cover the news overlooked by the mainstream press.

- ❑ **STAY CURRENT.** Find the latest court rulings, revivals, and cultural trends.

- ❑ **UPDATE OTHERS.** Easy to forward to friends and family with the click of your mouse.

CHOOSE THE E-NEWSLETTER THAT INTERESTS YOU MOST:

- • Christian news
- • Daily devotionals
- • Spiritual empowerment
- • And much, much more

SIGN UP AT: **http://freenewsletters.charismamag.com**

8178